Date Due

THE MAN IN THE PEW

Sʳ H. SLINGSBY.

From an Original in Posess. of Talbot

1   SIR HENRY SLINGSBY

A. Tindal Hart

THE MAN
IN THE PEW
1558 — 1660

HUMANITIES PRESS INC.

NEW YORK

©

A. Tindal Hart
1966
First published in the United States of America
by Humanities Press Inc.
303 Park Avenue South
New York, N.Y. 10010

Library of Congress Catalog No 66-28388

Printed in Great Britain by
Clarke, Doble & Brendon Ltd
Cattedown, Plymouth

A. Tindal Hart

THE MAN
IN THE PEW
1558 — 1660

JOHN BAKER

5 ROYAL OPERA ARCADE

PALL MALL, LONDON, SW1

©

A. Tindal Hart
1966
First published 1966 by
John Baker Publishers Ltd
5 Royal Opera Arcade
Pall Mall, London,
SW1

Printed in Great Britain by
Clarke, Doble & Brendon Ltd
Cattedown, Plymouth

Contents

List of Illustrations

LINE DRAWINGS IN THE TEXT

Preface

THIS little book is intended as a sequel, although the comparison should not be pressed too hard, to my *The Country Clergy in Elizabethan and Stuart Times*, which was published in 1958. But now it is not so much the man in the pulpit as his contemporary in the pew whom I am interested in; and if it is still the countryman that I am chiefly concerned with, his urban brother has not been entirely omitted from the scene.

At a time when the Ecclesiastical Establishment appears about to be tottering to its fall : faced as we are apparently today with the imminent collapse of the ancient parochial system, the demolition of the parson's freehold, the disappearance or at least the radical revision of the Book of Common Prayer and the Thirty-Nine Articles, and the steady whittling away of the Royal Supremacy as exercised through Parliament; it is perhaps not an inappropriate moment to try and assess what that Establishment, when it was first set up under the Elizabethan Settlement, meant to the people of this country as looked at through the eyes of the ordinary man in the street, who was also of course at this period, willy-nilly, the man in the pew.

As this study is intended for the general reader rather than the professional historian, I have kept my footnotes to a minimum. On the other hand I have included a full bibliography of all the works, published and unpublished, that I have consulted, and from which the bulk of my material has been drawn. For the rest I am indebted to a number of scholars, who have supplied me with the fruits of their valuable and continuing research. In particular I should like to take this opportunity of expressing my grateful thanks to Dr D. K. Barratt, Dr W. A. Pemberton, Dr Arthur Warne and the Revd. F. H. Linn for their kind permission to read and quote from their as yet unpublished theses. To Dr Ronald Marchant I owe an especial acknowledgement: since not only does Chapter VI on the Non-Conformist draw heavily upon his *The Puritans and the Church Courts in the Diocese of York 1560-1642*, but he has most kindly sent me from time to time items, which he thought might be of interest and help, from his more recent investigations into the archives of the Diocese of York at the Borthwick Institute of Historical Research. I am also most grateful to Miss Elizabeth Kitson for compiling the index.

Finally I must once again record the invaluable help rendered me by my wife, and for her steady encouragement at a time when, owing to illness and the insistent pressure of my normal clerical duties, it seemed as though this book would never be completed.

A.Tindal Hart

Appleton Rectory,
Berkshire.
September, 1965.

CHAPTER I

The Village Scene

'MEDIEVAL England', wrote A. H. Dodd in *Life in Elizabethan England*, 'has been called a community of communities; Elizabethan England still retained something of that character'.

This was particularly true of the average village in the late sixteenth and early seventeenth centuries, which was usually a small compact affair of no more than one or two streets, with a few back lanes that quickly petered out into open fields. The houses lay alongside, whether farms or cottages, presenting either a full front or at least a gable-end to the roadway, but with no gardens in between. There were none of those solitary farmsteads, surrounded by their own lands, which in more modern times have proved such an attractive feature of the English countryside. All were contained within a very narrow area, together with their outhouses, crofts of permanent pasture, vegetable plots and orchards, since both the arable and pasture lands that lay outside it were far too valuable to be needlessly encroached upon. In the centre of the village stood the stone-built medieval church with its rectory hard by; the village green complete with its pond, pound, ducking-stool and stocks; and possibly a freshly constructed Elizabethan manor house, with its formal garden. This last would probably have been built of brick; whereas the humbler dwellings that clustered so closely about it were, outside the stone-belt, timber-framed, mudwalled and thatched.

The village community itself was a closely knit and exclusive society, which did not take kindly to 'foreigners', and owed its allegiance first and foremost to its squire. For every lord of the manor, great and small, possessed his court leet, over which his steward presided, and where a jury of tenants considered grievances, laid down what rules and regulations were needed for governing village life and agriculture, and dealt with disputes between neighbours concerning the immemorial custom of the manor.

Classes in the country were not very clearly defined and tended to merge into one another. There was a complete lack of class consciousness and a complete dependence of one upon another, due to the overriding common need to survive and if possible prosper. Furthermore peoples' lives were directed, dominated and welded together for good or ill by the close and constant super-vision of Ecclesiastical and State Authorities, who enforced their sanctions through the Church Courts and at Quarter and Petty Sessions. On the whole it was a prosperous society, with an efficient agriculture, an expanding trade and a growing population, which was a good deal healthier, better-fed and less poverty-stricken than it had been a generation or two before. It was the day of the smaller gentry, the newly minted country squires, who as yeo-men or merchants had originally profited from the break-up of the old medieval manors, and the dissolution of the monasteries, to acquire land cheaply. Judicious marriages, patient industry, lucky speculations in buying up neighbouring freeholds or for-feited lands, the enclosure of open fields for either pasture or specialised crops, the raising of rents, and the apprenticing of younger sons into industry and commerce, all helped to swell the family fortunes. The Ishams and Brudenells in Northamptonshire, for example, excelled as sheep-farmers and wool-dealers; while others like Thomas Myddelton from Denbighshire in Wales profited hugely from speculations in privateering. A man began, perhaps, as a merchant in some prospering provincial town, or as a yeoman freeholding-farmer in a village, 'an honest man riding to market astride his sacks of corn', and gradually earned for himself the right to be called 'master' instead of 'goodman'; but who left behind him a son or a grandson living in a comfortable newly built Elizabethan manor, drawing rents from land, and putting 'gent' or even 'esquire' after his name. Such gentry were eventually to find their way on to the local bench and even enter Parliament itself as members for the county.

The yeoman freeholder, who did not quite make the grade as a gentleman, was none the less doing very well for himself out of his few hundred acres of arable and pasture. Their numbers during this period have been estimated in hundreds of thousands and their yearly incomes ranged from £40 to £200 per annum.

HAYMAKING
from *The Roxburghe Ballads*

Some left goods behind them valued at £500 and more. They
were in the relatively strong position of living on fixed expenses,
whilst selling their surplus produce at higher and higher prices.
Labour costs were indeed rising, but not as high as prices; and
where there had been a conversion to pasture the former were still
reasonably low. Almost inevitably then the 'little man' on the
land prospered, increased his flocks and herds, rented new acres
and made money hand-over-fist. They worked without ceasing,
except for the sabbath rest, from the rising of the lark to the
setting of the sun, got the very best out of their servants and
children, and relied on the equally strenuous labours of their
wives, who spun and wove cloth, kept poultry, turned the milk
into butter and cheese, fruit into preserves, and herbs into home-
made medicines. 'Most yeomen', wrote Maurice Ashley in *Life in
Stuart England*, 'were pretty well educated. They learnt their
lessons at the petty schools or on their own family hearths; they
attended the free grammar schools; many of them went to the
universities; some of their sons became clergymen. They read the
Bible and other religious books; sometimes they had modest
libraries. They left money to further education.' An outward
sign of a yeoman's success story would be the enlargement of his

old house, or even the building of a brand new one; although most of them probably preferred to stick to their original farmsteads and spent their new wealth on creature comforts, which took the form of pewter and silver in their cupboard, cushions to sit upon, feather beds to lie in, tapestry on their walls and glass in the lattice of their windows, besides of course a variety and abundance of good things to eat and drink. This position of affluence was not arrived at without a struggle, which entailed at once being militant, ruthless, cunning and efficient. The yeomen fought his squire in and out of the lawcourts and successfully challenged the latter's right to exact medieval dues and services; but all too often in alliance with his enemy he also ground the face of the poor. As the early seventeenth century poet, Taylor, wrote of him:

> Will give his landlord more
> Than he would ask, in hope that from the poor
> He may extort it double by the rate
> Which he will sell his corn and cattle at.
> 'Tis plenty makes this cormorant to whine
> To hoard up corn with many a bitter ban
> From widows, orphans and the lab'ring man.

The husbandmen, who possessed no land of their own but were dependent upon leases and copyholds, were also doing very well for themselves. Landlords, on the whole, were not extortionate and the fines, rents and services demanded of them, which were largely prescribed by tradition, were not as a rule unreasonable. They enjoyed security of tenure, and fixed rents, whilst selling their produce at the new high prices. However, the taint of villeinage still hung about them; and although some succeeded in raising themselves to yeomen status, the majority were still ranked among the small-holders and cottagers. Their wills and inventories certainly go to show that their standard of living was rising; and they too were increasing the internal comforts and sometimes the outward appearance of their homes.

This was certainly the great century of domestic architecture. Everywhere manor houses, farmsteads and cottages were arising; but as the majority of these had still to be crammed within the restricted area of the old village, and the population was likewise steadily mounting, the health of the community often became seriously affected. From 1609 onwards there were persistent epidemics of one kind or another, which helped to keep such growth in check. It has been estimated that the average-sized family during this period, excluding servants and apprentices, was in the region of four or five persons. Many children died soon after birth, often their mothers died in bringing them into the world, and, in any case, few people lived beyond forty or fifty.

The tenant-at-will and the landless labourer were in a very different position from either yeoman or husbandman; but none the less the day labourer with his own freehold-cottage—although usually no more than a one-roomed hut of clay and branches— four acres and a cow, possessed at least some stake in the community. He was among the fortunate few, since by an Act of 1589 such a cottage might not house more than one family at a time, and from lack of space their numbers were obviously limited in the average built-up village. Naturally enough the farmers grudged good land for the sake of erecting new houses; but it was sometimes possible to secure permission, or even without it, to erect a shack on the waste. This, however, would have little or no holding attached to it. Moreover even where the three acres existed they were not of themselves sufficient to keep a family in food all the year round; so the man would normally hire himself out by the day to some farmer, either for a money payment or in exchange for the things he needed : the use of a cart, plough or harrow, which he could not afford to buy for himself, produce that he could not grow on his own patch, some seed-corn and an extra acre or two on which to sow it, and permission to pasture his cows and sheep on his master's leys. His working hours were long : from 5 a.m. to 7 p.m. in summer, and dawn to dusk in the winter months. For meals he would be allowed $2\frac{1}{2}$ hours; but fined a penny for every extra hour he took off beyond that maximum. This sounded a hard life, but in practice it was mitigated by a lot of idling and work-dodging when the eye of authority was not upon him; for which the English, a fundamentally lazy people, have always been famous. Where he was paid in cash he received by the day 2d. in winter and 3d. in summer with food, or an extra 3d. in lieu of it.[1] On his own land he probably worked very much harder than on his master's, and here he could be greatly assisted by an energetic wife and a young but growing family. Between them they could produce enough barley, wheat and rye at least to keep the family in bread; while the small enclosed croft

[1] Maurice Ashley, *Life in Stuart England*, p. 27. Gives the average wage as 8d. or 10d., which would seem to be too high.

B

or garth at the back of his cottage would comfortably hold a cow
and her calves, besides a pig and a few hens. Furthermore he possessed grazing rights on the common, if he cared to use them, for
sheep or swine. This class of labourer naturally varied a good deal.
Some could boast of holdings ranging from five to twelve acres,
and others had little or no land of their own at all; just as the two-
roomed cottage, with its chimney, loft, and out-buildings of the
more prosperous and well-to-do, was so much more comfortable
than the one-roomed shack, with no outlet for smoke except
through the door, and a mere partition separating humans from
animals, which was the lot of the very poor.

Not so fortunate were the farm servants and single labourers,
who lived with their employer in the farm house. Under a
benevolent master they might fare well enough with plenty of rye
bread, cheese and bacon to eat, ale or perry to drink, 'hempen
homespuns' or kerseys to wear, a warm bed in the loft or barn,
and not be too over-worked. But it was difficult to escape from a
bad one. No hired servant, who had once accepted his 'godspenny',
could leave without a quarter's warning; and then where was he
or she to go? They might not leave the parish without testimonials
from the constable and incumbent; and no one else would employ
them in the village unless they had been honourably discharged
with a good character. An employee, indeed, who ran away and
found refuge on another farm could cause his new employer to be
summoned and heavily fined.

Farm servants might start as stubble-boys at 20s. per annum,
and graduate to driving an ox-plough for another ten shillings.
Others became swineherds, neatherds, cowmen and shepherds.
The highest paid agricultural worker earned from 50s. to 60s. a
year. He was known as 'the first man in husbandry': 'a good
mower and a goode fower horse-man . . . sowe, mowe, goe well
with a draught and bee a good ploughman, goe happerly with a
waine and lye a loade of corn handsomely'.

The average village, while still predominantly an agrarian
society, was by Elizabethan times also becoming a hive of rural
industry. The cloth industry flourished there, and on a winter's
evening the peasant and his family engaged profitably in the arts
of weaving and spinning. Mining and smelting were other valuable
supplements to farming; and, of course, there had always been
the traditional village craftsmen: the smith, the wheelwright, the
carpenter, the mason and the thatcher, who were constantly in

demand. Their wages, which were fixed by the local justices of the peace, averaged a shilling a day. However their employment was not continuous; and in winter especially out-door workers like thatchers, masons, bricklayers and others often found themselves out of a job. Consequently many of them also engaged in husbandry and some were even found in occupation of a farm. 'Just as the whole village had a balanced economy', wrote W. G. Hoskins, 'with the land as its basis, a balance of farming and of industry and trade within its own narrow field of activity, so the individual craftsman or tradesman kept a balance in his own economy, turning from his craft or his trade back to his farm in slack times and in busy times performing a function in the village economy which was indispensable. The village would have broken down without him.'[2] The Franklins of Ecton in Northamptonshire, for instance, owned a thirty-acre farm for three hundred years, yet they always apprenticed the eldest son of the family as a smith. Innkeepers were likewise farmers; hence the well-known public house names of 'The Plough', 'The Jolly Farmer', 'The Woolpack', etc.

Most households were self-sufficient, making their own clothes and producing their own food and drink. This last, among the poorer members of the community at anyrate, consisted chiefly of rye bread, cheese and ale; but an astonishing number of people ate meat at least once a day except in winter, when due to a shortage of salt it was impossible to preserve it. Bean soup, eggs and bacon were consumed in large quantities; and also coarse fish, conies and other edible vermin, besides game when and where it could be poached. After Christmas it often became a matter of tightening one's belt and praying for an early Spring. Vegetables and raw fruit were rarely eaten, although the latter was used to make preserves. The potato had only just put in an appearance; and a century or more was to pass before it became the staple diet of the indigent poor.

The yeomen and gentry, of course, fared very much better. Their tables groaned under enormous joints of mutton and beef, poultry, rabbits, pigeons and pheasants, venison when in season, and every variety of fish on the statutory fast days. 'The English have an abundance of white meats', declared Fynes Moryson at the beginning of the seventeenth century, 'of all kinds of flesh, fowl and fish and of all things good for food. . . . English cooks, in

[2] *The Midland Peasant*, p. 167.

comparison with other nations, are most commended for roast meats.' Such privileged families and their retainers certainly did not go hungry in winter time.

The Statute of Labourers and Apprentices passed in 1563 made sure that everyone, unless they were property owners, learned a trade, a craft or a job in agriculture and stuck to it. Apprenticeship lasted seven years, during which the pupil was expected to serve his master 'as a true and faithful servant ought to behave himself'; and the master on his part was expected not only to teach him his work, but 'in due manner chastise him, findinge unto his said servante meate, drinke, linnen, woollen hose, shoes and all other things to him necessary'. It was virtually impossible for the non-apprenticed to get either into industry, commerce or even agriculture.

The section of the community most hardly used was perhaps that of the working women, who were chiefly employed in domestic service, but also as day-labourers on the farms, as assistants in thatching and quarrying, and indeed in most labouring occupations. A cook or a dairy-maid could earn up to £2 or £3 a year; most others got no more than a penny or two a day. In the home they did all the housework, cooked, made the clothes and mended them, were experts on the production of home-made wines, preserves and medicines, supplemented the family income by spinning, the keeping of poultry and rabbits, and cultivating the herb garden; and above all produced a succession of children, most of whom died in infancy. Married in their early twenties, they were old women by thirty. It is reported that the Devonshire Justices of the Peace fixed women's wages only for those between the ages of eighteen and thirty, since they were convinced that no woman over thirty would be physically capable of doing a day's work in the fields or quarries.

Most English villages were still working the open-field mixed type of farming, where the arable acreage was about three-quarters that of the whole. It was largely subsistence farming, since all except the biggest farms were concerned more with providing food for immediate consumption than in supplying an adjacent town or neighbourhood, despite the tempting prices that were often paid for any surplus produce. The village was, in fact, a self-reliant community, not merely growing its own food and distilling its own drink, but also producing its own clothing, fuel, light and power. It would build its own houses from local materials and manufacture much of its own furniture and farm equipment. Some imports like salt, iron, and possibly coal and wine were essential : then, as the countryside grew more prosperous, luxuries of every kind, many of them of foreign origin, gradually seeped down from the manor house into the homes of the better-to-do yeomen and husbandmen.

Everywhere much good agricultural land had been turned over to pasture during the two preceding centuries, not only for the production of wool, but also to satisfy the ever growing demands of a meat-eating nation for bigger and yet bigger supplies of mutton and beef. However, despite much depopulation and alarmist fears voiced right down to Elizabethan times, when the movement had largely ceased, wholesale permanent enclosures were still mainly confined to highly cultivated counties such as Kent, which with its abundant capital and highly specialised crops of hops and fruit, that found a ready market in a rapidly expanding London, made them pay big dividends. It was far otherwise in the Midlands and the North, particularly in areas distant from large centres of population, where the open-field farmer with his traditional mixed husbandry continued to predominate. The open-field village was still the typical village in 1600, and remained so until after 1660.

Furthermore the traditional three-field cropping system persisted in the majority of rural communities : namely that peas, beans or oats were sown in one field; wheat, rye or barley in another; while the third lay fallow. But as the seventeenth century went on this rigid rotation gradually became more flexible, and rich individual farmers began to exercise their own initiative and ignore the custom of the past.

An ever pressing problem in village society was the growing number of indigent poor, who had come into being owing to the steady rise in population—nearly four million by Elizabeth's reign —without any corresponding increase in cultivatable land, industry or a colonial expansion sufficient as yet to absorb them. There were, too, the crowds of vagabonds and sturdy rogues, the bye-product of such revolutionary upheavals as the agrarian revolution that had converted so much arable into pasture and depopulated whole villages, the dissolution of the monasteries, the disbanding of private armies and the ending of recruiting for the seemingly never-ending French wars. These men and women flooded the roads, lurked in the greenwood, and terrorized the whole countryside. Harrison reckoned that there were something like 10,000 of these vagabonds at large in England; a 'rowsy ragged rabblement of rakehells', who constituted, in the absence of any regular standing army or police force, an ever present menace to Society as a whole.

> Given a crisis—a famine, large-scale unemployment, a breakdown of government—disorder might occur as it did in 1607 when there were 'Levellers' in Northamptonshire and 'Diggers' in Warwickshire. In 1622 Gloucester unemployed went in groups to houses of the rich, demanding money and seizing provisions. There were minor revolts in the south western counties in 1628-31.[3]

The problem gave rise to a series of Poor Law enactments, culminating in the famous Act of 1601, under which Overseers of the Poor were to be elected by each parish Vestry and then confirmed in office by the J.P.s at Quarter Sessions in order to carry out their provisions. In this task they were to be closely associated with the churchwardens, who themselves were *ipso facto* overseers. A special rate was levied, which if necessary could be compulsorily enforced by the magistrates, and was to be used for four main purposes : to give weekly relief, normally in money, to the sick, the aged, and the impotent; to set up a workhouse or house of correction for sturdy rogues and able-bodied vagabonds, together with a stock of raw materials for their labours; to build houses where possible on common or disused land for homeless and destitute families; and to see to it that the children of the very poor, orphans and waifs were properly educated, i.e. apprenticed out from the age of seven upwards as domestic or farm servants. Every substantial householder was expected to accept at least one of these children into his employ and to teach him or her their trade or craft.

Vagabonds, who included vagrant women, players of 'interludes', fiddlers, pedlars, and wandering scholars—anyone, in fact, who was unable to account for himself by producing some kind of testimonial or licence—were not as a rule treated very humanely. The petty constables were expected to round up such people; and, if they were 'foreigners' i.e. not native to the township, to have them whipped and placed in the stocks. A little later, armed with a testimonial from the head constable and incumbent

---

[3] Christopher Hill, *The Century of Revolution*, p. 27.

of the parish, they would be handed over to the former's opposite number in the next village, where the process was repeated and continued *ad nauseam* until the luckless victims, sore alike in back, buttocks and feet, reached their 'settlement' or place of origin, when they would be sent to the house of correction, little better than a prison, and set to hard labour. Twice a year, during the days immediately preceding a meeting of the J.P.s, the head and petty constables, assisted by the churchwardens and overseers, would institute a search of their village for any such undesirables, put them in the stocks and then carry them before the magistrates.

'Rogues' were in rather a different category: a more criminal class, liable to terrorise people living in lonely places and constituting a perpetual, if unorganised, element of revolt against Authority. The more dangerous were gaoled, transported or sent to the galleys; but the vast majority, against whom no definite crime could be proved, were treated hardly less savagely by being branded on the left shoulder with an 'R', whipped, and admitted to the hard labours and scanty rations of the house of correction. These wandering sturdy beggars and rogues were all the more disliked because they brought disease in their train, infected with the plague villages that had hitherto boasted a clean bill of health, and often inflicted considerable damage on property of every kind before they could be caught. The timid householder would sometimes give them food, money and even a night's lodging in the hope of getting rid of them quickly and relatively peacefully; despite the fact that anyone found harbouring or assisting these outcasts was liable to a very heavy fine. All good citizens, indeed, were expected and in honour bound to come to the aid of the constables in helping to apprehend such rogues and turn them over to the Justices.

Most country parishes were controlled by a Vestry. Theoretically this was a meeting of the whole village held either within or immediately without the church during Easter week; but in practice it had normally been reduced to a small group of prominent inhabitants, twelve or twenty-four in number, who retained office for life and had the power to co-opt new members when necessary to fill vacancies caused by death, resignation or departure from the neighbourhood.

At their annual meeting the churchwardens were appointed and their accounts examined; other parish officials such as the overseers, the surveyors of the highways, and the head and petty constables, elected; and the church and poor rates levied. The incumbent was the traditional chairman and his authority was needed to confirm its proceedings; while the church clerk, if sufficiently literate, usually acted as its scribe. The churchwardens were responsible for upholding moral standards and enforcing a religious discipline; but the constables had the even more invidious task of seeing that the multitudinous mass of Tudor and Stuart statutes were duly observed. Both these sets of officials will be dealt with in later chapters.

During the course of the year on the initiative of either the incumbent or the churchwardens the vestry could be summoned to a special meeting to decide some important matter that had arisen in connection with church or village; and whether so summoned or not it none the less exercised a powerful, if largely hidden and latent, supervision over the affairs and servants of the parish year in and year out.

Villagers, by and large, were kept on a very tight rein; much tighter than anything previously experienced in pre-Reformation days or to be later encountered in the more tolerant era that followed the Restoration, and culminated in the *laissez faire* philosophy of the eighteenth-century. The risings of the peasants, whether for religious or economic reasons, in East Anglia, the West and the North during the reigns of Edward VI and Queen Elizabeth; the permanent background of discontent in the early seventeenth century fostered by rising prices, fixed wages, unemployment; and the sharp and growing distinction between the 'poor', whose beastly, brutish and short lives were on a permanent semi-starvation level, and the prospering gentry, yeomen and better-class husbandmen, who were rapidly acquiring a taste for luxury; all impelled Authority, whether in the Privy Council or the Parish Vestry, to be firm and even brutal at times if it was to govern successfully or even survive.

> People were frequently accused on mere suspicion; men were held responsible for their wives' misdeeds and were expected to see that their children behaved circumspectly. No one was allowed to waste his estate by card-playing or riotous living, no feasts or banquets were to be given after nine o'clock at night and no person might behave in such a manner as to cause inconvenience to the community.[4]

'E. Trotter, *Seventeenth Century Life in the Country Parish*, p. 178.

Informers were encouraged by being given a third or even half the fine imposed for the offences that they had reported. Yet even they were expected to be licensed.

For six days a week men, women and children over the age of seven, worked or idled, if given half a chance, in field, house and institution or at some trade and craft as long as their health and strength permitted. There were no old age pensions. This was necessarily a young England, with the teenagers greatly out-numbering the grey-beards; since owing to so much famine, pestilence and sudden death among the poor, few could hope to reach the Biblical maximum of three-score years and ten. Fire caused a great deal of damage every year in these tightly packed village areas, where wood and thatch largely predominated; and left a trail of blackened ruins and destitute, homeless families behind it, who could only be relieved by some form of private or public charity. There was no insurance. The 'surveyors of the highways', who had come into being during Queen Mary's reign, were saddled with the invidious task of calling upon every inhabitant of the parish possessing land to supply carts, horses and other equipment needed for repairing the roads which linked their township with the next. The rest of the village, armed with spades, mattocks, picks or other sharp implements, did the manual labour on the six days immediately preceding the Feast of St John the Baptist. This work was most unpopular. No one felt under the least moral obligation to maintain the Queen's highway; and it was only the fear of heavy fines that kept them grudgingly to their task. Even then the work was scamped, consisting of little more than hacking down some of the undergrowth in order to keep the track open at all, filling in some of the larger holes with stones, and smoothing over a few of the deepest ruts with loose earth. Very soon the road was as bad as ever. The smaller bridges were also a local responsibility; but were usually so badly serviced that they constantly collapsed under heavy waggons or were toppled over by flood or storm. In most cases it was safer and more convenient in the long run to make use of the nearest ford.

⚹On Sunday mornings every parishioner was expected to attend divine service in his parish church or pay a shilling fine; while children, apprentices and servants were obliged to come again in the afternoon to be catechized. The remaining male population then practised archery at the butts on the village green; despite the fact that with the arrival of the hand-gun its value in real warfare was steadily diminishing. On the other hand games, especially bowling, football, cards, backgammon, dicing and shuffle-board, were heavily frowned upon. Queen Elizabeth herself took the pre-Reformation viewpoint that having once made a formal attendance at church, she was free to spend the rest of the day enjoying plays and masques or doing business. This was certainly not the opinion of her much more protestant Government. Sunday, it was felt, was none other than the Jewish sabbath, and all the shibboleths of the Fourth Commandment should be strictly applied to it. It was that seventh day wherein no ordinary work should be done which was not strictly necessary; and no part of it might be used for purely pleasurable purposes. It must be spent in worship, in prayer and meditation, in Bible-study, learning and being examined in the Catechism, in visiting the sick and feeding the poor, and in rest of body and mind. The mass of the people, however, remained strangely unconvinced and paid scant attention to such sabbatical exhortations: they bought and sold on a Sunday; wrestled, fought and played football often in the very churchyard itself; feasted, drank and gambled in the alehouses or at one another's homes. For these misdeeds they could be brought before the Archdeacon's Court or Quarter Sessions, and either admonished, fined, compelled to undertake a penance or even given a prison sentence. In 1574 the homily 'of the Place and Time of Prayer' was appointed to be read in all churches, which castigated in no uncertain terms

> The wicked boldness of those that will be counted God's people, who pass nothing at all of keeping and hallowing the Sunday . . . they must ride and journey on the Sunday; they must drive and carry on the Sunday; they must row and ferry on the Sunday; they must keep markets and fairs on the Sunday . . . they will not rest in holiness, as God commandeth; but they rest in ungodliness and filthiness, prancing in their pride, pranking and pricking, pointing and painting themselves, to be gorgeous and gay; they rest in excess and superfluity, in gluttony and drunkenness, like rats and swine; they rest in brawling and railing, in quarrelling and fighting : they rest in wantonness, in toyish talking, in filthy fleshiness; so that it doth too evidently appear that God is more dishonoured, and the devil better served on the Sunday than upon all the days in the week beside.

The Thirteenth Canon of 1604 forbade any profanation of Sunday; and this was reinforced by a royal Proclamation of James I's that declared: 'We do strictly charge and command that no bear-baiting, interludes, common plays, or other like disordered and unlawful exercises be frequented, kept or used . . . upon the Sabbath day.'

None the less Justices of the Peace, churchwardens and constables had their work cut out to prevent people from working, drinking or playing on a Sunday, even during the hours of divine service. When they enforced the law too strictly there was often a riot as happened in Lancashire during the year 1617, and the local authorities both in Church and State were defied. James was wise enough to see the red light, and published his famous Declaration of Sports the following year, which, after re-affirming the need for compulsory church attendance on Sundays, the illegality of carrying offensive weapons, and the prohibition of certain 'unlawful' pastimes already named, went on to concede the public's right to 'any lawful recreation, such as dancing, either men or women, archery for men, leaping, vaulting or any such harmless recreation, nor from having of May-games, Whitsun ales, and Morris dances, and the setting up of May-poles and other sports therewith used, so as the same be had in due and convenient time, without impediment or neglect of Divine Service.'

The puritanical House of Commons strongly resented this Declaration, and took its revenge in the early years of the next reign by passing a series of measures aimed at restoring the sabbatical 'rest': in particular discouraging the wakes, revels and church ales that many parishes organised on the festival of their patron saint or at Whitsuntide in order to help their finances; but which sometimes led to unseemly behaviour, serious disorders and even bloodshed. In 1633 Lord Chief Justice Richardson and Baron Denham, then on the Western Circuit, ordered that 'revels, church ales, clerk ales and all other public ales be henceforth entirely suppressed'. This caused an uproar and resulted in the personal intervention of the powerful Bishop of London, William Laud, who forced Richardson into making a public recantation. Then, on Laud's prompting, Charles I re-issued his father's Declaration and compelled the clergy to read it from their pulpits. The pleasure-loving public was not slow, of course, in taking advantage of such royal support. 'In the village where I lived', recorded Richard Baxter in his *Autobiography*, 'the reader read the Common Prayer briefly, and the rest of the day, even till dark night almost, except eating time, was spent in dancing under a may-pole or a great tree not far from my father's door'. As a puritan, Baxter naturally disapproved of this profanation of the Lord's Day, at any rate in theory; but as a hot-blooded youth himself he was carried away by the general enthusiasm. So instead of sitting at home with his family and reading the Scriptures, he ruefully admitted : 'I broke loose from conscience and joined them.' This conflict between the puritan conscience and human frailty, encouraged by Anglican laxity, widened and deepened during the eleven years of Charles's personal rule, and provided yet further fuel for the inevitable explosion.

Under the Commonwealth and Protectorate the pendulum swung in the opposite direction, when every kind of game, sport, pleasure and feasting, unnecessary work and Sunday travel, were prohibited; and a proper observance of the sabbath enforced. An Ordinance of 4 January 1654, for instance, said of Sunday :

> That what time is vacant between and after the solemn meetings of the Congregation in public be spent in Reading, Meditation, Repetition of Sermons (especially by calling their families to an account of what they have heard) and catechizing of them, holy conferences, prayer for a blessing upon Public Ordinances, saying of psalms, visiting the sick, relieving the poor, and such like duties of piety, charity and mercy, accounting the Sabbath a delight.

The festivals of Christmas, Easter and Whitsuntide were abolished, with all their jollifications; but at the same time the Government wisely provided a safety valve in yet another Ordinance that expressly decreed : 'That all scholars, apprentices and other servants shall, with the leave and approbation of their masters respectively first had and obtained, have such convenient reasonable recreation and relaxation from their constant and ordinary labours on every second Tuesday in the month throughout the year.' Judging from the records of Quarter Sessions the implementation of such a Sunday discipline was not easily achieved; but by the Restoration it had become so stamped upon the public mind that puritan legislation in this field was never revised.

Ale-house keepers in particular had always been carefully supervised, since their establishments provided a natural centre for intemperance, disorder and lawlessness. Consequently they had not merely to be licensed, but must produce a number of substantial neighbours to stand surety for their good behaviour. Outside the door of each inn stood its pole, with a bush on top if wine as well as ale was licensed to be sold there. But if for one reason or another that licence should be withdrawn, then the constable would be sent for to cut it down, sometimes in the face of fierce opposition. In 1613, for instance, the innkeeper's wife at Cockeswold in York-shire was committed for trial before Quarter Sessions, '. . . for cominge forth of her house with a pitchforke and beating awaie a man that was cutting down her Ale-rodd, he being soe com-maunded to do by Sir H. Belassis Knt Barronett.'

Women, as has already been noted, played a very important part in village life during this period. They took their full share in bread-earning; and were self-assertive, litigious, quarrelsome and even physically violent over what they considered to be their own peculiar rights, privileges and possessions or those of their husbands and families. At a public washing-place in Winchester in June 1569 a squabble took place between two ladies, resulting in a public brawl, and culminating in a court case between them the following month, when it was alleged :

> Churcher's wife came out from her house with two kettles and said to Mistress Clerck then being there, 'Dost thou thrust my maid from the washing place?' and immediately went to the said Godsland's wife (who was helping Mrs Clerck wash her clothes) and thrust her into the water. And then Mistress Clerck demanded of the said Churcher's wife why she did so. And she sware that she would thrust her in also, which immediately she did as soon as Mistress Clerck set her feet upon the board (by the water's edge) and thrust her back twice.

At Andover in July 1602 one of the churchwardens referred to a certain Elizabeth Ayres as being 'as froward as other women are when they are angry and one time the cucking stool was set against her door'; adding somewhat incongruously, but no doubt sincerely : 'yet she is accounted an honest woman.'

Sometimes they were greatly feared. It was a serious matter to call a woman a witch; but most villages possessed one, in the sense that it was believed that she could exercise powers whether for good or ill above the ordinary, cast the evil eye, over-look her neighbours' livestock, bring on mysterious illnesses or effect miraculous cures and bestow good fortune. In a cruel and superstitious age, particularly in the days of the Commonwealth, many an old and relatively inoffensive woman was 'nosed' out by informers, charged with witchcraft before the Church Courts or at Quarter Sessions, and often condemned to be drowned or burnt alive. Occasionally the villagers would take the law into their own hands, with ugly and even murderous consequences, of which a vivid, if fictitious account, of the burning of a local sorceress is portrayed in Rosemary Macaulay's *They were Defeated*. The witches themselves were partly responsible for their own sufferings, since they deliberately set out to build up their reputations and excite the awe and fear of their neighbours. Out of the innumerable cases dealing with witches or so-called witches, the following taken from the Winchester Consistory Court depositions well illustrate the kind of things which were believed of, spoken to or about, and perpetrated on these unfortunate women. In June 1573 Mistress Dingley said to one of her employees: 'Get thee hence thou witch and clear thyself . . . for I will never take thee for other than a witch till thou hast cleared thyself . . . get thee hence from my staff thou rogue and scold or else I will make my servant beat thee out of my shop.'

After morning prayer in Farley parish church on the first Sunday in August 1575 a husbandman, John Whyte, asked Stephen Spering, 'whom he meant to be the witch he talked of'. Spering replied: 'I cannot tell. I can no sooner pound Hunt's cattle but I have a shrewd turn afterwards.' But, on being pressed, admitted that he believed it to have been caused by 'old mother Hunt'; and added: 'I can no sooner shake a pig of hers or pound her cattle but presently I or my master have a shrewd turn.'

Thomas Daw of Pamber attributed his loss of cattle in 1577, particularly a sow that 'died great with pig upon a sudden' to 'Howse's wife'; and in the same year Alice Trenell told Jane Gay: 'thou art a witch and I have a servant at home fallen sick, and if she do otherwise than well I will make thee burn a stake.' However it was no light matter to accuse a person of being a witch. In each of these last three instances the maligned lady in question brought an action against her traducer and won it; and many escaped because the constable or would-be informer was unsure of his ground, afraid that the case might be dismissed either in the Archdeacon's Court or at Quarter Sessions, and the outraged

witch's wrath then descend upon his own head. The enemies of
Elizabeth Cooke of Thirsk, for example, must have shaken in
their shoes, when they learnt that in July 1611 the Justices
had acquitted her of 'being a common scold and disquieter of
her neighbours with continual banning and cursing of her neighbours and their goods, in as much as the said goods and themselves whom she curseth oftentimes presently die by her said ill
words.'

An amusing story of almost incomprehensible credulity came
from Takeley in Essex. A certain Reuben Bowier, a Suffolk man,
was travelling on foot between Elsenham and Takeley accompanied by his dog, when the latter began to chase a pig belonging
to Helen Dish of Takeley. In great wrath she told Reuben 'hee
should have noe greate joy after it.' As a result, or so he declared
on oath before the Justices of the Peace at Quarter Sessions,

> . . . hee hath had exceedinge stronge and many painfull fittes
> to ceize on him att severall times; [and one morning] there
> came a thinge uppon his bedd, like a blacke catt . . . another
> thinge like a hedgehogge satt uppon a sticke neere his bedd
> side . . . and immediately after the sight of those thinges his
> fittes ceized on him very stronge and painfull, and hee feeleth
> some thinge runne upp into his body, whilest it comes to
> his throate and then hee is almost strangled and is in great
> torture and misery.

Judging from the records that have come down to us from the
Church Courts and the findings of Quarter Sessions, the average
male and female parishioner must have felt that their lives were
continually under inspection from the cradle to the grave : in their
working and leisure hours, in their sexual relationships, in the
kind of company they kept, in the times and manner of their
worship, and in the upbringing and training of their families, by
the all-seeing eyes of Church and State as personified in the incumbent and churchwardens or the parish constables and the
local Justices of the Peace. Their slightest mis-demeanour : a little
bit of extra washing done on a Sunday, a few angry words, a glass
of ale or a hand of cards taken at the wrong time or with the
wrong people, the occupation of a pew other than the one allotted
to them in church, the mistaken charity of offering a slice of bread
or a glass of water to a luckless vagabond, and countless other
offences innocuous in twentieth-century eyes, could well land the

late sixteenth- or early seventeenth-century villager in court, and
bring down upon his head an admonition, a fine, even a penance.
It might well have been thought that such conditions would have
reduced the mass of the Nation to the status of cowed and
dispirited serfs. Far from it. Churchwardens and constables, clergy
and Justices, with the full majesty of the Church, the Law, the
Crown and the militia behind them, found it quite impossible to
suppress the natural instincts of a vigorous, flourishing, prospering
and intensely independent English countryman. Wisely they
tempered the wind to the shorn lamb; and although, of course,
law and order, religious observance and moral behaviour must
at all costs be upheld, yet each individual case could be and
usually was treated on its merits, in a common-sense and neigh-
bourly spirit, which at once safe-guarded human rights, whilst
upholding the Sword of Justice.

During the latter half of the sixteenth century a great and be-
wildering revolution had been wrought in the worship and
appearance of the village church that must have upset many a
parishioner and increased the already strong anti-clerical spirit
in the English countryside. In 1570, to choose a date at random,
not a few of the clergy possessed more than a little of the Vicar
of Bray's philosophy of life in their make up. One's parson, for
example, might perhaps have started as a religious in some monastery, from which he had been ejected at the Dissolution, but
awarded a pension and given his present benefice. During Edward
VI's reign he married and settled down, cheerfully taking the
Prayer Books of 1549 and 1552, with all their accompanying in-
novations, in his stride. But he may as hastily have repudiated
his wife and children and returned to the old liturgical ways and
the Latin mass as long as Queen Mary occupied the throne. When
Elizabeth introduced her compromise Settlement he accepted that
too; for was not the doctrine being established all over Europe :
cujus regio ejus religio, and where the 'godly' prince led the way
his subjects must faithfully follow him. Besides he was glad to
get his lady back on any reasonable terms, to continue to draw
his pension and to collect his tithes rather than to go out into the
wilderness with some of his more uncompromising brethren, who
either starved quietly in obscurity or at great risk to life or limb
went on ministering to the faithful few that steadfastly adhered
to the Old Faith.

His church had been thoroughly cleansed of all 'superstitious

The Angell to the Virgin tidings brings
That she shall beare the glorious King of Kings,
Elizabeth our famous Queene did dye,
Whose place our Soveraigne Iames did supply.

MARCH

MARTIVS AGROS. NVNC VITEM AC SALICES PRÆCIDO ET BALNEA QVÆRO ARQ SECO VENAS ET SEMINO

2 PLOUGHING AT THE BEGINNING OF
THE SEVENTEENTH CENTURY

3   Early seventeenth-century beggars

4   Malefactors in the
stocks, 1651

5 Old Scarlett, Peterborough Gra
digger, buried Queen Catherine
Aragon, and Mary, Queen of Sc

relics', which included images, shrines and the rood screen. Chantry chapels were either destroyed or converted by the local squire-archy to their own use, where with the help of large and com-modious pews they could worship God comfortably in this world, and find a dignified resting place for their human remains when they passed into the next. Soon these chapels became filled with family tombs and monuments. Vestments, ornaments of every kind, and church plate disappeared; but were often carefully preserved by the faithful against another swing of the pendulum or turn in fortune's wheel. Certainly many bowed down in the House of Rimmon only under the mistaken if not unnatural assumption that, as in the recent past, there would be a return to Roman Catholicism, possibly by the triumph of Mary, Queen of Scots, or the eventual succession of her son, James. This did not happen. Instead there was another and yet more iconoclastic out-break of violence during the Commonwealth, when what had escaped the Elizabethan 'gospellers' succumbed to the even fiercer Cromwellian soldiery.

Church walls were white-washed in order to rid them of the medieval paintings, particularly the great 'Doom' over the chancel arch; stained-glass gave place to plain glass; the stone-altar was taken down and in its place stood a wooden table covered with 'silk, buckram or other such-like', which, according to the Royal Injunctions of 1559, must be moved down into the chancel or nave and clothed in a fair white linen cloth for the communion service. Here, in practice, it usually remained in a table-wise rather than an altar-wise position.

> As for our churches, [wrote William Harrison] belles . . . remain as in times past . . . all images, shrines, tabernacles, rood-lofts, and monuments of idolatrie are removed, taken down and defaced; onlie the stories in glasse windowes excepted, which for want of sufficient store of newe stuffe . . . not altogether abolished in most places at once, but by little and little suffered to decaie, that white glasse may be provided and set up in their roomes[5]

So now only the Ten Commandments, the Lord's Prayer and possibly other scriptural texts, besides the Royal Arms and what-ever stained-glass yet remained, broke the monotony of those whitened church walls. The chief Sunday service was still at

[5] *Description of England*, VOL II, p. 32.

C

9 a.m.; but it differed vastly from the Latin mass. For the priest no longer stood at the east end before the high altar, separated from his flock by the whole length of the chancel, where clad in the eucharistic vestments he had once offered up in a dead language a sacrifice on behalf of a congregation that played little or no part in the worship. Instead he occupied a desk at the top of the nave or possibly just within the chancel screen, facing his people, who could not only see and hear him speaking to them in their own idiom, but might themselves join in what Archbishop Cranmer and his fellow-compilers of the Prayer Book had especially designed as a Biblical and congregational service. Cranmer had originally envisaged a Holy Communion Service, attended by large numbers of communicants, as the central act of Sunday morning worship, to which Morning Prayer would be no more than an introduction. But this hope, and indeed expectation, was defeated and extinguished by the average Englishman's obstinately conservative determination not to communicate more than a few times in the year. Morning Prayer was therefore succeeded by the Litany and ante or 'dry' communion, and was rounded off by a sermon or a homily and a psalm. The whole service could well last for two or more hours, especially if it also happened to include a baptism; but eventually freed its worshippers in time for their main meal of the day at noon. In the afternoon children, apprentices and servants were catechised for an hour after the second lesson at Evening Prayer.

Following on the laxity of the pre-Reformation Sunday the compulsory attendance and uniformity of worship imposed on the whole community without exception, must have been galling in the extreme: to the secular-minded, who wished to be about their business or recreations; to the extreme puritan, who desired a much simpler and even more Scriptural type of service; and to the Roman Catholic recusant, who favoured the old Latin mass. But such objectors met with scant sympathy. They must either attend Divine Service in their parish church or pay a fine or, for persistent absenteeism, be sent to prison.

There was on the whole little organised opposition even among the recusants; but a good deal of individual evasion and sometimes down-right defiance. Men and women of means could comfortably afford the shilling fine, and probably possessed enough influence in their own locality to escape a public prosecution. There was no penalty as yet for hearing mass in secret or con-

ducting private devotions at home, whether of a papist or Protestant type. The return, however, to a more colourful and reverent
catholicism, together with a tighter discipline and a sterner persecution both of puritans and recusants during the early years of
the seventeenth century, and particularly in the Laudian era,
when churches were restored, their interiors re-beautified and
some of the old ceremonial re-introduced, also led to a greater
opposition. The subsequent destruction of so much of beauty and
antiquity in the churches and the persecution of the Anglican
clergy in the days of the Great Rebellion, certainly stemmed as
much from a dislike of paying tithes, the oppressive clerical
authority wielded by many incumbents in their parishes, and
the enforcement of a cut-and-dried uniformity, as from any particular love for Presbyterianism.

Above all, the whole of village society, from the squire down-
wards, was profoundly influenced and shaped in late Tudor and
early Stuart times by the English Bible. Ever since Henry VIII had
introduced the chained Bible into the parochial churches, there
had been a widespread urge to read it; and this urge was even
strong enough to make the illiterate desirous of learning their
letters. By the fifteen-eighties the family Bible had arrived, which
quickly became the register of family births and deaths; and by
the middle of the seventeenth century England had become the
'Nation of the Book'—the Authorised Version of 1611—which
was largely to determine the ordinary person's attitude to life for
centuries to come, along the lines that success or failure was
governed by Divine Forces outside his control, and one's fate was
predestined either for good or ill from the beginning.

None the less despite the tremendous upheaval in Church and
State occasioned by the Reformation and its aftermath, the village
remained fundamentally an unchanged and unchanging society—
a peasant society dependant upon its own resources and physical
labours, where everyone had and knew his place, and nothing was
wasted.

    If the peasant of Henry VIII's day could have returned
to the streets and fields to visit his great-grandson, he would
have felt at home, back in a timeless world in which all the
fields had their familiar names; in which many of the
families that he had known still carried on the remembered
trades or cultivated the ancestral acres as of old; and in

which all the familiar boundaries and landmarks were still to be found where he had always known them, the same mills, wells, springs, lanes and hedges. There were the immemorial sights and sounds that he had always known, and the rich smells of living in a busy arable-farming village.[6]

W. G. Hoskins, *The Midland Peasant*, p. 190.

CHAPTER II

The Squire

THE most important person in the countryside was usually the squire, except in parishes like Wigston Magna in Leicestershire, where after the break-up of the medieval manor an entire peasant community had taken over command, headed by substantial yeomen, tradesmen and the farmers of the rectory. This last was a type of village not uncommon in the Midlands and East Anglia, but rarely to be found in the South or the North, where normally the squire would be at once the chief landowner, the patron of the benefice, the lay-impropriator of most of its tithes and the local Justice of the Peace. Many of these men were new-minted, the sons or grandsons of successful opportunists, who had taken advantage of the Tudor politico-economic revolution to lay the foundations of their fortunes. These were greatly increased by the favourable economic conditions prevailing during the reigns of the first two Stuarts, when rents, prices and profits were all increasing, while wages were relatively steady. The growing practice of enclosure, the custom of primogeniture, the laws of entail and the careful marriage settlements arranged between families, strengthened and extended their grip on land and doubled or trebled their incomes.

Naturally there were numbers of extravagant or improvident gentry, who disappeared as quickly as they had risen in the first instance; but on the whole they were a hard-headed, industrious, far-sighted and acquisitive race, who sank their roots deep and built for posterity—

A combined profit-seeker and social climber [wrote E. Wingfield-Stratford] whose authority was set at nought by the yeomen farmers, but who was not above conspiring to evict cottage farmers from their holdings in order to exploit the land to better advantage. He himself might have had one son at an apprentice's bench in the City, and another taking his part in some voyage in distant seas in which motives of patriotism, commercial gain and sheer piracy were blended in undeterminate proportion; and either or both of them married to a daughter of some City Tradesman with enough money to provide her with a fat dowry.[1]

The most visible symbol of this newly attained prosperity was the erection of a substantial Elizabethan or Jacobean mansion, stone or brick-walled, with a slate or tiled roof according to the materials most easily available.

> He that wyll builde [wrote Borde in *A Compendyous Regyment*, published in 1567] let him make his foundation upon a gravaly grounde myxte with clay, or else let him buylde upon a roche or stone . . . or els upon a hylles syde. And order and edyfye the house so that the pryncypall and chiefe prospectes may be east and weest, especyally north east, or south east, and south west . . . Make the hall under such a fashion that the parler be anexed to the heade of the hall. And the butterye and pantry be at the lower end of the hal, the seller under the pantry . . . the kychen set somwhat a base from the buttry and pantry . . . the pastry house and the larder house annexed to the kychen . . . let the pryve chambre be anexed to ye chambre of astate, with other chambers necessarie for the buyldynge, so that many of the chambers may have a prospecte into the Chapell . . . the bake house and brewe house shulde be a distaunce from . . . other buyldynge.

Some twenty years later William Harrison noted a change of style, 'The ancient manours and house of our gentlemen are yet, and for the most part, of strong timber . . . howbeit such as be latelie builded are commonlie either of bricke or hard stone or both; their roomes are large and comlie, and houses of office further distant from their lodgings.'

The normal Elizabethan manor house of any size was constructed round a series of quadrangles, and contained a large number of rooms pierced with mullion windows and lined with oak-pannelling. At Paulerbury in Northamptonshire, the home of

[1] *The Squire and his relations*, p. 67

THE FAMILY MEAL
from *The Roxburghe Ballads*

Arthur Throckmorton, such wainscot came from Kenilworth and was set up at a cost of 20s. per yard. Unlike the medieval castle or fortified manor-house of the past, its primary object was no longer war but comfort and even elegance. So, instead of reducing the living quarters to a minimum in order to provide for a defence in depth, there was to be ample space for civilised living. On the ground floor the rooms, which led one into another, would have included a dining-hall and private chapel, the with-drawingroom, the winter and summer parlours, and, of course, the fashionable picture gallery. Overhead were plenty of large bedrooms; and a sprawl of servants' premises at the back consisting of kitchen, pantry, buttery, brewhouse, bakehouse, laundry and dairy, with long dormitories to house sometimes as many as a hundred men and women. At Paulerbury, Throckmorton employed seven female and twenty-four male servants; while Sir Henry Slingsby of Scriven in Yorkshire wrote in his diary during 1638 : 'The number we are at this time in household is 30 persons whereof 16 are men servants and eight women, besides ourselves . . . good faithful diligent servants, so yt at least I spend every year in housekeeping £500.' John Evelyn, however, spoke of his father keeping '116 servants in liveries, every-one liveried in green satin' at Wotton in Surrey; but they were not there simply for display, since such great houses were at once courts in miniature, centres of culture, and hives of industry, providing for an almost totally self-sufficient community. Throckmorton's retainers had included a miller and cooper; and it was the manorial water-mill and saw-mill, the brewhouse and bakehouse, together with the looms and spindles of the women folk that transformed the raw materials, whether grown on the desmesne lands themselves, or paid in kind as rents or impropriate tithes, into the food and drink, the clothes, the farm-instruments and other necessities of comfortable if not luxurious living, not merely to provide for the family itself and their retainers, but to feed and entertain innumerable friends and acquaintances, and possibly even Queen Elizabeth herself if she decided to pay them a visit: a visit that could well prove ruinous however vast the estate or ample its supplies. Normally, in addition to the squire himself, his lady, unmarried children and servants, the mansion might contain several married sons as well, each with his own quarters: a number of families dwelling together amicably under the same roof-tree. During the Great Rebellion Sir John Bramston recorded in his *Autobiography* how his father had welcomed the whole family to the ancestral home at Skreens, near Chelmsford:

> To Skreens [came] my brother and sister Palmer and theire children, the warr beinge sore in those parts where his estate lay. . . . My brother Moundeford Bramston, his wife and children were there alsoe at my father's charge. But the warr continuinge my father found himselfe not well able to beare the charge of soe great a familie (wee were above fiftie); wherefore he required us to contribute toward the table, and to find oats for our horses; fier we all had for noethinge, and hey and grass for our horses. . . . Thus we hearded together for the most part of the tyme after the warr began.

The interiors of these mansions were often most luxuriously furnished, in contrast to the spartan simplicity of a generation or two earlier. For, with the rise of English sea- and trading-power all sorts of foreign goods were now flooding the market and were being bought up by a prospering squirearchy. Throckmorton, for instance, noted in his diary that between 1 January and 13 December 1610/11 he spent some £1,597 17s. 6½d. in furnishings. These might well have included Eastern embroideries, Italian marble statuary and mantelpieces, French tapestries, and Dutch and

Flemish paintings. Heavy home-made oak tables, chairs and carved chests, four-poster beds with their ponderous canopies and soft feather mattresses, silver spoons, candlesticks and dishes, cushions and cupboards, were rapidly taking the place of primitive boards and tressels, truckle beds, forms, stools, pewter and earthenware. Neither was interior decoration neglected.

I have agreed with Christopher Watts, freemason and carver [entered the Earl of Cork in his diary] to make me a very fair chimney, also for my parlour, which is to reach up close to the ceiling, with my coat of arms complete, with crest, helmet, coronet supporters, mantling and foot-pace. . . . He is also to make twelve figures each three foot high, to set upon my staircase.

Most gentlemen had their own deer-parks, and were busy converting their crofts, garths and orchards into pleasances or gardens on the French or Italian model and consisting at first of tall trees, box-hedges and a variety of shrubs set out in geometrical patterns; but gradually the flower garden was introduced, together with gravel paths bordered by long avenues of trees. Neither were orchards, kitchen gardens and herb plots forgotten, which would keep the dinner table continually stocked with fresh fruit or vegetables, and supply the medicine chest with simples :

If you looke into our gardens, [wrote William Harrison] annexed to our houses, how wonderfullie is their beauty increased, not onlie with floures . . . but also with rare and medicinable hearbes . . . so that in comparison of this present, the ancient gardens were but dunghills . . . I have seene in some one garden to the number of three hundred or foure hundred of them [herbs] . . . And even as if it fareth with our gardens, so doth it with our orchards, which were never furnished with so good fruit nor such variety as at present.

Through their letters, memoirs or diaries families like the Verneys, Throckmortons, Cecils, Harleys, Grenvilles, Blundells, Osbornes, Evelyns and Falklands are well-known. Their large and splendid homes, whether at Great Tew or Stowe or Burleigh or Wotton or Claydon, became centres of cultured and civilised living that shed their beneficient rays over the adjoining countryside. Here were men of learning and breeding, who had travelled widely, and often played their full part at Court and in Parliament, in war and in diplomacy. But this kind of family was the exception rather than the rule. A far commoner type was the bucolic squire, who stayed at home most of the year round, hardly ever visited London, and concerned himself primarily in farming his own land, keeping his tenants up to the mark, sitting on the local bench, entertaining his friends and neighbours generously if rather coarsely, indulging freely in the pleasures of the table and the chase, and finding in the Bible, the Prayer Book, and possibly Foxe's *Book of Martyrs* sufficient reading matter for a lifetime. Sir Thomas Overbury sketched his portrait in an essay entitled 'the Country Gentleman' at the beginning of the seventeenth century :

> He speaks statutes and husbandry well enough to make his neighbours think him a wise man; he is well skilled in arithmetic or rates; and hath eloquence enough to save his twopence. . . . His travel is seldom farther than the next market town, and his inquisition is about the price of corn : when he traveleth, he will go ten miles out of the way to a cousin's house of his to save charges, and rewards the servants by taking them by the hand when he departs. Nothing but a sub poena can draw him to London, and when he is there he sticks fast upon every object, casts away his eyes upon gazing, and becomes the prey of every cutpurse. When he comes home these wonders serve for his holy-day talk.

One such gentleman, who was described by his friend Sir Anthony Ashley Cooper, afterwards the first Earl of Shaftesbury, as 'an original in our age', was Mr Henry Hastings, a younger son of the fourth Earl of Huntingdon. Hastings, who lived to be almost a centenarian and died in 1650. He inherited Woodlands Park in Dorset from his wife, where he devoted himself to every form of sport. 'He was', wrote Cooper, 'low, very strong and very active, of a redish flaxen hair, his clothes always green cloth, and never all worth, when new, five pounds'. His fine park was stocked with deer; while near the house were fish-ponds, and breeding grounds for rabbits and pigeons, besides a bowling green. 'He kept all manner of Sports-Hounds that ran, buck, fox, hare, otter and badger, and hawkes long and short winged'. He was also a keen fisherman. In addition to Woodlands he owned the manor of Christchurch and a 'walk' in the New Forest, where he hunted the red deer and angled for fish. 'Indeed', we are told, 'all his neighbours' grounds and royalties were free to him; who bestowed all

his time in these sports, but what he borrowed to caress his neighbours wives and daughters.' Curiously enough this latter addiction
added rather than detracted from his popularity, since he made
a point of 'speaking kindly to the husband, brother or father', and
invited them to treat his house as liberty hall, where they would
always find an abundance of good things to eat and drink. Certainly this was no place to shame their rusticity. The Great Hall
was strewn with marrow bones, its walls hung with the skins of
fox and pole cat; while hounds, spaniels and terriers roamed the
floor, and hawks screamed from their perches. The Great Parlour
was in like confusion, with litters of kittens in the great chairs,
bows and arrows lying in the window recesses, and hunting and
hawking poles standing in the corners. At the upper end of the
room stood a large desk bearing the squire's entire library that
consisted of the Bible and Foxe's *Book of Martyrs*; but also contained dice, cards, backgammon boards, used tobacco pipes, and
green hats with their crowns knocked out in order to hold pheasants eggs, of which Hastings was very fond. Immediately opposite
was an oyster table, 'which was in constant use twice a day all
the year round; for he never failed to eat oysters before dinner
and supper through all seasons.'

Next the Parlour lay a disused Chapel, whose pulpit had been
converted into a larder, never lacking in beef, venison, bacon or
a 'great apple pye, with thick crust, extremely baked'. His table
was, indeed, always well, if cheaply, supplied by the produce of
his own lands or the fruit of his hunting, hawking and fishing.
His friends were quick to note that 'it was good to eat at'; particularly on fast days, when the very best fish then available, both
fresh and salt, were served.

Hastings himself, and this may well have accounted for his good
health and long life, was no glutton or drunkard; and he did not
intend that his guests should be either. The strong beer and wine
were housed in a small closet off the Parlour, 'which never came
thence, but in single glasses, that being the rule of the house,
exactly observed; for he never exceeded in drink nor permitted
it.' On the other hand he did not despise the good things of life,
and was a hearty trencherman, wielding as he ate, a round white
stick to defend his food from the cats that followed him everywhere. At his elbow there always stood a tun glass of small beer,
which he stirred with a sprig of rosemary. On the whole he was a
jolly, good natured man, who was kind and generous to his

servants and familiar with everyone; but with a temper that was quickly aroused, when he would roar away like a bull of Basan, calling his male employees or tenants, 'bastards or cuckoldy knaves; in one of which he often spoke truth to his own knowledge, and sometimes in both, though of the same man.'

Despite his apparent indifference to either morality or religion, he was a stout Kingsman and had his estate sequestrated in consequence during 1641; but secured its return from the Parliamentarians on the payment of a £500 fine. At the age of 80 he was still climbing on to his horse unaided, riding to the death of a stag or fox, and able to read and write without spectacles.

Another squire of a rather different type, but of the same general pattern, was Nicholas Assheton of Downham Hall in Lancashire, who was an equally hard rider to hounds, expert fisherman and bowman, and loved to engage in horse-racing, foot-racing, dancing, dicing and singing. But his brief journal, which covers the year 1617/18, also shows him to have been a strongly religious man of puritanical sympathies, who was constant in his attendance at church or lecture, where in the course of a few months he listened to forty sermons, three of them by bishops. More than once he dined at the parsonage, which he supplied with fish and game; and was not averse to engaging in theological arguments. But none of this prevented him from passing straight from the church to the ale-house, where he would be 'very merrie' or even 'more than merrie', or 'hunting the stagg of a Sunday.' On Sunday, 28 September 1617, he recorded: 'Word came to me that a stagg was at the spring: Walbank took his peece and Miller his, but hee was not to be found. Miller shot with Walbank at a mark and won.'

It was his practice every evening when at home to take what company he had with him after dinner down to the village ale-house, where he stood them and any parishioners he found there drinks. His dinner table was famous, sometimes providing as many as forty dishes, 'forty mess', at one time; and he feasted the King himself when he came to hunt at Hoghton Tower. He drank hard and gambled often. Such entries as the following were not uncommon in his journal: 'July 1 [1617] . . . to Shodeborne; back again: here tipled till afternoon'; 'July 9. To the Ale-house . . . When I laide me downe, I was sicke with drinke'; 'August 19. All the morning wee plaid the bacchanalians . . . Tabled all night'.

But there was another and much more serious and edifying side
to his nature, as when he wrote on 16 February, 1617/18,

> My wife in labour of childbirth. Her delivery was with
> such violence, as the child dyed wthin half an hour, and, but
> for God's wonderful mercie, more than human reason could
> expect, shee had dyed, but he spared her a while longer to
> mee and tooke the child to his mercie; for which, as one of
> his great mercies bestowed on mee, I render all submissive
> hartie thanks and prayse to the onlie good and gracious God
> of Israel.

John Bruen of Bruen Stapelford in Cheshire, of whom we shall
be hearing more in a later chapter, was even more religiously inclined. He neither drank nor gambled; regarded hunting as the
work of the devil; and devoted himself to religious exercises, feeding and clothing the poor, and bringing up his own household, and
such of his neighbours' children who were sent to benefit from his
instruction, in the knowledge and fear of the Lord.

Sir Simonds D'Ewes described the character of his grandfather,
the squire of Coxden in the parish of Chardstock, Dorset, who died
27 June 1611, as follows :

> He was aged at the time of his death about sixty-one years,
> of a most comely aspect and excellent elocution; so that he
> ordinarily gave the charge at all the sessions where he met
> with other Justices of the Peace in the county of Dorset. . . .
> He was a man of personage proper, inclined to tallness, in his
> youth violent and active. . . . Sound and sure he was of his
> word, true and faithful to his friend, somewhat choleric, yet
> apt to forgive, cheerful in his journeys or at his meals, of a
> sound and deep judgement with a strong memory, giving
> good examples to his neighbours by his constant hospitality,
> earnest he was and sincere in the right cause of his client,
> pitiful in the relief of the distressed, and merciful to the poor.
> The misspent time of his youth was, in a great measure,
> recompensed by the laborious studies and practice of his
> maturer years; having little academic learning, but great
> knowledge of the municipal laws of the realm.

In fact D'Ewes then went on to allege that his death was due to
his grief at seeing 'the causes of divers of his clients adjudged
against them, contrary to law and justice.'

At a court leet of his own tenants at Lavenham in Suffolk on 27 April 1631 Sir Simonds assured them that 'I value the love of my tenants beyond my profit' and would do his best to reduce their rents and fines. In return he expected 'a threefold obligation and bond': an oath of fealty, the full and cheerful rendering of all 'the customs or services due unto me', and a punctual payment of their rents and fines. 'So', he concluded, 'I expect three things from you: true fidelity against the backbiter, due presentment against the delinquent and just payment against the defrauder'.[2]

From these various living portraits we may now venture upon a composite one of the average country squire: Like Nicholas Assheton or Sir John Bramston he would probably have been educated at the local grammar school, the university and one of the Inns of Court. Then, like Arthur Throckmorton, who did the Grand Tour of Europe, or Marmaduke Rawdon of York, who visited many strange lands, he would travel for a year or two before settling down in the ancestral home, to help his father manage the family estate prior to its passing into his own hands. His amusements were varied: a mixture of country pursuits and the more sophisticated pleasures he had learned to enjoy at Oxford or on his travels. These included violent but healthy physical exercise such as hunting, hawking and coursing, together with the more placid and time-consuming pastime of fishing. He might well lose more money than he could afford at dice, cards, horse-racing, cock-fighting and bowling. His evenings would be passed either in heavy drinking, dicing and card-playing, or strumming upon the lute or viol, and watching fiddlers and dancers who had been invited into the manor house in order to amuse its guests.

But he could well have a more serious side to his nature: conduct religious exercises every morning and evening for the good of his household, attend his parish church twice of a Sunday, and prove a good friend to the poor, the sick and the unfortunate. He was usually a Royalist and turned out with his tenantry like Sir Bevil Grenville and Henry Hastings to fight for Charles in the civil wars, at the cost often of losing both life and estate like Sir Henry Slingsby.

The squire's lady, besides bringing innumerable children into the world, most of whom did not survive infancy, at great risk to her own life, was expected to supervise the conduct of the

[2] *Autobiography of Sir Simonds D'Ewes*, ed: J. O. Hollinell, 1845. VOL. I, pp. 41-2; VOL. II, pp. 31-7.

whole household, and particularly the kitchen quarters, since dinner played an all important part in the manor's daily round. She must also look after the herb-garden, distill its contents into medicines, and administer them if and when they were needed.

Her boys would be sent to the local grammar school or tutored by a private chaplain at home; but the education of the girls, such as it was, lay in the hands of their mother. Children on the whole were not unkindly treated. Discipline was strict and the rod was not spared; but their's was a healthy, vigorous out-door life, with plenty of servants at their beck and call, and a happy round of varied activity. Certainly parents took the liveliest interest in their offspring and displayed as a rule the greatest concern for their welfare. In the biography of Marmaduke Rawdon of York, for example, we are told :

> His father had once thought to have made him a scholler, and had a livinge promised him of 200 pound a year, nere Barton, in Lincolnshir, which was in the guift of Squier Barton, his mother's brother; but he was, beinge a child, soe extreame studious, readinge night and day, and best pleased when he was pouringe uppon a booke, which was very prejudiciall to his eiesight, which his father percievinge did alter his resolution, fearinge if he should follow that call-inge, he might come to be blinde before he came to be aged.

As a Justice of the Peace, like Sir Nathaniel Bacon, who was J.P. at Stiffkey in Norfolk from 1580-1620, the squire would sit on the bench at Petty and Quarter Sessions, where in return for 4s. a day to cover his expenses he dispensed a rough and ready, but on the whole impartial justice. He was appointed to that office by a Royal Commission, held it only during the sovereign's pleasure, and was expected to take an oath of obedience to the Royal Supremacy. Generally speaking the country squires, particu-larly those in the least urbanised parts of the country like the North and West, turned out with their tenantry and servants loyally if reluctantly, for they were essentially men of peace, to fight for Charles in the Great Rebellion, to provide the material for Rupert's dashing cavalry squadrons, and to hand over their plate to the Royal Mint. A good example of such spontaneous and whole-hearted loyalty is to be found in the conduct of Richard Shuckleburgh, a Warwickshire squire, who, while out hunting one day, ran into the King's Army on its march southwards, joined it there and then, and was knighted for gallantry at the battle of Edgehill.

The squire was the chief authority in his immediate vicinity, exercising control over constables, churchwardens, Overseers of the Poor, and other parish officials. Even the incumbent might well have to look to him for his stipend, and was often treated by him as little better than a superior servant. Should, however, a Laudian rector with an independent mind inflict a rebuff upon his squire, who entertained Non-Conformist sympathies, the latter in reply might well install a chaplain of his own religious opinions, both to officiate in his private chapel and act as tutor to his children.

At special or Petty Sessions, held twice a year, the squire would be mainly concerned with applying the Statute of Labourers and Apprentices; but if a quorum of two or five magistrates was present in addition to the Sheriff's Deputy, then they could in conjunction with a jury try any offences except felony. Normally, however, all major cases were determined in Quarter Sessions against whose decisions there was no appeal. But even a single Justice could exercise a great deal of power on his own responsibility : confiscate flesh in Lent,[3] cause vagabonds to be whipped, gaol sturdy rogues, fix prices, sentence witches, fine or imprison the unruly, and impose oaths on Roman Catholic recusants. On his warrant churchwardens levied fines for absenteeism from Sunday worship; and if offenders persistently refused to pay up he could commit them to prison. But it needed at least two Justices to licence an ale-house or order it to be closed.

The chairman at Quarter Sessions was the Lord Lieutenant of the shire, and he could usually rely upon a quorum of legally-trained J.P.s, since most squires sent their eldest sons to complete their education at the Inns of Court. A knowledge of the law was indeed an idispensable part of any gentleman's equipment in such a notoriously litigious age. They were, on the whole, an impartial, fair-minded body of men, concerned primarily with fact-finding and the administration of the law in a common-sense manner; in no way oppressive, and with considerable sympathy for genuine distress; but none the less prepared if necessary to put the well-being of the local community as a whole, of which they had been

---

[3] A letter from the Privy Council to the Sheriff and Justices of the Peace in Norfolk, dated 10 December 1613, reminded them that in this matter : 'It is required and expected that in your owne familyes and persons you make such demonstrations of conformity herin as may serve for examples unto inferior persons '

appointed the guardians and watch-dogs, above the claims of any particular individual. Nathaniel Bacon, for example, lent a ready ear to the petition of the inhabitants of Holton, who desired that one Bartholomew Barneby, a poor man, should be allowed to build a house on 'a certaine waste peece of ground', which would be 'in no way pejudicall to any person'; although a 'foreigner', George Dowson, who had 'buylt an howse adjoynynge to that waste place' desired it for himself. Foreigners were never popular; and it was alleged of Dowson that he 'is neyther tennent unto yor Wo: nor any way beneficiall unto our parishe, for he payeth all his taske tythes and herboge unto the towne of Halliworthe'.

Yet where their own private interests were concerned Justices were not always so accommodating; and when during the Great Interregnum the power of the Church or the Crown to intervene on behalf of the common man's rights and liberties through the Courts of the Star Chamber and High Commission and thus protect him against the tyranny of the local gentry, had been swept away, together with the jurisdiction of bishop and arch-deacon, and the J.P.s were left supreme and unfettered in their own field, they not infrequently abused their privileged position. Their duties, indeed, multiplied and included among other things : the billeting of soldiers, the keeping of the peace locally (not an easy matter) and the prevention of crime at a time when civil and social unrest, religious strife, and a strong anti-clerical, anti-class spirit was abroad, which took full advantage of an often chaotic situation to create as much trouble as possible. None the less they also found time to feather their own nests. 'England had become an ideal country for the owners of great possessions to live in. The Great Rebellion had been successful to that extent.'

Even in the spacious days of James I private wars were not entirely unknown. Nicholas Assheton related how on 4 June 1617 Sir Thomas Medcalfe, having gathered his retainers together, besieged Raydall House, the home of the diarist's aunt. 'This eveng [5 June]', he wrote in his journal, 'abt sunsett or after, was shooting at ye house, and one Jas Hodgson, one of the rash bar-barians of Sir Tho. coming upon ye house, was shott and slayne.' Eventually the Law arrived in the persons of Mr Midlome J.P., the Sergeant of Mace and a pursuivant from York with their officers, who 'took Sir Tho wth some five or six of his companie; the rest dispersed'.

Certainly the position of J.P. was much sought after, because if

D

its duties were onerous, it carried with it a status that was highly honourable and privileged. In 1603 and again in 1622 the King actually ordered those J.P.s in London : 'to return to their houses in the country so that they might relieve the poor by their ordinary hospitality, take action for the prevention of plague, and keep order in their districts,' a striking proof of the important part they played in local administration, and of their outstanding value to the Government of the day.

In two other respects at least the squire often exercised influence and control over his parish : when he was also patron of its benefice and the lay impropriator of a large proportion of its tithes. The dissolution of the monasteries had greatly increased the number of advowsons in lay hands; for the Tudors had quickly disposed of the booty, including advowsons and appropriations, to their courtiers. But the process did not end there. Many of these men were already in debt, and they sold out cheaply to those smaller gentry and rich merchants, who possessed bursting money bags. Others became involved in treason, when their estates were forfeited and once again thrown upon the market; and some died without heirs, whose property was then divided up amongst a horde of poor relations. The sum result of this vast redistribution of land from 1536 onwards was that by late Elizabethan and early Stuart times a very considerable number of advowsons were in the hands of the squires. Another movement was likewise at work. At first a few men owned many livings, with whose parishes they had little or no connection; but as the nation settled down under the new Eastblishment there was a notable and natural tendency for the squire of the village where he lived or at least owned land, to seek to acquire the advowson and thus reunite it with the original manor.

Canon Law and Common Law were both agreed that it was illegal to sell an advowson apart from the estate to which it was attached, or to make a grant of the next presentation when a benefice lay vacant. None the less there appeared to be no objection, judging from the large number of cases involved which included bishops, colleges and even the Crown as well as private lay patrons, to selling the next presentation or series of presentations during an incumbency. It was, of course, an easy way of making some quick money; and the nearer the sitting parson was to death or resignation, the higher the price. A benefice, for instance, worth only £10 per annum could fetch between £40 and £100 in the open market, where there were always plenty of bidders particularly among the more substantial yeomen farmers and tradesmen.

However, the bargain could sometimes prove disappointing to the buyer, when :

> The jolly old Rector whose death would delight him
> Lived on if only on purpose to spite him.

Such was the case with the vicarage of Beoley in Worcestershire. For when John Hutton of Claines paid £105 for the next presentation in 1616, the then incumbent had already enjoyed the benefice for forty years, but refused to die until 1622! 'Almost all advowsons', writes Dr D. M. Barratt, 'except those which belonged to the Crown or the Colleges, were owned by nobility, gentry or higher clergy. Many of the grantees of the next presentation on the other hand were yeomen, tradesmen and parish clergy.'[4] Most of these last were primarily concerned with providing for a son or some near relative. In 1577, for example, Richard Brokelich was presented to Acton Beauchamp, Worcestershire, by John Brokelich 'agricola'; or Thomas Pridie some five years later to Birlingham in the same county by his father, John Pridie. The squires themselves on the other hand usually had different and worthier motives in mind when they presented; since the age had not yet dawned when the younger son of the manor house automatically took over the family living. They were concerned to find a 'godly' minister, 'a preacher', who could be relied upon to expound the Word of the Lord 'purely', and to bring the spiritual benefits and consolations of true religion, undefiled by corrupt superstitions, to the hearts and minds of their parishioners. Conscientious patrons like Sir Nathaniel Bacon of Stiffkey in Norfolk not only refused to sell their next presentations, but allowed the parishioners themselves to have a voice in the selection of their own parson. Bacon's choice for Whissonett in the fifteen-nineties did not meet with the approval of its inhabitants, seventeen of whom signed the following tactful petition to him :

> We acknowledge great thankfulness . . . that yor worp is pleased to appoint unto us soe worthie and learned a man for or minister and teacher . . . But entringe into a Consideration of or unfitnes for him in regard to the poverty of or towne and or want of howseromth for his intertainement, and

[4] *The Condition of the Parish Clergy between the Reformation and 1660*, p. 375.

ffyndinge not only or Towne but alsoe the Country nere about greatly affectioned to a brother of or late minister Mr Swallow, a man approved unto us to be noe less qualified with good giftes, and furnished wth like faculties, then his said Brother was, whoe in regard he is a single man and is suer to retaine the same Schollers wch his brother had (for that he alsoe teacheth singinge and musicke).

Bacon's reply to the men of Whissonett is unknown; but was probably in similar terms to that given in response to a request from 'yor wrps tenants of Hemsbie', who desired him to appoint that 'zealous protestant' of 'honest parentage', i.e. the son of a constable, John Boulte of Ludham, to assist and eventually succeed their sick incumbent, Mr Green. This declared: 'I shall willingly upon his (Green's) resignation present Mr Boult to you and satisfy yor desires'.

How far Bacon was a typical patron it is hard to decide; but undoubtedly many a learned puritan divine, who would never otherwise have acquired a living at all, did so under James I and his son due either to the patronage of a conscientious Protestant squirearchy, or to the greed of the profit-hunting, hard-headed, business gentleman, who encouraged this unsavoury and near simoniacal practice of selling the next presentations to his livings —a method of money-raising that was abolished during the Commonwealth and Protectorate, when the Trustees for the Maintenance of Ministers and later the Protector himself presented to all benefices previously in the gift either of the Crown, the cathedrals, the bishops, or of those private patrons, who had fought against Parliament and forfeited their estates.

The purchasers of monastic lands likewise succeeded to their appropriated rectories as lay rectors, claiming as of right the major share of their tithes, and allowing the wretched vicars no more than the small tithes, and sometimes only a tiny fixed stipend. In cash terms the clergy as a whole were probably little worse off than they had been under the monks; but the latter at least provided spiritual blessings and material hospitality, whereas their lay successors all too often thought of their new possessions simply in terms of rents and services, for which, if necessary, they or their farmers could sue in the ecclesiastical courts.

It had once been possible to justify tithes by the argument that they paid for communal functions—for the village boar

or bull or dovecot which the priest kept, for the hospitality
and charity which it was his duty to dispense, as well as for
his spiritual services to the community. But no impropriator
could pretend that the community received any return for the
tithes which he collected.[5]

Such a dictum did not necessarily apply to the resident squire,
who farmed his own land, took a friendly interest in his tenants,
was charitable and hospitable to the village as a whole and to his
own parson in particular. Richard Harlakenden of the Priory
at Earls Colne in Essex, for instance, was exceedingly kind to his
Vicar, Ralph Josselin, the son of a Roxwell yeoman, from the first
moment he arrived in the parish during March 1641. Josselin
entered in his diary: 'Well, I stayed with Mr R. Harlakenden
untill Apr. 1641, when we went to board with Mr Edw. Cressener
. . . I began to prepare my house . . . I layd out my £20 and Mr
Harlakenden £20'. The following year the squire was one of the
witnesses at the christening of the Vicar's daughter; and also began
to help him in other and more material ways. 'Sept. 17. 1644.
My good ffreind Mr Harlakenden sold one bagge of hops for mee
wherin I was advantaged £1 15s. This was God's good providence'. Two years later the squire lent Josselin £100 to help him
to purchase 'widdow Bental's' land; and when in 1658 the Vicar
contemplated retiring from Earls Colne altogether because of the
unsatisfactory stipend, he further recorded in his journal:

> Mr Harlakenden of the Priory entertained it very heavily,
> and when I told him I would not leave it for means, he
> offered mee an £100 to apend in 5 yeares as a further
> addition; but Feb. 1. he came up and left against my will
> £50 with my wife, as mine if he or I died, but if we lived as
> an engagement for 2 yeares and halfe until Sept. 29.61, and
> then if he did not purchase £20 yearly and adde to my
> means, if living, he would raise and pay out of his estate
> £20 yearly,—an act of love not easily matcht, evidencing his
> zeal to God and love to my ministry.

No wonder when Harlakenden died the following year, Josselin
declared: 'I buried my deare friend with teares and sorrow and
laid his bones in his bed'.

Such a relationship between the squire and his parson was not

---

[5] Christopher Hill, *Economic Problems of the Church*, p. 135.

infrequent. None the less the contrast between what the lay rector collected in tithe and the miserable stipend he paid to his vicar was often all too glaring. A puritan survey of the Church's plight in Staffordshire during 1604, long after the Elizabethan Settlement had got into its stride, highlights this discrepancy : The market town of Leek, for example, was 'a Parsonage Impropriate held by the most of the parishioners, having bought each one of their own tithes; worth £400 per annum. The Vicarage worth £10.' Here, evidently, the lay impropriator, Thomas Rudyard Esq., had allowed the local inhabitants to redeem their tithes; but in the vast majority of cases they were still in the hands of one man— the squire.

Biddulphe, a Parsonage Impropriate held by John Bowyer Esq. worth £20 per annum. Vicarage worth £10 per annum.

Ellastone : Impropriate to Thomas Fleetwood Esq. Vicarage in the R. bookes £4 12s. Parsonage worth £120.

Mafield or Matherfield, Parsonage Impropriate to Sir Walter Aston, worth £200 per annum. Vicarage in the K. booke £5 is worth £30 per annum.'

In fact practically all these 120 livings were impropriated either to a private patron, a college, a bishop or the Crown; and the small tithes paid to the vicar ranged normally from £8 to £20 a year. Where a fixed stipend replaced tithe it was even lower, in the region of £6. "Barlaston Parsonage. Improp. held by Mr Wells, worth £30 per annum. Stipend £6."[6]

In other parts of the country conditions could be even worse. Leigh in Lancashire was valued at £632 per annum during 1636 by its lay rector; but worth no more than £18 1s. 4d. to its vicar; and two West Country vicars told Laud that whereas their patrons received £400 a piece from their respective rectories, they themselves obtained less than £30 each. Further examples could be quoted almost *ad nauseam* from practically every county in the kingdom; since by 1603 it had been estimated that out of a total of 9,284 livings at least 3,849 were impropriated and most of these were in lay hands.

At one time the puritans clamoured for their restoration, as that appeared to be the simplest and cheapest way of providing the clergy with a living wage and thus secure a well-educated

---

[6] *The English Historical Review*, XXVI, 1911, pp. 338-52.

'preaching' ministry. But experience taught them that the gentry of England, whether Cavalier or Roundhead, would not lightly abandon their rights in this respect any more than they had been willing to restore their monastic lands at the invitation of Queen Mary. For as Archbishop Whitgift shrewdly surmised: 'This is a certain and sure principle that the temporality will not lose one jot of their commodity in any respect to better the livings of the Church; and therefore let us keep what we have; for better we shall not be, we may be worse, and that I think by many is intended.'

By the beginning of the seventeenth century impropriations had become a vast vested interest which cut right across classes, politics and religion; and only a very much more radical upheaval than the Great Rebellion and Interregnum, something along the lines of the French Revolution of 1789 that triumphed over landowners and the Church alike, could have successfully dealt with them. The Long Parliament, which met in November 1640, contained far too many men who owned or profited from impropriated tithes in one way or another to be a convincing advocate of their total abolition; so it contented itself with the destruction of Archbishop Laud and the replacement of one religious order by another, equally intolerant, but geared to the same economic and social system.

Squires, who knew their people well and valued their good will, were not averse to consulting them before choosing a new incumbent; unless, of course, they had themselves incurred personal obligations that they felt bound to honour. A private chaplain or the clerical tutor of his children, who had served their master well in the manor house, had not unnaturally a strong and justifiable claim to first refusal of any advowson in his gift, or in that of his friends. William Child Esq. of Northwick in Worcestershire during the fifteen-eighties recommended the Revd. Robert Hill to his friend Ralph Sheldon, the patron of Tredington Rectory, because 'he did about ten yeares past teache two of my sons', and 'demeaned himself very honestly'. Hill secured the appointment. In the sixteen-thirties Ralph Verney similarly sought to provide for his old tutor, John Crowther, who expressed his grateful thanks as follows:

I understand by your unkle of that care you have taken for me since in seeking to procure for me some convenient place, and that more particularly you have now aimed at my good in preferring me to Mr Poulteney . . . the doctor tells me you have proposed my living with him, under this con-dicion, that he shall give me an advowson of his next living that falls. I know not the valew they are of, nor what age the incumbents are of, but I am persuaded that you will doe the best for me herein, and therefore in this I will repose myself on you.

Often the parishioners themselves would take the initiative and petition on behalf of a 'favourite son'. The Mayor and six in-habitants of Lynn in Norfolk wrote to Sir Nathaniel Bacon, 'This beror [the Revd. William Rooke] a neighbor's child have bene brougyt upp in Lernynge and procedide Mr of Arte in Cambridge beinge very well stayde and of honest behaviour have Requestede us to desyre yor Lawfull favor in helpynge Hym with yor ffavor-able Letter in his behalfe to my Lorde Keper, for a benyfyce called Wigynhall St Marie'.

Neither were the clergy slow in asking for themselves. The Revd. Thomas Doynes wrote to Sir Roger Townsend on 21 November 1622:

My being in Beckles is on the termes of meane stipendarie allowance with to many inconveniences of troublesome stand-ing. My suite is that if god shall give opportunity of a church place by you to be bestowed you will be pleased to thinke on me or myne for my sake and gods especially. Not doubting but that the flocke over whome god shall set hym or me shall have cause to praise god for yowre christian care.

On the whole the Elizabethan and early Stuart country squire, unlike the more sceptical and worldly-wise courtier of the type of Sir Walter Raleigh, was, whether Anglican or puritan, a man of deep religious convictions; a thrifty level-headed business man; a go-ahead farmer, who strove not unsuccessfully to improve and modernise his estate, sometimes by enclosure but more often in co-operation with his neighbours; a housebuilder and layer out of gardens; a conscientious Justice of the Peace; and one who took his full part in country pastimes and pursuits. He was moreover, if not exactly a scholar himself, at least sometimes a man of culture, who collected books and MSS and, like Lord Falkland at Great Tew or the Vaughans of Golden Grove, helped to foster learning

in others by his generosity and hospitality. When Sir Simonds
D'Ewes died in 1650 he left to his heir :

> . . . my precious Library, in which I have stored up for divers
> years past, with great care, cost and industry, divers originals
> and autographs, ancient coins of gold, silver, and brass,
> manuscripts or written books. And it is my inviolable injunc-
> tion that he keep it entire, and not sell it nor divide or dissipate
> it, neither would I have it locked up from furthering the
> public good, but all lovers of learning, of known virtue and
> integrity, might have access to it at seasonable times.[7]

Above all he was singularly lacking in that overwheening family
pride and ostentatious, not to say luxurious living, which was one
of the hall marks of his successors in Restoration England and
caused them to separate as a class from their neighbours. For he
was essentially a simple and homely man, neither unconscious nor
ashamed of his own humble beginnings, who was prepared to
associate freely with both yeomen freeholders and his own tenant
farmers, to treat the clergy with a reverence and respect befitting
their cloth, and to be readily accessible to the poor, whose distress
would at once touch his heart and open his purse strings.

[7] *Autobiography of Sir Simonds D'Ewes*, VOL. II, p. 151.

CHAPTER III

The Churchwarden and His Accounts

THE oldest parish officers were the churchwardens, who had been in existence as early as the thirteenth century. They were the *oeconomi* or stewards, the *guardiani ecclesiae*, whose powers were greatly increased after the Reformation, particularly in Elizabeth's reign; when, in addition to their normal church duties, they became responsible for a vast number of secular matters as well. They were ordered to provide arms for the militia; made responsible for the maintenance of hospitals, roads, bridges, ponds, stocks and whipping-posts; and, assisted by overseers and constables, were turned into relieving officers for the sick and poor, and helped to round up rogues and vagabonds.

In accordance with the Canons of 1571, reinforced by those of 1604, the wardens had to be elected at the annual Parish Vestry Meeting during Easter week, either within or immediately without the church, by the unanimous consent of incumbent and vestrymen, whose principal executors they then became in dealing with church and parish affairs, and to whom they were expected to render an account of their stewardship at the end of their year's office. Should there be any disagreement over their appointment, then the Vestry chose one and the parson selected the other.

None the less such elections often engendered a lot of friction between incumbents and their parishioners. In April 1593, for example, the Vicar of Mansfield, Nottinghamshire, alleged before the Archdeacon's Court that his two new wardens, William Walheade and Richard Wheate, had both been elected solely by the parishioners, although 'the election of one of the churchwardens belonged by law or by virtue of a reasonable and lawful custom to the Vicar for the time being'.

He put forward his own candidate, Robert Spencer gent.; but John Hacket, who acted as proctor for the Vestry, quickly shewed 'that Robert Spencer was not an inhabitant or parishioner of Mansfield or resident there and so was not eligible for the office'. He further claimed that by immemorial custom the wardens were always elected by the parish. Walheade and Wheate were thereupon sworn in as churchwardens. But the following year the Commissioners for Ecclesiastical Causes, sitting in the Chancel of the Collegiate Church of Southwell, decided that for the future six candidates were to be nominated at Mansfield : two by the vicar, and two by each of the out-going wardens; from whom the Vestry would then choose the new churchwardens. This method, however, worked no better. There was another disputed election in 1595; and Mansfield eventually had to accept the ordinary Canonical ruling in this matter. At the end of their year of office the churchwardens were entertained by the Vestry to a sumptuous banquet, known as the Audit Dinner, which must have cost the parish a pretty penny and where the chief delicacy was a calf's head, as at least some small token of their fellow parishioners' appreciation of their arduous labours.

In these last they were sometimes assisted by 'two or three discreet persons' known as sidesmen or questmen; but, judging from an entry in the Childwall Parish Books at the beginning of the seventeenth century, the services of these gentlemen were of doubtful value :

> To ken and see and say nowt
> To eat and drink and pay nowt;
> And when the wardens drunken roam
> Your duty is to see them home.

This final obligation was no means always a theoretical one. At Sutton in Sussex during 1625 it was reported of one of the churchwardens, Robert Ford alias Pullen, that he 'is very often drunke. Since hee was churchwarden, hee was drunke at Petworth, and lay abroad all night in the streete. And little before that he was drunke, and lay all night uppon the hill going to Arrundell, and lost his corne that he was carrying to market'. But the sidesmen themselves were in no better case. The Vicar of Arundel presented one of his 'upon knowledge and without malice', who had been discovered sick and intoxicated 'in the middest of the towne'. As for seeing and saying nowt : Thomas Welpham and John Cramborne, questmen of Climping, were cited in 1628 'for that they did not deliver in a register bill the last Easter, neither have been willinge to joyne with us (churchwardens) in making our presentments this year past'.[1]

Occasionally the churchwardens were drawn from the smaller gentry. As has already been seen the Vicar of Mansfield put forward as his candidate Robert Spencer gent.; and at Crondall in Hampshire Mr Giles Powlett and William Fauntleroy gent. were the wardens for the year 1587. But generally speaking they were chosen from tradesmen or artisans in the towns, and farmers or village craftsmen in the countryside. Women could and did serve as churchwardens. Staplegrove in Somerset appointed a pair of widows in 1645, 'Widdowe Farthinge and Widdowe Shartocke'; while earlier in the same century St Budeaux in Devon regularly chose one warden from each sex. There was no property qualification, and even non-residents who held land in the parish were eligible for election.

It was not a popular office, one more onerous than honourable, which however could not be evaded without incurring considerable penalties. In 1561 the wardens of Spelsbury, Oxfordshire, were fined 'ii stryk of mawlt' for refusing to stand; and Thomas Bowyer of Vinnetrow farm, North Mundham, Sussex, who 'being lawfully chosen by the parish' in 1625 but 'hath since from tyme to tyme refused the office', was cited before the Consistory Court 'as a matter requiring due reformation'. Some five years later the cash fine demanded from similar defaulters at St Thomas Sarum was as much as seventy shillings.

Occasionally it was possible to wriggle out of the nomination on the grounds of some technical disqualification : Adam Arnold of Elston in Nottinghamshire, for example, who was presented 'for refusinge to use the office of a churchwarden' in 1577, successfully pleaded 'that the house wherin he dwelleth ys not charged to serve eyther the office of churchwarden or any other office'; while Edward Wylson of Lowdham in the same county also escaped in 1584 because he alleged that he had no house of his own, lived

---

[1] When another Sussex churchwarden tried to economise by buying up an old Maypole and making it into a ladder for the use of his church, one of his sidesmen, together with a friend, broke into the shed where it was stored in the middle of the night and cut it to pieces. See,*Churchwardens Presentments*, PART I, Archdeaconry of Chichester, xxxix.

with his mother who supported him, and was servant to a certain
Mr George Vaux, who was domiciled outside the parish. Certainly a reluctant warden could often be a hindrance rather than
a help. It was said of William Morley, for instance, who was
'elected and chosen churchwarden' of Sutton in Sussex for the year
1622 'by the mutual consent of the whole parish', that 'after nomination and election the said Morley, being sworne for the true and
due execucion of his said office . . . doth altogether refuse for to
ioyne with the said Richard Beale, churchwarden, his partner, in
the executing of the office, but doth lay the whole burden and
charge on his partner Richard Beale to his great charge, cost and
trouble.'

Theoretically the churchwardenship was of only one year's
duration, but it none the less became customary for the junior
partner to be re-elected for another term, together with a fresh
colleague. Such a two-year term did not, alas, exempt a man from
being chosen again at a later date. In some parishes, to help lighten
the burden, the principal householders agreed among themselves
to serve on a rota basis, whereby each held office once in so many
years; but in a village this was not always possible, and here, for
want of suitable alternatives, a man or a woman might be elected
time after time without the power to decline the honour, if such
it could be called. Certainly as Dr W. A. Pemberton shrewdly
surmised :

> No one would seek the position with any kindling spark of
> enthusiasm; but anticipated with dreadful gloom the day of
> election or turn on the rota, and having been elected looked
> forward with eager expectation to the festive dinner when,
> having emerged from the suffocating armour of responsibility,
> he could enjoy the sumptuous repast with an easier conscience
> and a better digestion.[2]

Inevitably in very small benefices illiterate labourers had sometimes to be appointed, who were incapable of making up accounts.
These had then to be done for them either by the Church Clerk
or the minister himself. A good example of the latter is to be found
at South Newington in Oxfordshire, where from 1579-94 the
Vicar, Oliver Orrell, kept the books in an excellent hand and with
a consistent spelling approximating to modern standards. At the

[2] *Studies in the Ecclesiastical Court and Archdeaconry of Nottingham.*
p. 748.

visitations, no doubt, the Archdeacon's Registrar, in return for a small fee, would write up the presentments, while the wardens added a mark at the bottom of the page against their names. But although the Archdeacon himself might well consider this type of churchwarden socially, intellectually or doctrinally unfitted for his task, yet he had no legal right to refuse him admission to office or to evict him from it.

It was possible for a churchwarden, who possessed sufficient influence or could plead exceptional hardship, to nominate a deputy acceptable to the Vestry to carry out his duties for him. But even in such rare instances the original nominee was expected to serve his own turn at a later date. A churchwardens' troubles did not necessarily come to an end with his two years of office; since during that period he had probably acquired a host of enemies, who were only too anxious to get their own back. For although he was safe-guarded from retaliation whilst conscientiously performing his duties, once he had retired into private life his successors, the incumbent, or any parishioner who felt he had been wrongly penalised under his rule, now had the right to present him in their turn before the Archidiaconal Court. Furthermore, should he have turned a conveniently blind eye on the misdemeanours of his neighbours and some informer thought it worth his while to give him away, then the Archdeacon himself or his deputy could cite him to appear before them on the score of neglect, fine him, or even in a bad case, pass a sentence of excommunication and refuse absolution until his fault had been made good. On 23 August 1585 Christopher Sprawton of Balderton in Nottinghamshire had said, 'that there ys no faltes presentable that he knoweth of'; but at a later date one of the Apparitors named Inkersall alleged 'that the parishioners dyd worke on Swensons bridge upon Sonday the fyrst daye of August beinge the saboth daye', and subsequently Sprawton was fined 20s. for the poor box.

Newly elected churchwardens were sworn in by their rector or vicar in the face of the whole congregation at Morning or Evening Prayer on the Sunday immediately following the Easter Vestry, when they had to subscribe to 'the Othe, which the parsons, Vicars and Curates shall administer' to their churchwardens, namely :

Yow that be chosen churchwardens of this churche or chappelle for this next yere doe swere by God and the holly

Gospell before yow laide that yow shall execute the said office effectuallie and diligently to the advancement of Godde's glorie and the commoditie of this churche and parishe. The Quene's Injunctions and the Ordiniare's monicions ye shall observe, and in so far as in yow liethe cause others to observe; and the violators of the same yow shall duely and without all parcialitie present and detect to the Quene's Highnes Commissioners for causes Ecclesiastical within the Dioces or to the Jurates and sworne men or to the Chauncelor; and yow shall yeilde and give up at the yere's ende a faithefull and true accompte of all somes of money church implementes furniture and bookes as then shall remayne and delyver to your successors. So God you helpe by Jesus Christ.[3]

Then, after they had sworn, the minister solemnly read out to them 'the Quene's Iniunctions and the Ordinarie's monitions'.

Twice a year after Easter and Michaelmas the Archdeacon held his visitations, to the first of which both sets of churchwardens, the out-going and the incoming, were cited to appear: the former to exhibit their presentment bills; the latter to be sworn in, to pay the necessary fees, and to receive from the Registrar, together with a charge explaining their meaning, a book of articles upon which to ground their future presentments. These articles were divided into seven sections, six for the churchwardens and the last for the minister, and dealt in great detail with every aspect of village life. After demanding to know whether the church was properly furnished, the number of recusants recorded, and the churchyard, parsonage house and glebe kept in good order, they went on to inquire into the lives and practices of the parson and his people. Did, for example, the minister perform the statutory services in the prescribed clerical attire, catechise and instruct the youth of the parish, visit the sick, bury the dead, baptise infants, pray for the monarch, and 'diligently drive away all Erroneous and Strange Doctrines contrary to God's Word?' Were any of the parishioners guilty of such misdemeanours as adultery, fornication, blaspheming, swearing, stirring up sedition or discord, refusing to come to church, indulging in unlawful work or recreation of a Sunday or holyday, contending about or erecting pews without a licence, brawling in church or churchyard, and above

[3] *Injunctions of Bishop Barnes of Durham*, (Surtees Society) pp. 26-7.

all : 'Do you know of any that have abused the churchwardens
of the parish, by giving them evil words for executing their office,
or have endeavoured to dishearten them or deter them from doing
it, as by oath they are bound?'

The minister, for his part, was asked whether the wardens had
been properly elected, had presented their accounts, prevented
disorders in church and churchyard, and made out their presentments. Such articles, unlike the queries sent out to the clergy by
the bishop before primary visitations, required no formal replies,
but were simply supposed to provide an official guide to help the
churchwardens in the efficient performance of their duties and to
frame the accusations which they must make at the following
Michaelmas visitation, when they had once again to appear either
before the Archdeacon or his official or one of his surrogates.

The 1571 Canons had ordered the churchwardens to keep their
churches : 'diligently and well repaired . . . that neither the minister nor the people be troubled with tempestuous weather . . .
clean and holy that they be not loathsome to any by dust, sand or
any other filthiness'. From time to time the walls should be
'whited', i.e. whitewashed; the artistry of the Middle Ages carefully obliterated; and then decked 'with chosen sentences of the
holy writ', including the Ten Commandments and the Lords
Prayer. They might also be ornamented with the royal arms,
which were set up in most churches during Elizabeth's reign : At
St Mary's Devizes the church accounts for 1576 contained a payment 'to the painters for writing the X Commandments on the
church wall . . . xvs'; while those of Tavistock recorded during the
year 1567/8 that 'the quenes armes and my Lord of Bedfordes'
had been set up in the church, there, a striking illustration of the
fact that the nobility and gentry were not to be slow in following
the royal example.

In general the churchwardens were expected to 'cleanse' their
churches of all images, altars, vestments, rood screens, and other
'superstitious relics'. The following accounts taken from Mere in
Wiltshire are typical of the kind of destruction that was going on
throughout the country at this time :

1559/61.   for takynge downe of the Rode in the Churche
            . . . vid.
            for warshyng oute of the Rode and the trynyte
            . . . viiid.

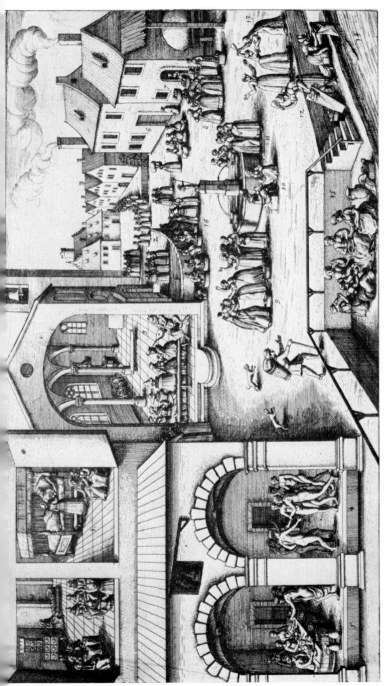

6   THE MARKET PLACE, 1603

A Health to all Vintners, Beer-brewers and Ale-tonners,

Tapsters, Bezlors, Carrowsers, and Wine-bibbers, Bench-Whistlers, Lick-wimbles, Down-right Drunkards, Pety Drunkards, Bacchus Boyes, Roaring-boyes, Bachanalians, Taverne Antients, Captaine swaggerers, Fox-catchers, Pot and halfe-pot men, quart, pint half pint men, fhort winded Glaffe-men, and in generall, to all and every privie Drunkard, Halfe-pot Companion, indenturians, &c.

And to all either Good fellowes of this our Fraternitie, whom these Presents may concerne, GREETING.

K NOW yee that wee Ralfe Red-nofe of Ring-fpigget, in the Countie of Fill-por-lane, together with our deere and wellbeloved Friend, Francis Fiery-face, of the fame Towne and Countie, two of our moft deere and loving Company and Well-willers to any that profeffe any of the fore-named facultie, as well Male as Female, by vertue of our Letters of great permiffion and charge, given

> for lime for the same . . . viid.
> for the defacynge of the Images of the xii
>   Apostles, which were paynted in the Face of
>   the Rode lofte . . . xiid.

1562/3.   for the takynge downe of the Rode loft by the
>   commandment of the Byshop . . . xd.
> for lyme to amende the same place ageyn . . .
>   xvid.
> for the amendynge of the same ynewe . . . iiis iiiid.
> for lathes to amende the Rode lofte . . . xvid.

In South Newington church the images were torn out during 1563 and sold for 22d; while a mason was given 5d. 'for pollynge stones in the churche where the images dyd stand'. About the same date the organ loft in St Martin's Leicester was pulled down, the stone altar removed, one 'yreland' paid xxd. 'for cuttynge downe the ymages hedes in ye churche', and a further xiid 'for takynge downe the angels wynge and remoynge of his fether'.

In place of a stone altar at the east end, a wooden communion table was set up either in the chancel or nave, for which 'a Clevar carvar' received iiis iiiid. In the West Country at Patton, Somerset, reforming wardens were also at work :

1559/60.   for takyng downe the Roode . . . vd.
> In expenses at the plucking down of the Images
>   . . . vid.
> for foldyng the vestments . . . iis.
> for takyng downe the altar . . . iis.

Included in such 'superstitious relics' were the stained-glass windows; but owing to the scarcity of good white glass many of these were suffered to remain, until they fell victim to the zeal of the seventeenth-century puritan. At Toft in Norfolk one 'Ruseles the Glaysher' was paid 1s. 6d. in 1643/4 to take down the painted glass there; and in the same year a glazier of Lowick in Northamptonshire 12d. for putting plain glass into the church windows 'when the Cruicifixis and scandalous pictures' were removed.

Having once cleared their churches the churchwardens must then provide the necessary new furnishings : a pulpit and reading-desk for the minister, a font and communion table, a Bible and

E

Prayer Book, a special edition of the Psalter, Erasmus's *Para-phrases*, Bishop Jewel's *Apologia* and Foxe's *Book of Martyrs*. In conformity with the 70th Canon they were expected to see that a register of baptisms, marriages and burials was kept; and, together with the incumbent, sign their names at the bottom of each page. A copy of each year's entries must also be sent to the bishop for preservation in the episcopal archives. Another indispensable item was the Preachers' Book, where the names of 'strange preachers' could be recorded, and so, if necessary, their *bona fides* investigated at a later date. Order was to be kept in church and churchyard, of which, in conjunction with the incumbent, the churchwardens enjoyed the freehold. But their authority in this respect did not extend beyond the lych gate.

'Vintners and victuallers' should be warned not to open their taverns and shops in time of divine service; any unseemly enter-tainments either within or immediately without the church sternly suppressed; and all unlicensed pedlars, fiddlers, players of inter-ludes, merchants, packmen, beggars and vagabonds rounded up, punished on the spot or presented at the visitation. Their principal task, however, was to ensure that the villagers came to church every Sunday and made their communion at least three times in the year; that mothers were churched and in due course brought their infants to be baptised; and that parents or employers who failed to send their children, apprentices and servants to be cate-chised were heavily fined.

Inevitably, then, they became the village snoopers, nosing out any irregularities, misbehaviours, omissions of duty or unlawful activities, and seeing that the culprits were properly punished : sexual offenders, both before and after marriage; drunkards, cursers and slanderers; those who desecrated the sabbath or holy day; the parish clerk, schoolmaster, physician or midwife who practised without a licence; the petty usurer who sought to extract excessive profits; and anyone who was suspected of witchcraft or sorcery. Perhaps never before or since in English history has village life been subjected to such an unrelenting totalitarian regime, part religious, part political and social, as prevailed during the late sixteenth and early seventeenth centuries, when all activities of body, mind and spirit were wide open to a merciless probing and regimentation, of which the churchwardens were the chief instru-ments. For willy-nilly they must inquire into and supervise every aspect of parochial life from the spiritual ministrations of the parson down to the dubious secular practices of whining beggars and sturdy rogues.

Further more they have left behind them in the income and expenditure items of their Accounts a vivid and accurate picture of what was happening in their parishes, for the benefit of posterity. One of their main sources of income was the church rate, which was levied by order of the Vestry upon all landowners,[4] whether resident or not, who owned property in the parish; and this order included the right, exercised through the churchwardens themselves, of distraining by warrant upon the goods and chattels of defaulters. Those who still declined to pay could if necessary be prosecuted and, if they remained obdurate, excommunicated.

In Elizabethan times many parishes hesitated long before they recognised the need for such compulsion, frantically endeavouring to meet their obligations through voluntary efforts. Hampshire churchwardens' accounts, for example, even as late as 1600 only record one such compulsory order: that at Crondall in 1599, where the parishioners were assessed and rated 'to gyve and allowe a certeyne rate of money yerely towards reparacions and mantenaunce of this church'. But, judging from the receipts in the next few years, its collection proved slow and difficult. This was likewise true of Melton Mowbray in Leicestershire, where some 188 rate-payers in 1596, who had been assessed at sums ranging from 6d. to one penny, produced a total sum of only £4 5s. 10d. between them.

However early in the next reign it had come into general operation in most parts of the country, and had been accepted as necessary if the church buildings were to be properly maintained. During the Commonwealth and Protectorate it became a legal obligation, enforcible through the Civil Courts, whereas formerly it had possessed no statutory authority and was only cognisable in the Ecclesiastical Courts. The primary purpose of the rate was to ensure enough money for the repair of the church fabric, although it could be and usually was used in other ways as well. It was fixed at a special meeting of the Vestry summoned for that purpose by the churchwardens, who, even if no one else but themselves attended, were still empowered to act on their own. In fact to refuse to do so, and to leave their church unrepaired could lead to their own excommunication. The Repton wardens, for instance, who disregarded an injunction of 1595 to replace a number of

[4] At South Newington it was charged at 1s. 4d. per yardland in 1617.

broken windows, were thus punished. The eventual outcome is frankly stated in their accounts :

> Item.   Geven to Thomas Beldde for bryngyng a certyficatt
>   for us being excommunicate . . . viiid.
> Item.   Att Derby when we sartyfyed that our churche was
>   glassed;

and then, presumably, they at last received absolution.

Inevitably there was a good deal of opposition to paying this rate, especially on the part of those landowners not domiciled in the parish, who were sometimes compelled to contribute two or even three times over to separate churches. Occasionally recusants or extreme puritans objected on religious grounds; and others pleaded poverty or disputed the legality of their assessments. To get in the full rate was one of the churchwardens' worst headaches; but get it in they must, for the money was badly needed.

The alms collected at Holy Communion, on the other hand, were used to relieve the sick and poor of the parish. These included the 2d. fee paid by every communicant to the churchwarden on delivering up the lead or metal token, the proof of his attendance, which he had received on signifying to the clerk the week before that he would be partaking of the Lord's Supper. Two entries in the Sarum accounts for 1622/3 and again in 1651/2 record respectively : 'Tokens to deliver to the communicants 12d.' and 'brasse tokens and for a box to put them in and two steele stamps 18s. 2d.' But the 2d. due from every member of a householder's family at Easter from sixteen years and upwards, was the perquisite of the incumbent. Fees paid to the Church at the Occasional Services were very valuable, particularly those from 'pit-money' i.e. burials within the building itself. These graves, known as lairstalls and to which every parishioner had a legal right, were so popular that many churches became little better than pest houses, being packed tightly from end to end with dead, uncoffined bodies in shallow earthen graves. Furthermore as they were constantly disturbed in order to make room for fresh arrivals, it is scarcely surprising that there were recurring epidemics of plague, typhoid or similar diseases among the congregations. Surplus bones displaced by new internments were put into a 'bone-hole' or charnel house in the churchyard. A lairstall, with its lairstone over it, cost 6s. 8d. for an adult and 3s. 4d. for a child; a coffined burial in the churchyard from 18d. to 4s. in accordance with the type of coffin used or the status of the person interned; but an ordinary uncoffined funeral no more than 4d. to 8d. The wardens also received payments for the use of the bells, since knells were charged at the rate of 8d. per three bells; but 20d. for five or more, and an extra 12d. for 'lyenge in ye churche'.

All these fees were, of course, in addition to what was officially paid to the incumbent and his clerk. The passage of an important corpse through the parish likewise required a fee. The Basingstoke accounts included the following items :

1623. Received for the passage of the corpse of a knight ... 6s. 8d.

1627. Received for the passage of the corpse of the Bishop of Bath and Wells ... 6s. 8d.

1631. Received for the passing of Lord Pembroke's corpse through the town ... 6s. 8d.

Such fees as those above for 'buryalles, christenyngs and banes', payable to the churchwardens, began in Elizabeth's reign and continued until the Commonwealth; but the burials brought in far the largest sums. At St Edmund, Sarum, in 1575/6 they totalled £3 14s. 3d. as against 5s. 10d. for baptisms and 4s. 6d. for banns. Moreover these last, together with the wedding offerings, that commenced in 1611/12, and varied from 1s. 6d. to 4s. per couple, were almost certainly voluntary gifts, which were by no means always forthcoming and could not be enforced in any way.

Pew rents were a steady source of revenue to the church; although they could often be a cause of controversy, and occasionally of open violence. They were rented on a graduated scale, and people were seated according to their sex and social status. Front seats were sometimes worth as much as 20s. or 30s. per annum; but the average price was 12d. or 8d. a year, with the seats at the back or in the side-aisles and the forms occupied by the youth of the parish fetching only a penny or two. Much depended upon the preacher. For at a time when church attendance was compulsory on pain of a shilling fine for every Sunday's absence and the sermon was of more than an hour's duration, there might well be a considerable amount of competition for the better and more comfortable seats, and prices were charged accordingly. But at

St Michael's, Worcester, where from 1595 to 1602 some 116 seats were let out for hire, none cost more than 1s. or less than 4d. The seating of the well-to-do could be most elaborate. The Earl of Huntingdon, for example, possessed a pew in St Martin's, Leicester, which was padded all over in red leather and cost the churchwardens xvid; but what rent he paid is not stated. Very occasionally a pew was sold outright, but for life only, and then the wardens were not able to lock its door unless especially licensed to do so.

Included among other small sums taken in church were the offerings for the holy loaf and the holy ale, a medieval custom that was continued in some parishes until the seventeenth century. Bread and ale baked in the Church House were blessed by the parson and then sold by the churchwardens to the congregation at the church door after morning service, who carried away slices of the bread and jugs of the ale to consume in their own homes. In 1560 and again in 1588 the Melton Mowbray wardens entered the following items among their receipts :

for ye holly loaf v sondays in Lent . . .xvid.
Received for the holye loffe in lxii days at iiiid the day . . .
    xxs viid.

As late as 1590 similar entries appeared in the Mere account books; while in 1618 every householder attending St Mary's, Reading, agreed to pay 2d. per head 'for the holle loffe every yere according to the Olde Custome'.

Money, of course, could be realised from the sale of superfluous church goods or 'superstitious' relics, a regular jumble sale of odds and ends : 'a olde lanterne', 'a peece of bellrope', 'an old bible', lead remaining over after 'the gotter was mended', or elm and ash trees out of the churchyard. The roodloft at Northill in Bedfordshire was taken down in 1563 at a charge of 1s. and sold together with the church plate, its chest and some furnishings to the local inhabitants. These last included two 'latten' candlesticks (16d.), a 'latten' pyx (6d.), a 'latten' cross (12d.), an Easter sepulchre and two cruets (14d.).

Copes and other vestments were also disposed of in this way or used for such practical purposes as covering cushions or erecting canopies. 'A cope and a Vestemente and three stooles' from St Ewe's church in Cornwall fetched 50s. during 1598. Bramley in Hampshire received one pound for its medieval challice in

1569/70; and Patton in Somerset, 'for plate being sold by consent of the wardens . . .£xii xiis.'

The hiring out of church property, equipment or furnishings was not uncommon. The Church House itself could be let for private entertainments along with its ovens and brewing apparatus. In many churches the wardens stored garments and scenery for the acting of plays, and often loaned them out to other parishes. Chelmsford, for instance, that owned an abundance of such things, hired them out to Colchester (53s. 4d.), Billericay (26s. 8d.), Walden (10s.), Stratford (£3 6s. 8d.), and Little Baddow (26s. 8d.) between the years 1567 and 1576.

Then there was the church livestock: flocks of sheep and geese, herds of cows and swine, poultry or hives of bees, which devout parishioners had bequeathed to it. Bassingbourn in Cambridgeshire depended very largely for its income upon its cows; St Columb Major owned 'a but of bees with three swarmes' that was very profitable, as also did Culworth and Fordwich, selling their honey locally. Profits from sheep were considerable. At Stoke and Wootton in Hampshire two thirds of their annual income was derived from their flocks; but whereas the Stoke wardens pastured their own, the church sheep of Wootton were let out to a number of other parishioners. Some Hampshire villages, like Bramley and Ellingham, also hired out their kine. Crondall was given a cow by William King that brought in a rental of 1s. 4d.

Substantial revenues were sometimes obtained by renting out church lands and houses. A few acres at Clifton in Bedfordshire during Elizabethan times brought in an income of between one and two pounds per annum. But many such church 'lands', few in numbers, small in acreage and widely scattered, tended to become 'lost', particularly where enclosure was prevalent, the squire a man of substance and influence, and the churchwardens subservient. Houses were safer. Andover possessed at least one cottage that brought in an annual rental of 4s.; while at Wootton the wardens were busily building one in 1565/6 for 'Hewesesys wyfe . . . in ye lane at Ramsdell'. A still better endowment was a financial bequest either for some special object, general church repairs or simply to swell church funds. Thomas Coach, husbandman, of Shillington, Bedfordshire, left 5s. in 1590 'towards the byinge of a decent clothe for the communion table'. There were many more like him among a prospering farming community. From time to time a brief or letter of request might be read in church by the parson to the assembled congregation. This had been issued either by the Crown, the Privy Council, the Bishop or some local magistrate in order to help a particular cause or person : a church destroyed by fire or flood, people stricken by plague or some other natural calamity. Then the wardens would stand at the church door at the end of Morning Service and make a collection, which did not as a rule amount to a very great deal. In 1583 South Newington made such a collection for one, Thomas Browne, and paid the Apparitor 4d. for its 'carriage'. Browne, apparently, was considered a worthy object of charity by the bishops because of 'his honest conversation and special service not many years since to the great benefit of this realm by the discovery of some things and dangers hanging over this state.'

Lastly, but by no means least, there was the church ale. It originated in the holy loaf and holy ale, that, baked and brewed in the Church House, blessed by the rector, sold by the wardens, and carried home from the church door by the parishioners, gradually in Elizabethan times gave place to other more elaborate, and less 'superstitious', social activities, which none the less continued to centre in the church. These ales were usually an annual event either held at Whitsuntide or on the day of the local patron saint, when the parson early announced their coming from the pulpit, invitations were sent out to neighbouring villages, and the festivities themselves were kept up for several days.

Cuchoo kings and princes were chosen, or lords and ladies of the games, ale-drawers were appointed. For the brewing of the ale the wardens brought many quarters of sack out of the church stock, but much, too was donated by the parishioners for the occasion. Breasts of veal, quarters of fat lambs, fowls, eggs, butter, cheese, as well as fruits and spices were also purchased. Minstrels, drum-players and morris-dancers were engaged or volunteered their services. In the church-house or tavern, a general utility building found in many parishes, the great brewing crocks were furbished and the roasting spits cleaned. Church trenchers and platters, pewter or earthen cups and mugs were brought out for use; but it was the exception that a parish owned a stock of these sufficient for a great ale. Many vessels were borrowed or hired from the neighbours or from the wardens of nearby parishes, for . . . provident churchwardens derived some in-

come from the hiring of the parish pewter as well as money
from the loan of parish costumes and stage properties.[5]

People flocked in from near and far, sometimes led by pipe
bands; the church bells rang out; long tables were set up in the
churchyard or on the village green if it were fine, or in the church
itself if the weather turned wet; and then the serious business of
eating and drinking began. 'Well is he', we are told, 'that can get
the soonest to it and spend the most at it, for he that sitteth the
closest to it and spendes the most at it, hee is counted the godliest
man of all the rest . . . because it is spent upon his church for-
sooth.'
When everyone had eaten and drunk his fill, the games and
entertainments followed : races of all types, wrestling, single-stick,
archery, football on the village green and sometimes in the churchyard, traditional plays, and, of course, dancing. Inevitably there
was much drunkenness, some horse-play, and a good deal of general
disorderliness, which gave a handle to the Puritans, who consistently pressed for their abolition. This was finally accomplished
during the Great Interregnum, their place being taken by a
quarterly offering collected by the wardens at the church door
on Easter Day, Midsummer's Day, Michaelmas and Christmas.
Entirely voluntary, in theory, it quickly became, for all practical
purposes, a further assessment or rate on the landed inhabitants
of the parish, and could even be sued for in the courts.
Besides the general church ale, there were also 'bridal ales' to
help celebrate the weddings of those too poor to pay for their own
wedding breakfast; 'clerk ales' to make up the church clerk's
stipend; and 'bid ales' to succour some deserving pauper. Church
ales were certainly very profitable. One held at Mere in 1607
raised as much as £23 6s. 8d. The young men and women
chosen to be 'lords' and 'ladies', 'cuchoo' kings and queens, were
liable to be heavily fined if they shirked their duties. A memorandum attached to the churchwardens accounts of Wing in Buckinghamshire declared :

> . . . that S. Wylliam Dormer knyght . . . with the consent of
> the churche wardens thr beyng and the rest of the parryshe
> have agreed and taken in order that all such yonge men as

shall hereafter by order of the hole parryshe be chosen for to
be lords at Whytsontyde for the behalfe of the churche, and
refuse so to be, shall forfeyt and pay for the use of the churche
iiis.

Every 'mayde', who likewise offended, had to pay xxd. Harry
Kene, who was 'chosen lorde and refused' in 1565 'payde to the
churche' 3s. 4d. Apart from the 1s. due from all absentees from
divine service, there were a number of other similar small cash
forfeits that helped to swell the church coffers. By a sumptuary
statute of 1570, for example, every male of six years old and over,
who was not also a gentleman, was compelled to wear on Sundays
and holydays 'a cappe of wool knit, thicked and dressed in England'; in default of which he could be fined as much as 3s. 4d. per
day, although normally the amount demanded was a good deal
smaller. At Milton Abbot in 1588 the wardens accounts recorded :
'to John Cragge for the fyne of wearing of hats this year . . . xiid'.
Occasionally, as happened in South Newington some eight years
later, the blind eye would be turned; but then, if informed against,
the churchwardens themselves could be cited into court and fined
for failing to do their duty : 'Item. spent at Woodstock when we
were called thither for wearing of caps . . . xiid.' This Act was
repealed in 1597/8.

Many money-making medieval customs lingered on well into
Elizabeth's reign. Hocktide celebrations, which originated in the
Massacre of the Danes on St Brice's Day 1002, continued to be
held on the Monday and Tuesday of Easter week, when first the
men and then the women captured as many of the opposite sex
as possible 'in a merry way', releasing them only after the payment
of a small sum to the church. It should be noted in passing that
in this game the woman usually had considerably more success
than the men. Plays at Christmas, Corpus Christi and on other
festivals were staged in the church nave and were slow to die out;
so too were the morris-dancers, who would tour neighbouring
villages from Whitsuntide to Midsummer, collecting money at
each performance and giving it to their own church funds. They
were usually limited to six men and 'a fool', their bells, shoes and
coats being provided by the wardens. May Day was still kept up
with much of its traditional splendours, as also Midsummer
Night with its bonfires : the profits from the feasting finding their
way into the annual receipts. But gradually a more puritanical

spirit prevailed, and such pastimes were frowned upon as superstitious. Chelmsford, for instance, a great centre of this type of
religious drama, had from the beginning of the fifteen-sixties onwards to set a guard over its stage properties to prevent malicious
damage. In 1562 'a certain Lawrence was paid 4d. for 'watchinge
in the churche when the Temple was adrying'; and after the last
performance of all in 1570 8d. had to be given to a glazier, 'for
mendinge of x broken holes in the church windowes which was
done at the late play'.

A year later Archbishop Grindal was asking in one of his visitation articles: 'Whether the minister and churchwardens have suffered any Lords of Misrule or Summer Lords or Ladies . . . in
Christmas or at May-games or any Morris-dancers . . . to come
unreverently into the church or churchyard and there dance'. None
the less as late as 1595 at St Ives and St Colomb Major in Cornwall the morris-dancers were still active; and the wardens of Great
Marlow, Buckinghamshire, 'received of players for playinge in
the churche lofte . . . 2s. 4d.'

Judging from the long expense columns in most churchwardens'
ledgers their out-goings were even more varied than their receipts.
First there was the cost of the two annual visitations, for which
money was needed to cover their travelling expenses, the making
of their presentments, and fees of various kinds. These last would
include 14s. at their swearing in, plus a further 2s. at Michaelmas,
together with the customary payments to the Apparitors, who
delivered the citations. Next came the Pentecostals, those sums
claimed from each parish by the mother church of the cathedral
as of ancient right. Repairs to the fabric of the church building
itself constituted in most years the bulk of the expenditure. For
they were not only costly, but well illustrated how arduous a task
it was to keep the whole structure, within and without, water-
tight, decent and shipshape. 'Those numerous and necessary items
of the purchase of lead, tiles, slates, glass, iron, sand, stone, lime,
ropes, wire and nails for the reparation of the roofs, walls, windows, bells, bell-frames, doors, benches and pulpits, together with
the cost of the carriage of the same over miles of earthen roads
and tracks.'[6]

The rapidly soaring wages of the craftsmen, who used these
materials, had also to be taken into consideration: glaziers,
masons, carpenters, smiths, plumbers and tilers, many of whom

[6] W. A. Pemberton, op. cit. p. 230b.

might well have to be imported from some neighbouring town, thus inflating their value.

Then, as has already been noted, good money had to be paid away in order to 'cleanse' the church's interior of its superstitious relics, to white-wash its walls and refurnish it with the necessary articles and ornaments prescribed by Authority. The clerk must be paid his quarterly or half-yearly wages and the bellringers provided with ample quantities of ale to sustain their strength and interest. Undoubtedly the bells figured largely in the accounts in one form or another : whether for repairs to existing ones, the installation of new-comers or for their ringing on local and national occasions. Queen Elizabeth expected all bells to be rung on her birthday and day of accession, and indeed for every important event during her reign such as victories or the births and deaths of famous people. At Minehead in Somerset it was recorded in February 1586/7 : 'Ringers for joy when newes reached us of beheadinge of quene of scottes . . . xiid'. Nearly sixty years later the ringers of St Benedict, Gracechurch, received 2s. 6d. for a merry peal in 1642 : 'when the bishops were voted downe by Parliament'.

Normally, however, they were kept busy on local matters : ringing for the regular services, weddings, knells and funerals; welcoming visitors to the church ales or marking unusual happenings in the parish. In the year 1646/7 3s. 6d. was paid out by the wardens for 'ringinge the race day that ye Erll of Pembroke his horse woon the cuppe.'

Among other small items of interest in most church accounts are the frequent entries for repairs to clocks and sundials, and the provision of the all-important hour-glass in the pulpit, which cost about one shilling.

On 'sacrament Sunday' the floor and pews of the church were strewn with fresh rushes; while on Christmas Day, Palm Sunday, Easter Day and at Midsummer boughs of box, yew, rosemary, bay, birch and holly, together with such flowers in season as roses, lillies and gilly-flowers, must be provided to 'garnish' it. The practice continued even after the Puritan revolution, for although the great festivals were now abolished, the Roundheads were only too pleased to strew herbs and hang up garlands and flowers in the church in order to celebrate their days of victory or humiliation. The wardens' accounts at St Petrock in Exeter read as follows :

1615. for bys and flowers in church . . .2s.
1634. for flowers and herbs in church . . . 1s.
1645. for rosemary and bay to put aboute the churche at
Christide and Easter . . . 2s.

Furthermore sweet-smelling herbs, frankincense, benzoin and juniper were greatly needed to fumigate what otherwise would have become an intolerable church atmosphere, which was composed largely of the odour of closely packed unwashen humanity and freshly interred, uncoffined, corpses decomposing in shallow earthen graves.

The annual Rogationtide perambulation, encouraged by Archbishop Laud, required a generous allowance from church funds for bread, wine and ale. The little Nottinghamshire village of Upton-by-Southwell was typical of many another when it inscribed in its account books :

1604. for bread and ale in Rogation week 1s. 8d.
1615. paide for bread and drink in Procession week 5s.
1616. for breade and drinke at the perambulation about ye
feildes 6d.

The South Newington ledgers contain some very similar entries :

1600. Item for bread and drink at the Rogation day . . .
12d.
1589. Item to John Eedes for drink bestowed on the Rogacion week . . . 20d.
1598. Item for bread and ale at church in Rogacion weeke
. . . 2s.

Another item that constantly recurred in the expense columns was the bread and wine required for the Communion service : for the best wheaten bread and fine fermented wine had to be provided by the wardens if not once a month then at least quarterly. Usually enormous quantities of wine were consumed. At Exning in Suffolk the wardens 'paide for bread and a gallonde of Malmessye agaynste Easter Daye' 1590; while the communicants of Hartland in Devon drank as much as twelve gallons and a quart of canary during Easter 1614. The wines most used were claret, malmsey and muscatel. Sometimes an odious distinction was made between the rich and the poor : the masters and mistresses imbibing a rich and expensive muscatel, while their employees and families had to make do with a cheap and nasty claret. How-

ever, when 'sacrament Sunday' only occurred three or four times
a year, provision was often made out of the rates to give the old
folk attending it a dinner. Leek in Staffordshire used regularly
to pay out 7s. for seven such meals.

Most parishes, too, could produce a miscellaneous list of small
out-goings which all help to light up the picture of village life at
this time : the payment of 3s. made 'to the strange singeing man
of Steple Ashtone yt dyd labour for the S'vice'; the 7s. 4d. set
aside to clothe the organist in 'a coat and a pair of hosen'; the six-
penny piece given 'to John Baillie for whipping dogges forth of
the church'; the sum of 11s. 6d. collected and 'payd unto the
waytes at Christmas for a carroll'; the xvid 'payde for the ingoing
to Burfield to the cunnyng woman for to make enquire for the
communione clothe and the ii outher clothes that were lost out of
the church'; and the well-spent vid earned by 'Goodwyfe Wells'
'for salt to destroy fleas in the churchwardens' pew.' The churchwardens were also responsible for seeing that the necessary instru-
ments for a penance were forthcoming when they were needed :
namely, 'a convenient large sheet and a white wand to be had
and kept within your church and vestry to be used at such times
as offenders are censured for their grievous and notorious crimes'.

As part of their more secular duties they must enforce the
Vermin Act of 1566 (8. Eliz. c. 15), which meant buying a parish
net to catch predatory birds such as crows, choughs, rooks, hawks,
buzzards and ravens; compelling landowners systematically to
destroy 'noyfull fowles and vermyn'; and making the necessary
public funds available for rewarding those who brought in the
heads of proscribed birds and animals, 'to be burned, consumed
or cut in sunder before the churchwardens and taxours'. The
payments ranged from one penny for the heads of three to twelve
small birds and another for 'everie syxe egges of them unbroken',
to a shilling for a fox's head. This Act, renewed in 1572 and
again in 1598, was vigorously enforced in the countryside where
so much valuable food could easily be lost from the inroads of
such pests. In some places like Bishop's Stortford a permanent
vermin destroyer was employed by the parish and paid according
to results. Between 12 April 1569 and 12 April 1571 Edward
Waglley received £2 12s. 7½d. in exchange for 141 hedgehogs,
53 moles, 6 weasels, I polecat, 1,476 mice, 80 rats, 202 crows'
eggs, 128 magpies' eggs, 154 crows' heads, 24 starlings, 5 hawks
and 5 kingfishers. In the West Country foxes were so numerous

that a professional catcher had to be employed. At Tavistock in 1566/7 'kyllyng of foxes' cost xs; and seven years later had risen to xiis for the half-year.

Under the Great Statute of 1597 responsibility for poor relief was placed fairly and squarely upon the shoulders of the church-wardens, assisted by four Overseers, who were empowered to raise funds by a compulsory rate, and ordered to keep an account of the disbursements in a special register. In most cases payments were made in money, but sometimes in clothes, food or firing. At South Newington, for example, there were a number of entries specify-ing that help was given in the form of such things as boots, shoes or a coat. Licences to beg, passports enabling their bearers to proceed from one place to another, certificates of character and letters of request for charitable assistance, were issued to all sorts of people including widows, maimed soldiers returning from the wars, vagabonds of every type, poor wandering scholars, poor ministers and Irishmen. Sometimes a needy person could make a collection in church. At South Newington an item of 4d. is entered in the 1597 out-goings as having been so collected by 'a poor woman who gathered in the church on St Simon and St Jude's Day'.

In many parishes the churchwardens were responsible for the communal armoury, which was often housed in the church itself. Between 1559 and 1581 there are several references to it in the wardens' accounts for the Hampshire villages of Ellingham, Wey-hill, Stoke and Crondall:

for scorynge of the tythynge harnesse . . . 1s. 6d.
towards making the butts . . . 5s.
buyinge of a tithinge harness . . . 15s.

The Bedfordshire village of Shillington is remarkable for the number of hospitals it supported, most of them originally founded for lepers, from Cambridge to Canterbury, including of course the local one at Dunstable. Collections were also made for prisoners in the country gaol, besides those in the London prisons of the Marshalsea and Queen's Bench, in accordance with the statutes of 1572 and 1597/8; not forgetting another of 1592/3 directed towards helping maimed soldiers.

On the whole the Elizabethan and Stuart churchwarden received far more kicks than half-pence. During his two-year's office he would be kept so busy maintaining law and order that he could have had but scant leisure for his own business or domestic concerns; yet he earned much more abuse than thanks, and sometimes violence or the threat of it. Joan Lewer of Slinfold in Sussex, 'a malicious and contentious woman' caused 'the unjust vexacion of George Fearne, one of our churchwardens, in abusing him in his speeches; caling him beggarly and runnagate knave and otherwise scorning and mocking at him, his wife and children'.

John Cooper, a so-called 'gentleman of Felpham', told one of the sidesmen the following year that he would 'spend his blood with him'; while another man named John Bennet challenged a warden of Bramber, John Lutman, 'to come out of dores if thou darest' and fight him. At Coldwaltham the churchwardens were actually waylaid in the churchyard by a furious mob of parishioners, led by Thomas Smyth and Roger Brookfield, who 'did give us the churchwardens evill speeches'. It was certainly no joke to be a conscientious churchwarden or sidesman.

Bishop Redman's Visitation Returns of 1597 tell us, for instance, how careful he had to be in making up his accounts lest he should give an occasion for offence: At Heacham in Norfolk William Joyner and William Noake, churchwardens, were presented 'for not geveing upp a sufficient accompt'; and it was alleged of William Andrewes of Cromer: 'He was this last year's churchwarden, but hath not given up' i.e. his accounts. The sins of husband and father could even descend upon his luckless wife and family: Elizabeth Harte of Bradfield in Suffolk, 'lately relict of William Marret, lately churchwarden' was accused of 'witholding xiii part of the church stock'; and Thomas Gooch of Mettingham in the same county, 'administrator of his father's will', was taxed with 'detaining vii and more of the church stock, which was taken forth by the deceased when he was churchwarden'. In each case the facts were strongly denied and the accused dismissed by the Consistory Court, which no doubt felt morally obliged to uphold its parish officials against vindictive neighbours and even the parson himself.

In 1584 William Horne and Robert Chamberlyn, gardianos de Wootton in Oxfordshire, were charged with 'not presenting of evell rule done in the church by the Lord and Lady on Midsomer day'; to which they replied: 'that theare was noe lord or lady this yeare in Wootton parisse, but on Midsomer day laste at evening prayer the youthe were sumwhat meerie together, in crowning of

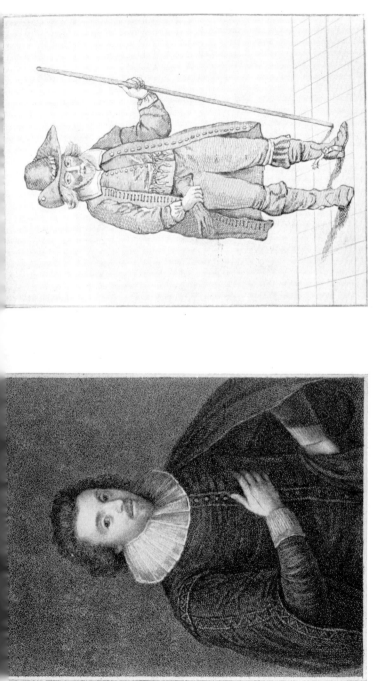

8 NICHOLAS FERRAR

9 HENRY HASTINGS

10 PAGE FROM THE CHURCH REGISTER OF APPLETON IN BERKSHIRE COVERING THE YEARS 1589 TO 1593

lordes, and otherwise they knowe no disordre at all'. Their plea was accepted and the case dismissed. So too was that brought against John Dancaster and Hencruffold, 'gardianos de Sowthstooke', for supposedly 'sufferinge dauncinge in the churchyard and digging thereof wth swyne'. In 1608 The Archdeacon of Oxford received the following articles made out by the Reverend Richard Jones, curate of Towersey, against his wardens, John Thornton and Philip Barnard :

> Imprimis the sayd John Thornetone hath misuseth me the Curat of Towersey beinge a minister of the word of god and a bachelere of arts by callinge me jackesauce and welsheroge . . . callinge me yow saucie pratlere . . . because I had takene the reversione of the wyne that remayned aftere the communione the sunday before . . .
>
> Item. that he on most sundays and holy dayes from christmas to Easter had gamesters playinge cards in his house . . . they played there and com not to churche afore I had read the 2 lessone. . . .
>
> Item. In the wintere tyme did put one his hatt in the tyme of divine service and suffered others to do the same. . .'

Other accusations included their failure to provide a carpet for the communion table and a chest for the Vestry; while the 'church mounds are not made accordinge to the lawe'. However, on investigation it was discovered that all this was in retaliation for the churchwardens' presenting him for not wearing a surplice and not holding services on 'Saynt lukes even and saynt lukes day and weddensedaye fredaye and satarddaye followinge'. The parson at Graffham in Sussex was more disinterested when he presented his two churchwardens, John Even and John Philpe, in 1621 because

> . . . uppon Sunday the second day of September last the said churchwardens in the afternoon, in tyme of divine service and the sermon, took away the keyes of our church-dores; and after evening prayers were ended, being demanded the keyes by the minister and parson of the church, they would not restore them, but they took away the keyes . . . and the bookes out of the vestry and left them at a lawelesse alehouse over against the church; and they left the church dore open from Sunday at night.

Certainly their conduct was not always impeccable: Thomas Hopkins and Richard Pawling, 'gardianos' of Great Bourton in Oxfordshire, were caught red-handed 'bowlinge and dauncinge in the churchyard'. They admitted the bowling but denied the dancing: 'that sume tymes they doe use to boole in the church-yard, especialie in Whitson weeke, but for dauncinge there hath beene none at all'. Even worse was the behaviour of the Caver-sham wardens, John More and John Whithill, who were found to be 'sufferinge a howse of bawdrie,' or that of their counterparts at Duns Tew, John Castell and Robert Mesie, who were 'keping interludes and players in the churche, and brawling in the churche abowte the same wth one old Polton . . . and allso for shoting and gamning in the churcheyarde upon theire wake-daye at evening prayer'. It was this very kind of thing, of course, which they were commissioned to prevent.

Elizabethan women, as has already been noted, and their Stuart sisters could, when roused, be equally violent both with their tongues and their hands, particularly in standing up for what they believed to be their rights. This was particularly so, as the churchwardens found to their cost, in the matter of their seating in church. The exchanges between Margaret Smyth and Ann Cripps in Blackthorne Church, Oxfordshire, were kept com-paratively civil. Margaret claimed that Ann had usurped a pew that really belonged to her father-in-law, Geoffrey Smith, but had not been used because his wife was dead. Ann retorted that she had sat in that seat for thirteen years and that it went with the house she lived in. However, on the churchwarden's advice, rather than create a scene 'she departed the church and used noe words'. In return she was allowed to continue sitting there 'untill she heare further' i.e. the whole matter had been thoroughly investigated.

At St Nicholas's Church in Oxford, on the other hand, one of the wardens named Gibbon appeared to treat a certain Marga-ret Ridley in a high handed manner when 'he came to her in the churche and there placed ii othere boddies into her seat and saithe that . . . iii did ever sett in the said seate'. No doubt Mr Gibbon was pressed for pew-space and made the best use of what he thought was reasonably available; but Margaret's wrath is none the less understandable, and there was some sort of scene, although she later pleaded 'that she did not contend at enytime in the churche'. Other ladies, who did so contend, were Elizabeth Robins, Emma Comber, Margery Hopkins and Barbara Nicholles of St

Ebbe's, each laying claim to the same pew as 'belonging to her house'. Emma was accused by Elizabeth of 'casting forthe of her seat her matt and would not suffer her to entre in'; while Barbara, refusing to give way to Margery, was told 'yf yowe will not let me come into mye owne seat I will sit upon your lappe'. There then followed 'words of inconvenience' between them 'as whore and basterd and such lyke'. All four ladies were subsequently presented and cited into the Archdeacon's Court; where also appeared George Grigge and his wife of Eastergate, Sussex, who in 1623, or so the churchwardens alleged, were 'letting out seates in our church and taking money for them and for placing girles in theire seates and therby displacing ancient men an women'.

It was a rough and irreverent age where a word could rapidly be followed by a blow even in the most sacred of edifices or at the most solemn of services. When Stephen Smith, churchwarden of Burford in 1584 reproved Walter Graingeman 'for his lewd behavoiur in the church', he received a buffet on the ear for his pains; and in Acaster church, after a reprimand, Simon Tanfield 'a drunkarde drue his knife and porred with it at Ambrose Jackson'. It was of course the churchwardens' job to put a stop to any such brawling whether in church or churchyard, and in this they were usually assisted by the incumbent. It is to be hoped, for example, that they went swiftly to the assistance of the curate of Deighton, who, when he rebuked Robert Fubarn and Christopher Hudson for bowling in the churchyard, was attacked 'and bett . . . grevowslie'. Behind them stood the Ecclesiastical Courts, which were prepared to punish abuse and shouting by suspension, and to excommunicate if an affray developed. This alliance between the parish priest and his lay officials, however, sometimes broke down over the question of churchmanship. In five Norfolk and sixteen Suffolk parishes, towards the end of the sixteenth century, the churchwardens discovered that their puritanical incumbents were encouraging lay preachers, for which they were promptly presented : At Blyford William Skott, a blacksmith, held forth without either surplice or Orders; and in Levington Church, under the auspices not only of the parson but also of 'Mr Richard Brooks gent', a certain 'John Skete, he being a laye-man and a wever by occupation serveth the cure and readeth devine service'. The parson himself did not always wear the surplice, a parish garment provided out of church funds. On one famous occasion the wardens forcibly clothed him in what they rightly considered to be an official garment, and for whose provision and use they were primarily held responsible. Sometimes the boot was on the other foot. It was the conformist Anglican rector, Alexander Huish, who compelled his puritanical wardens, Wheeler and Fry, to put back the communion table in the east end of the church 'where the Altar did stand'; but not until they had first been excommunicated and imprisoned. Eventually compelled to submit, they had to perform a public penance in their own church of Beckington, Somerset, at Frome and in Bath Abbey. That was in the sixteen-thirties; but some years later an Ordinance of the Long Parliament commanded all churchwardens "to demolish all altars and tables of stone : to remove communion tables from the east end to the body of the church, taking away rails and levelling the chancel'. This last order referred to the steps leading into the chancel from the nave; and some puritan-minded churchwardens were especially zealous in carrying it out. Richard Durden of Radwinter, for instance, a particularly sharp thorn in the side of his vicar, Richard Drake, was one of them. Without in any way consulting Drake he removed 'the communion table, which anciently stood above the ascent in the chancel . . . and set it below the steps, crowding one end into a hole and close to the north wall, so that the parson could not stand at the north end thereof, according to law to officiate'.[7]

He also refused to supply bread and wine for the monthly communion, which he regarded as a popish practice. He further suggested to Drake that he should appoint a curate of his, Durden's, choosing and pay him a £100 per annum out of his own pocket. Naturally the vicar refused such a request; whereupon he was subjected to more persecution. 'On 21 September', wrote Drake in his Latin *Autobiography*, 'Richard Durden took away the church door keys and so hindered the parson from coming to church to read divine service that day, being the feast of St Matthew, and so all the week after; which he is bound by the rubric to read daily and which he did till thus interrupted'.

Finally on 15 January 1642/3 matters came to a head when Drake was literally and brutally thrown out of his church, and Durden locked its doors :

'19 February, Being Sunday, in the morning the keys of the church door being in the possession of Richard Durden,

---

[7] H. Smith, *The Ecclesiastical History of Essex*, pp. 70-3.

the door was not opened nor a bell tolled, and so no service nor sermon, notwithstanding Mr Smith and Tho. Banes pressed that the congregation being met should not be disappointed.'[8]

Some few years earlier the boot was very much on the other foot in the case of the puritanical churchwarden James Wheeler of St Botolph's, Colchester, who was ordered by Dr Aylett, the Commissary, to rail in the communion table. But this he refused to do 'unless Dr Aylett would save him harmless'. 'For this [attitude]', ran his widow's petition to the House of Lords in February 1640/1, 'he was twice excommunicated and then the High Commission sent a messenger named Stockdale to apprehend him'. Stockdale, rightly anticipating trouble from Wheeler's many supporters in the parish, first enlisted the strong arm of the Mayor, Robert Buxton, 'who caused Wheeler's house to be broken up and ransacked'. That was done twice, and on each occasion apparently without a warrant. Wheeler himself fled into hiding, but two of his children were carried before the Mayor and imprisoned for three days and nights before being released on bail. Eventually the wretched churchwarden was caught, 'driven from his calling whereby he maintained himself and his family', imprisoned for three years, and then obliged to flee to Holland where he died, 'leaving his family ruined'. However, his widow's petition succeeded and both Aylett and Buxton were compelled to pay heavy damages.

Such incidents show at once to what extremes each side was prepared to go in the turbulent years immediately preceding and following the Great Rebellion, and of the ill-feeling existing between the parson and his people, even his own lay officials, at that time. There are well authenticated stories of wardens who personally led attacks on the parsonage and were formost in the rabbling of their incumbent and his family; but also of others who bravely stood by him and even hid him during these troublous years.

By-and-large the churchwardens in this period of change and upheaval shouldered their manifold burdens courageously, conscientiously, and, when not carried away by the heat of religious fervour, impartially. Certainly both Church and State found in them, as in the Justices of the Peace, a type of voluntary but indispensable service that was essentially English in its homeliness and lack of formality, yet functioned with remarkable smoothness and efficiency whether under the Crown, the Commonwealth or the Protectorate.

APPENDIX I

In making up their accounts churchwardens had to be particularly careful lest they be charged with undue extravagance during their year of office. There was an interesting case of this at Chingford in Essex, when in 1636/7 the parish, i.e. the select Vestry, criticised certain expenditure by the wardens and incumbent as unnecessary, and refused to pay for it.

The churchwardens produced the following expense sheet :

The accompt of John Burnett, churchwarden of the parish of Chingford, for his expenses about the church and chancell; for bread and wyne for the communion, for the maimed soldiers and for a new communion table and for rayles and barresters, from Easter 1636 until the fiveth of June 1637 :

Imprimis. for his oath, two books for the fast and charges at the two visitations . . . 10s. 8d.

And for a latch for the church gate, for whipping dogges out of the church, for glasing windows and for the paritos ffee . . . 4s. 7d.

Item. to the mayned souldiers and for searching a dead corpse . . . 10s. 6d.

Item. for a peece of tymber used about setting the communion table . . . 10s.

Item. for bread and wyne spent at communion . . . £2 0s. 3d.

Item. payd for a communion table . . . £2 0s. 0d.

Item. for rayles, ironwork and 2 deales and setting up . . . £5 3s. 0d.

Item. for tyles and carriage and for lime and sand . . . £2 5s. 6d.

Item. to the bricklayer and labourers for laying ye tyles in ye chancell . . . 11s. 6d.

Item. to the bricklayers for a day's work about the church, 5 junii . . . 1s.

summa . . . £14 6s. 8d.

To which Accounts the Vestry appended this memorandum :

> The exceptions to the accompts by the parish : ffirst for the communion table and rayles he bought without advisinge with the parish, and being surveyed by workmen they give under their hands that the table which he gives in the cost xls is too deare by xs. That the rayles which he gives in with two deales to cost £5 3s. 0d., that they are to deare by xxxvis iiid. The expense for tyles lyme and sand and workmanship was as well for beautifying the chancell as to erecte ye table, and ye bigger halfe of the chancell is without the rayles and ought to be done at the parson's charge . . . the moytie of which charge come to xxviiis vid. Soe the rest of the accompte allowed, and allowing him . . . and the two deales unspent for setting up the rayles, the remainder for which a Rate is made, comes to :

> £10   11s.   10d.

> (signed)   The mark of : Robert Leigh, Francis Tavener, John Burton, Robert Sawyer, John Young, John Gladwin, Robert Snell, Francis Hopton, Edmund Tewe, Tho. Gondrey, Walter Searle, William Dodson.

All these gentlemen, of course, were members of the select Vestry and substantial rate-payers.

APPENDIX II

The following case of the presentment of the churchwardens of Yedingham in Yorkshire, John Cooper and George Bell, by the curate, John Marshall, and their subsequent prosecution, conviction and sentence to perform a public penance in 1638, is of interest as showing that even at the height of the Laudian reforms gross irreverence even by church officials was by no means uncommon. For this was certainly no isolated or unusual offence. Many other instances might be quoted.

John Cooper's penance, as deceed by Chancellor Easdall, ran thus :

> 28 April 1638. A declaration of penance appointed to be done by John Cooper one of the churchwardens of Yeding-

ham of the dioces of Yorke. He is appointed to be present in the parish church of Yeddingham, aforesaid upon Sunday next comeing, where imediatly after the readinge of the Second lesson for morninge prayer, he shall stand before the place where the Minister readeth prayers, and say after him, with an audible voice, as followeth :

Whereas I (good Neighbours) forgetting and neglectinge my duety to Almighty God, the humble and reverent respects due by every good Christian to his heavenly Majesty and the blessed Sacraments of the lords Supper, did immediately after the holy Communion was ended in the Churche upon Easter Day Last, goe up to the Communion table and in undecent manner take parte of the consecrated bread and eate the same and did take some of the consecrated wyne remaineing, and spill parte thereof upon the ground, and carryed other parte thereof away to my owne house. And did bringe the bread provided for the said holy Communion undecently in my pockett to the Communion table, and there pulling forth the bread sett the same thereon to the great offence of Almighty God and the Congregation then assembled the dainger of my owne Soule and evill example of others. I am hartily sory for my saide offences, and desire Almighty God and you my Neighbours here present to forgive me, and you to take example by this my punishment, and here I promise never to offend in the like againe.

CHAPTER IV

The Parish Clerk
and other Village Worthies

THE office of Parish Clerk was likewise a very ancient and honourable one. Bede tells us that it dates back to the time of St Augustine's arrival in Kent, when a letter from Pope Gregory concerning the order and constitution of the newly founded Church made certain regulations about the Clerk's marriage and way of life; while King Ethelbert decreed that any property stolen from a Clerk must be restored threefold. The office at that date ranked of course as one of the minor orders in the Church, and the Clerk was expected to assist the priest in most of his duties, including the regular church services. One of the Canons promulgated by King Edgar bade each priest come to the Diocesan Synod attended by his Clerk.

By the thirteenth century the office had become a freehold, with specific fees and duties attached to it. 'In every church', runs an injunction of Bishop Grosseteste of Lincoln, 'which hath sufficient means there shall be a deacon and subdeacon, but in the rest at least a fitting and honest clerk to serve the priest in a comely habit'. Licensed by the Ordinary he was normally appointed by the incumbent, but paid by the parishioners; who, however, might sometimes demand a voice in his election. In the fourteenth century John Athon recorded a case where 'the clerk appointed by the parishioners against the command of the priest wrenched the book from the hands of the clerk who had been appointed by the rector and who had been ordered to read the epistle by the priest, and hurled him violently to the ground drawing blood.' He assisted the parish priest in a variety of ways such as ringing the bell for the services, leading the people in their responses, sprinkling them with holy water, and always preceded the incumbent, carrying a lighted candle and ringing a bell, in the visitation of the sick. He might also read the Epistle and Lessons; and, if literate, keep the village school. The clerkship, indeed, was often the first step in the career of a promising young scholar, who was aiming at the priesthood. The famous fifteenth-century canonist, William Lyndwood, wrote of him in *Provinciale Anglicana*:

> He is a clerk not therefore a layman, but if twice married he must be counted among laymen, because such a one is deprived of all clerical privilege. If, however, he were married, albeit not twice, yet so long as he wears the clerical habit and tonsure he shall be held a clerk in two respects to wit that he may enjoy the clerical privilege in his person and that he may not be brought before the secular judge. But in all other respects he shall be considered as a layman.[1]

At the Reformation, when most minor orders were abolished, the clerk's office increased considerably in prestige, since in effect he gathered to himself the combined rôles of sub-deacon, acolyte, door-keeper, exorcist and rector-chori. He shared with the incumbent the right to wear the surplice; read the Epistle at Holy Communion, and the lessons at Morning and Evening Prayer; led the people in the singing of the metrical psalms; and was responsible for seeing that the church, its furniture and ornaments were kept: 'faire and cleane . . . against service-tyme'. He might even be asked to catechise the younger children on a Sunday afternoon. 'If', as Archbishop Grindal pertinently reminded his clergy, 'he be able to do so.' He continued very often to conduct the village school; but only when he was licensed to teach. Christopher Harries, Parish Clerk of Trull in Somerset, for example, was presented during the archidiaconal visitation of 1623 'for keeping a school without a licence'; but after a reprimand was dismissed on paying a 12d. fee.

The 91st Canon of 1604 ordered that the Clerk be chosen by rector or vicar, 'which choice is to be signified to the parishioners the next Sunday' in time of divine service. During the seventeenth century, however, he was normally appointed by the select Vestry, and then confirmed by the parson, whose servant in any case he

[1] p. 392.

remained canonically.[2] As regards qualifications : he had to be
'twentie yeeres of age at the least', of honest conversation, and
known to be 'sufficient for his Reading, Writing and also for his
competent skill in Singing (if it may be)'. The Clerk of Radding-
ton, Somerset, was cited before the Archdeacon of Taunton's
Court in 1623 on the charge that 'he is not xxi yeares of age'. In
point of fact he was 'of the age of xiiii or thereabouts', and frankly
admitted 'that he answered the Minister as Parish Clerk three or
fower Sundaies untill the parishioners could get another.' The
court prohibited him from exercising the office any longer and
ordered the wardens, (not the incumbent!), to find someone else.
A similar case was reported during the Metropolitical visitation
of the Archdeaconry of Winchester in 1607/8, when a certain
Joan [sic] Hammond of St Peter's Colebrook, Winton, was said
to be 'psh clerk and not above 14 yrs old and ought not to serve
by the Canons'. But he or she was 'not cited', for the matter was
settled amicably out of court.

The Clerk had regularly to appear at the Archdeacon's Easter
visitation, pay a court fee of 4d. or 6d., and exhibit his licence.
The 91st Canon also laid down that 'the said Clearks . . . shall
have and receive their ancient Wages without fraud or diminution,
either at the hands of the churchwardens at such times as haith
beene accustomed, or by their owne collection according to the
most ancient custome of every Parish'. Usually the wardens paid
him a small fixed wage. Richard Dalton of South Newington, who
was Clerk there for the greater part of Elizabeth's reign, got 8d. a
quarter at Christmas, Easter, Midsummer and Michaelmas,
although occasionally he received two such quarterly payments
at once :

> 1561. Item. for Daltone's halffe yeares wagys . . . 16d.
>
> Item. to Richard Dallton for hys quarterege at
> mydsummer . . . 8d.
>
> Item. to Richard Dalton for hys Mychaelmas
> quarterege . . .8d.

---

[2] '. . . in 1611 Coke and the whole bench adjudged the Canon contrary
to common law, and denied that the incumbent or the ordinary had any
right to set aside a clerk chosen by the parishioners. The clerk's was a lay
office and the church courts had no power to deprive a man who executed a
lay office. The abolition of the hierarchy's control during the interregnum
saw the triumph of the common-law view' C. Hill, *Society and Puritanism in
Pre-Revolutionary England*, p. 437.

There is a curious entry in the Patton accounts for 1560 that reflects the depreciation in the value of money, 'Be it remembered that we provided to pay the clarke his part wagis, and to pay John Meryfelde for scowrynge the harnes xiis viiiid, and before the day came the moneye fell, be meanes whereof we loste iiis iiiid.' But in addition to his ordinary wages the clerk was entitled in respect of his office to certain fees and dues established by custom and tradition.[3] At Cropwell Bishop in Nottinghamshire, in accordance with local usage, the Clerk was paid as follows:

Every oxgate of land, yearly, 2 wheat sheaves in harvest. Every husbandman or woman having a husbandrie farme at Easter a dinner worth xiid or xiid in money, and 2 loaves worth ixd and the like at Christmas, and everie May day, lamas, Martinmas and Candlemas a loaf worth ixd or ixd in money. Everie cottager iiiid at Easter vizt to everie quarter ut supra id.

The case of Payne versus Churcher tried in the Winchester Consistory Court during 1569 established that 'these 30 years past' the chief farmer of Bishopstoke in Hampshire, had always provided the Parish Clerk with his Sunday dinner.

[George Glaspole, a husbandman, declared:] Richard Munday late a farmer of Bishopstoke did continually pay the said dinner to Richard Hunte then parish clerk without any denial during his lifetime, and after him old John Churcher in like sort found the said dinners all his time unto one John Hale parish clerk without interruption, and after him John Churcher his son did find the said Lucas Paine his dinner every Sunday aforesaid for a certain time, but afterwards denied the same and would suffer him to have it no longer. And afterwards the said Joan Churcher [the widow] found the said dinner to the said Lucas Paine the space of three years but afterwards denied the same.

[3] This wage was often raised by means of a 'clerk ale'. William Piers, Bishop of Bath and Wells, wrote in his *Defence of Church Feasting*: 'In poor country parishes where the wages of the clerk are but small the people thinking it unfit that the clerk should duly attend at Church and gain nothing by his office, send him in provision and then come on Sunday and feast with him by which means he sells more ale, and tastes more of the liberality of the people than their quarterly payments would amount to in many years'.

In the same court on 7 November 1579 a certain John Woodison
in the case of Abraham versus Woodison declared: 'That the tithe
of hay of all old meads within the bounds of that hamlet of Rotherwick hath not at any time within the memory of man been paid
or due unto the parsonage articulate or their farmers, but only to
the parish clerk of Rotherwick for the time being for part of his
wages.'

Again at Clayworth in Nottinghamshire it was decided that:

> . . . everie householder within the said parish of claworth
> have used and ought to give unto ye parish clarke there (over
> and above his wages in money) at the feasts of Easter and
> Christmas yearly or at some other feasts of the year, yearlye
> in the name of an Easter dinner and Christmas dinner, a pye
> or a loafe and some certain rate or quantitie of corne in
> augmentation of his wages for the better encouraging of him
> in his services in the paid pish clarkes place.

The Parish Clerk of Rempston in the same county received in
1629 a penny for every yard of land held or occupied by every
husbandman at Easter; and a peck of barley from every cottager.
For a marriage he was paid 2d.; and given a dinner by each
woman churched. Most parishioners bestowed some eggs upon
him at Easter 'by coutesie'. The Vestry of Houghton-le-Spring in
County Durham decided during March 1611 that 'the clerk shall
have from henceforth of every plough within the said parish in
lieu and full satisfaction of his corn at Xmas 2d. in money, and
for his eggs at Easter one penny'. Such commutations became
increasingly common.

Most of these dues, fees and perquisites the Clerk had to collect
himself, which was not always either an easy or a pleasant task;
although as his office was a freehold he had the right to sue his
debtors for them in the Ecclesiastical Courts. Bartholomew Han-
nies of Headington, Oxford, confessed in 1584 before the Archdeacon's Court that he owed 'to the clarcke there iid and more';
while his fellow parishioner, Richard Alder, who was likewise
charged with witholding the clerk's dues, defended himself by the
plea: 'there weare never anie such pence demaunded before this
present yeare, and doeth not belyve that there was never anie
suche order made by the consent of the most of parisshioners, but
that such dues weare asked when men weare kneling at the com-

munion wch was an undecent and unreasonable request and therefore is not bounde to pay ennie suche dues.'

At a number of parishes in Somerset, including Bridgwater,
Petherton and Stockland, and Bristol, people were presented, and
when they remained obdurate were actually excommunicated,
during 1623 because 'they do refuse to pay Clarkes wages according to the most ancient custom of the parish'. Some of these folk in
fact had not paid over anything for 'divers yeeres past'; while
during the Metropolitical visitation of the Archdeaconry of Winchester in 1607/8 it was likewise discovered that quite a few rate-
payers, notably one Richard Heath of Yateley, were 'refusing to
pay Clark's wages at 20s. the yr for 3 yrs'.

Another perquisite of the Clerk's was his dwelling-house; but
it was sometimes difficult for a fresh nominee to get vacant possession. At Ecchinswell, for instance, the same visitation disclosed
that the wife of the former Clerk, Joan, was still 'occupying the
psh clerk's house' together with a freshly wedded spouse, John
Grene.

In small country villages and hamlets the Clerk might also
have to act as beadle or sexton, when he received additional perquisites at Christmas and Easter, besides of course fees for digging
the graves both within and without the church. But in the larger
parishes the offices were kept divided. The Vestry Books at Houghton-le-Spring record that in 1655 the then sexton, Nicholas Dobson, was to be sacked 'except he be more diligent in executing of
his place', and repay 4s. 4d. which he had expended on spades
and shovels out of 'his own proper charges'. However, on the inter-
cession of some of the more substantial rate-payers he was
reprieved 'for one yeare', provided he kept 'the spades and shovels
for the making of graves, for that use and no other; and carefully
and duly to do all things else belonging to his place, otherwise the
said Dobson is to be displaced, and a new sexton chosen in his
room'.

He was to be paid at the rate of 2d. for a grave in the
churchyard, 4d. for one in the church, and 6d. if in the choir.
In addition he got 2d. a year from every plough in the parish,
and an ob ($\frac{1}{2}$d.) out of each cottager. 'And upon good will each
householder to give him buns at Christmas and egs at Easter
yearely.'

Other duties of the Clerk might well include the keeping of the
churchwardens' accounts, when the latter were too illiterate to do

so themselves. Richard Dalton of South Newington certainly
wrote them up for some years, since there are repeated references
to 'my wages'; and the Patton accounts have an entry in 1560 :
'payd to the clarke for kepyng the booke . . . iis'. The Parish Clerk
was often the Vestry Clerk and kept the registers. In 1571 the
Vestry of St Margaret, Lothbury, paid him 3s. 4d. to :

> 'kepe the register of cristeninge weddinge and burynge per-
> fectlye, and . . . present the same everie Sondaie to the churche
> wardens to be perused by them.'

It appears to have been the custom in many places during the
whole of this period for the incumbent or Clerk to copy down
particulars on to a loose sheet or into a private memorandum
book at the time of the actual ceremony, and then later enter them
up into the Register. This practice could and did lead to dis-
aster, as the following confession of the parson of Carshalton on
10 March 1651 amply illustrates :

> Good reader, tread gently : For though these vacant years
> may seem to make me guilty of thy censure, neither will I
> excuse myself from all blemishe; yet if thou do but cast thine
> eye upon the former pages and see with what care I have
> kept the Annalls of mine owne time, and rectifyed sundry
> errors of former times, thou wilt begin to think ther is some
> reason why he that began to build so well should not be able
> to make an ende.
>
> The truth is that besyde the miserys and distractions of
> these permitted years which it may be God in his owne
> wisdom would not suffer to be kept uppon record, the special
> grounds of that permission ought to be imputed to Richard
> Finch, the p'rishe Clarke, whose office it was by long pscrition
> to gather the ephemeris or dyary by the dayly passages, and
> to exhibit them once a year to be transcribed into the registry;
> and though I have often called upon him agayne and agayne
> to remember his chardge, and he always told me he had the
> accompts lying by him, yet at last p'ceaving his excuses, and
> revolving upon suspicion of his words to put him home to
> a full tryall I found to my great griefe that all his accompts
> were written in sand, and his words committed to empty
> winds. God is witness to the truth of this apologie and that I
> made it knowne at some parish meetings before his own face,

who could not deny it, neither do I write it to blemishe him, but to cleere my own integritie as far as I may, and to give accompt of this miscarriage to after ages by the subscription of my hand.[4]

When the new 'register' was appointed under the Act of 1653, who held that office for three years, occasionally the old Parish Clerk was elected and thus to a certain extent preserved the traditions of the past. In some cases he actually continued to use the same Register, although in all too many instances these were lost, destroyed or carried off at the time of the plundering and sequestration of the parsonage. But it was the usual practice to select an entirely new-comer, a layman, who disclaiming all responsibility for the old books, would start a fresh one of his own. In 1657 the appointment of 'registers' was only continued for another six months, and after that time they quietly disappeared. The Parish Clerk then resumed his functions.

One of the famous deacon-clerks of Barnstaple, Robert Langdon, who held that office from 1584 to 1625, not only kept the register but made numerous entries of his own recording passing events, some of them in Latin. In this he was by no means unique. Michael Blakesley, sexton and Clerk for sixteen years at Chelmsford from 1609-25 wrote up a particularly fine and unofficial one of his own, which recorded such things as age at death, occupation and abode.

Parish Clerks, although the paid servants of the Vestry, were not therefore automatically exempt from nomination to the office of churchwarden when their turn came round, as it frequently might in a small country cure. Then, 'with such a combination of offices they would have exercised considerable authority and only the incumbent would have been in a position to charge them with breach of duty.'[5] Furthermore there was always the danger that they would exceed their duties and usurp the actual ministerial functions of the parson himself. In his Injunctions of 1571 Archbishop Grindal demanded:

> ... that from henceforth no parish clerk, nor any other person not being ordered, at least for a deacon, shall presume to

[4] Quoted by T. F. Thiselton-Dyer, *Social Life as told by Parish Registers*, p. 57.
[5] W. A. Pemberton, *Studies in the Ecclesiastical Court and Archdeaconry of Nottingham*, p. 736.

solemnise Matrimony, or administer the Sacrament of Baptism, or to deliver the communicants the Lord's cup at the celebration of the Holy Communion. And that no person, not being a minister, deacon, or at least, tolerated by the ordinary in writing, do attempt to supply the office of a minister in saying divine service openly in any church or chapel.

From henceforth there was a spate of such episcopal injunctions and articles attempting to keep the Clerk in his rightful place as the minister's humble assistant. Bishop Joseph Hall, for instance, asked in his visitation articles of 1638 : 'Whether in the absence of the minister or at any other time the Parish Clerk, or any other lay person, said Common Prayer openly in the church or any part of the Divine Service which is proper to the Priest?';[6] and a few years later he was echoed by Archdeacon Marsh of Chichester, who inquired : 'Hath your Parish Clerk or Sexton taken upon him to meddle with anything above his office as churching of women, burying the dead or such like?' These exhortations and commands were all too often ignored. Thomas Kulham of North Hales in Suffolk was presented in 1597 because 'he doth many tymes reade devine service there, but whether he be a minister or no they know not'. Kulham frankly admitted 'that he have manie tymes redd the procession in the said Church being clerke ther'; but he laid no claim to holy orders. Again at Selsey in Sussex, where the vicar, Robert Johnson, was a notorious non-resident, it was reported in 1625 : 'divers children had died unbaptised for want of a minster and divers corps have of necessity been buried by our parrish clerke'. The churchwardens of St Mary Overy replying to the Bishop's article on the Parish Clerk declared : 'Touching the Parish Clerk and Sexton all is well; only our clerk doth sometimes to ease the minister read prayers, church women, christen, bury and marry, being allowed so to do'.

Bishop Mountain of London was, indeed, perfectly prepared to smooth the path of the Vicar of Waltham Abbey by licensing his clerk, Thomas Dickenson, in 1621 to read prayers, church women

[6] During 1624 the Vestry of St Edmund's, Salisbury, voted 20s. to the Clerk per annum in order that he might read Morning Prayer in the church, 'for the ease of Mr Thatcher during his time, and likewise for the ease of his successor, being a preacher'.—Hill, op. cit., p. 427.

G

and bury the dead in an emergency; although there is no indica-
tion that the latter was ever ordained. The irregularity was excused
on the grounds of 'the largeness of the parish and the excessive
duties of the curate.' The Bishop of Exeter, William Cotton, took a
different and more orthodox line in helping John Trinder, Vicar
of Barnstaple, who was having a lot of trouble with a puritan
lecturer, Robert Smythe. He raised his Parish Clerk, Robert Langdon, to the diaconate, ordaining him in Silverton parish church
on 21 September 1606. Langdon held this combined office of
Clerk-Deacon for nineteen years, being buried on 5 July 1625,
when the entry in the Register recorded: 'Robert Langdon
deacon'. So successful had been this arrangement that the Vicar
chose another deacon, Anthony Baker, as his new Clerk. Baker, the
son of a yeoman family at Bowden in the parish of East Downe,
had actually been ordained some five years previously; but like his
predecessor he was never priested. It is interesting to note, however, that whereas Langdon always signed 'clarcke' only after his
name, Baker invariably put 'deacon'.

The experiment continued to succeed; for in 1632 there is an
item in the borough accounts that recorded: 'paid for a new
gowne bestowed on Mr Baker the deacon by consent of Mr Mayor
and his brethren 59s. 8d.; and paid for the making of the gowne
given to the deacon 4s.' Baker's own salary amounted to 6s. 8d.
per annum; but no doubt he received very much more in terms
of the customary dues, fees and perquisites. None the less if he
had been a regular assistant curate his stipend must have been a
good deal larger; yet another reason, perhaps, for the popularity
of the permanent diaconate! Baker kept the Registers until 24
April 1643, a disastrous year for the parish when the vicar, Mr
Blake, was suspended from office, plague broke out, and presumably the Clerk-Deacon died, although there is no record of his
burial. The next clerk, John Sloby, who was appointed in 1647,
the date of Blake's return to Barnstaple, was never ordained. The
times were obviously unpropitious. But he continued to keep the
Register, where he manfully endeavoured to fill in the vacant
years, caused as he himself said 'by the trouble and contagion',
from a well-stored memory. In 1654 he actually became the new
'registrar'; 'John Sloby was chosen and sworn regester of Barne-
stapell by Mr Thomas Horwood maior and the rest of his brethren.
October 2nd 1654.' And on the incumbent's second eviction in
1657, followed by the appointment by Cromwell of the intruding

Independent, Nathaniel Mather, Sloby hung on grimly to his job, welcomed Blake back once more in March 1659, and recorded in his beloved Register his joy at the Restoration.[7]

Sometimes during the period of the great Interregnum the Clerk was left as the only person in a parish available to carry out ministerial functions or to make important decisions, with the result that he could attain to such a position of authority as to become for all intents and purposes a little dictator, who bitterly resented a return to normality at the Restoration. Such a man was Thomas Symon of Languar in Nottinghamshire, who in the absence of an incumbent had got himself appointed Clerk, Schoolmaster, and general factotum of the township. On the return of the rector, Dr Featley, he openly and violently disputed his authority. On the other hand no man could be more faithful to his master. Isaac Walton tells us of the friendship that sprang up between the judicious Richard Hooker and his clerk at Bourne: 'He [Hooker] was of so humble a nature that his poor clerk and he did never talk but with both their hats on, or both off, at the same time'. The Clerk lived on into the Commonwealth, when an intruded minister started to make some drastic alterations in the church services:

> . . . to which end the day was appointed for a select company, and forms and stools set about the altar or communion table for them to sit and eat and drink; but when they went about this work, there was a want of some joint-stools which the minister sent the clerk to fetch, and then to fetch cushions. When the clerk saw them begin to sit down, he began to wonder; but the minister bade him cease wondering and lock the church door: to whom he replied, 'pray take your keys, and lock me out; I will never more come into this church; for men will say my Master Hooker was a good man and a great scholar; and I am sure it was not used to be thus in his days'; and report says this old man went presently home and died.

---

[7] It was a different matter, however, when the Clerk was illiterate: The Southwell Act Books relate on 2 June 1587: 'They do not refuse to come to the churche upon any contempte or dislykinge of the service now used; but that thaie have no mynde to come for that the vicar dothe not come to saie theime service as he oughte; but appointes one Pawle the clerke to reede service, who cannot reede; which is to theire great grieffe.'

When Richard Drake was finally driven from Radwinter in 1642/3, he smuggled back a letter to be read to the parishioners by his faithful Clerk, Daniel Minot :

> Daniel Minot [the rector wrote in his autobiography], the clerk of the parish, was desired by me to read the letter to the parishioners in some convenient place and time. He indiscreetly began to read it in the Church, where and when Mr Robert Reinolds, the Parliament man, and his brother Captain John Reinolds being present, the reading of it was interrupted by them, and so my charitable inclination was not communicated to the parishioners.

Perhaps on the whole this was just as well, since the bulk of the epistle consisted of demands for monies owed him by his flock, together with a scarcely veiled threat to resort to legal action if these debts were not immediately met. Sir Walter Besant in *For Faith and Freedom* drew a picture of an old Clerk hobbling into his church one day, as the Restoration drew near, taking out an ancient key and opening an oak chest, wherein reposed a yellowing surplice and mildewed Prayer-Book. 'Here you be', he chuckled, 'put away for a matter of twelve years or more, and bide your time; you know you will come back again'; and added truthfully : 'Parson goes and Preacher comes; Preacher goes and Parson comes; but Clerk stays.'

Clerks, none the less, were not always what they should have been. In the Chancery Court of York in 1620/21 Richard Burrowes, one of the churchwardens at Rotherham, brought the following charges against their Parish Clerk, Peter Gurrey : that he was 'a curser and common swearer, given to excessive drinkeing of ale, beere and wine'; deformed in body and mind; illiterate; had been elected when under twenty years; and under colour of his office 'committed diverse absurdities and disorders in the said church . . . in time of divine service and sermons'. This last included playing the organ so unskilfully and untuneably that on one occasion for very shame he 'desisted to play any longer and the Minister and congregacion enforced to sing the remainder of the Psalme without the Organes which moved many to laughter and other some better affected to great griefe'. On yet another Sunday he deliberately continued to play while the preacher : 'Mr John Newton . . . was in his prayer after his sermon . . . of set purpose to disturbe the said Newton . . . to the great dishonour of god'.

Consequently, Burrowes asserted, divine service at Rotherham had 'become ridiculous, the word of god lesse esteemed, and many of the inhabitants there occasioned to absent themselves from the same'. Finally, it was alleged that Gurrey already stood excommunicated because he had attended 'many unlawful and clandestine marriages in Rotherham parish'. Gurrey denied the whole indictment, apart from the fact that he possessed some natural deformities of body, had been elected Clerk when nineteen years old, and sometimes played the organ for the services; and since Burrowes's witnesses, although cited, failed to put in an appearance, the case was adjourned and, apparently, eventually settled amicably out of court.

Drunkenness, all too frequently accompanied by disorder, neglect of, or inability to perform his duties, were accusations hurled at the head of many an Elizabethan or seventeenth-century Clerk. Here are a few instances taken at random from an abundant supply: A certain Chas., Parish Clerk of Middleham, was arraigned before Quarter Sessions early in James I's reign 'for receiving divers persons into his dwelling house during the time of divine service, and permitting them to play at unlawfull games, viz shovell a board etc, and also for an assault in the parish church of Midleham on one Brian Sweeting. . . .' So too was Thomas Thompson, clerk of Kirby Misperton, 'for being drunk on the Sabbaoth daie on divers occasions and is addicated to quarrelling and disrder when he is drunk.'

Gurrey was by no means unique in his mishandling of the organ and want of any musical ability. The Elizabethan Parish Clerk of Holy Trinity, Kingston-upon-Hull, had the unfortunate habit of making sure that :

> when there is any sermon, as commonly and for the most part there is every Sonday and holy day, he so consume the tyme with organes plainge and singinge and furder in settinge forwarde the clocke, that there can be no convenient tyme for the worde to be preached, and where as the preacher and minister have rebuked him for the same, he dothe not amend but rather is worse and worse.

It was the same at funerals and weddings, 'for all his delite is in ringinge, singinge and organs plainge'. He was not alone in his obstinacy. Thomas Milbourne, clerk of Eastham, was condemned in the early seventeenth century because :

he singeth the psalms in the church with such a jesticulous
tone and altisonant voice, viz: speaking like a gelded pig,
which doth not only interrupt the other voices, but is altogether dissonant and disagreeing unto any musical harmony,
and he hath been requested by the minister to leave it, but
he doth obstinately persist and continue therein.

Of one such Clerk the Rector of Buxted in Sussex was unkind
enough to enter after his name in the burial register: 'whose
melody warbled forth as if he had been thumped on the back with
a stone'.

Others were criticised for the slovenly manner in which they
performed their task of keeping the church building, its furniture
and ornaments in a state of order and cleanliness or for their in-
subordination. When Methusaleh Sharpe of Bathealton was presented during the Archdeacon of Taunton's visitation in 1623 as
being 'parish clerk there . . . that he doth not make cleane the
church and keep yt in decent and cleanely manner as yt ought to
be', he defended himself in court on the plea 'that the Clark
ought not to make Cleene the Church'; and anyway stated his
intention 'to leave the Clarkshippe forthwith'. Technically he may
well have been within his rights, since the actual work of scrubbing
and cleaning would no doubt, in the larger parishes at any rate,
be carried out by the sexton or some other underling; but it was
unquestionably his job to see that it was done, and in this he had
certainly failed. His resignation was accepted and the Judge of the
court admonished the churchwardens 'to exercise the office of
clerk within a month'. In other words they were expected to find
a new Clerk within that period or else perform the duties themselves! Some years earlier Richard Halome, the clerk of Swyne
in Yorkshire, who was designated as 'a defender and mainteyner
of the Romish religion', was likewise presented because he 'doth
not his dutie in keepinge cleane the Churche nor anything in the
same that he is commaunded, neither doth resort to the churche
at the tymes appointed for service, neither will be obedyent to the
vicar at any time'. This last fault was, of course, in flat defiance
of Archbishop Grindal's Injunction of 1571 urging clerks always
to be 'obedient to the parson, vicar, or curate.'

At Barnham in Sussex the Clerk, Richard Blake, was reported
to be 'an aged man', who 'doth not doe his duty in diligent attendance about his office. He is unlearned'; while at Itchingfield in

the same county the clerk, George Kempsall, was accused in 1625 of 'cursing and swearing in the church . . . for giving the church-wardens evill words for doing theire duties . . . for laying fagots in the belfrey of the church, and being warned of it refuseth to remove them.'

But lest we run away with the idea that the majority of Parish Clerks were incompetent, insubordinate, drunken or illiterate, it should be borne in mind that, as indeed with the clergy, most of those about whom we know any personal details had been hauled before the Ecclesiastical Courts on one or other of these charges. The faithful, the conscientious and the efficient, alas, are usually no more than names, and even these have not always survived. Christopher Harvey, the friend of George Herbert, wrote of the ideally loyal and humble Clerk in *The Synagogue*:

> The Churches Bible-clerk attends
>   Her utensiles, and ends
>   Her prayers with Amens,
> Tunes Psalms, and to her Sacraments
>   Brings in the Elements,
>   And takes them out again;
>   Is humble-minded and industrious handed,
>   Doth nothing of himself, but as commanded.

'The Parish make the Constable', wrote John Selden in the section on 'People' in his *Table Talk*, 'and when the Constable is made he governs the Parish'. It was officially an unpaid post, although he could always claim his expenses from the Vestry and there were opportunities for fees and pickings of all kinds, which rotated annually among the farms and cottages of the township. Like that of churchwarden it was one of great authority, which touched practically every aspect of secular life in a parish, and so required from its holders, who all too easily and almost inevitably raised up enemies, qualities of personality and toughness of body and will above the ordinary, if it was to be successfully undertaken. James Gyffen, himself a village Constable in the reign of James I, wrote of him in *The Song of the Constable*:

> A Constable must be honest and just,
>   Have knowledge and good report,
> And able to strain with body and brain,
>   Else he is not fitting for aught.

His duties were, indeed, various and extremely strenuous, since he seemed to be at once at everybody's beck and call, and responsible for pretty well everything that went on in the parish. IIis main task, however, was to see that the innumerable Tudor and Stuart statutes regulating the life of the parish and that of its inhabitants were duly observed : that riots and affrays were stopped and their perpetrators brought to book; no foul or blasphemous language was heard in the streets or lanes; no unlawful games played on the village green; no undue tipling in the ale-houses; no secret eating of meat on fast days or in Lent in the farmsteads and cottages; and no profaning of the sabbath day by man, woman and child, either by neglecting their church worship or by engaging in unnecessary work and recreation. But more positively he must also insist on every able-bodied male possessing a long-bow and knowing how to use it; that parents bound out their children as apprentices from the tender age of seven and upwards; that wages, fixed by the Justices, were paid and received; that rogues and vagabonds were immediately apprehended, whipped and sent on their way to their place of 'settlement'; and that the ordinary parishioner performed his communal services. Henry Best of Elmswell wrote in his diary on 19 November 1642 : 'I made the sheepe dike in the towne backe by Howsamlane ende, and William Whitehead would not sende any helpe to make it, but gave the Constable, Richard Parrat, ill wordes, and called him a slave when he wished him to come to helpe'.

As the servant of the parish the Constable was expected to supervise the local market, enforcing the various trade regulations and insisting upon a proper system of weights and measures; as the servant of the churchwardens he helped to collect the church rate and small fines of one kind or another; and as the servant of the Justices he executed their warrants, delivered their writs, whipped sturdy rogues, ducked scolds and summarily punished offenders caught red-handed. One Hopkins, for instance, of Burnham in Norfolk at the beginning of the seventeenth century was thus dealt with, and the incident is described as follows :

> . . . a disturber of his Maties peace, a common makebate, an ydle lyver, a notorious raylor . . . refusinge to obey the constable, upon quarrellinge of a nomber being together by the eares, and did refuse to goe to his house. And the constable setting him by the heels Hopkins threw both stones

and a stoole at the constable, wherewith he [the constable]
stroke him upon the side of the head.

Closely associated with the churchwardens and the overseers in
the administration of the Poor Law and Statute of Labourers,
the Constable was also expected to help choose and then to supervise the activities of the surveyors of the highways. Every year
in Easter week a special meeting was called to elect such surveyors,
to decide what work needed doing, and to assign certain days for
its performance. At Bale in Norfolk during 1611 for example:

On Tuesdaie in Easter weeke Jacobi Ris the Cunstable and
the Churchwardens of the said towne (callinge together the
parochians of the said parish) did then elect and choose the
said Robt. Bulleyn and John Spurrell Supervisors and
orderers of the works in the High waies for this yeare then
ensewinge. Secondly that the said cunstables and churchwardens then did nominate and appointe vi dayse . . . for
the amendinge of the said high waies accordinge to the
statute in that behalf provided.

Naturally the Constable's was not a very popular job; and, as
in the case of the churchwardenship, many tried to wriggle out
of it on one excuse or another, but not usually in so high-handed
a manner as did John Colffer of Briston in Norfolk, judging from
the following complaint:

Right Worshipfull Sir, [wrote the officers of the court leet
concerned to their local J.P.]. So it is John Colffer of Briston
beinge yestrdaye at a Courte Leete there houlden for that
Mannor, chosen by generall consent of all the Leeters twelve
in number, for one of the constables there this yeare, and
being required and charged in his Maties name to take the
othe accordinglye the saide Colffer in contempt of that Jurisdiction and in evill example of all the then and there tenntes
more than thirty, did not only depart that Courte disdaine-
fully without licence, but utterlye refused to beare that office,
so imposed uppon him. And bycause inferior authorities
ought not to be made contemptible and elusorye in publique
affayres, but hath been supported and assisted alwaies by
superior powers they in their grave wisdomes and censures,
reprovinge suche scorners and forcinge them to conformitie.

> We your dutifull suppliantes Lord and Steward of the Juris-
> diction aforesaide do beseeche your assistance to compell by
> your superior power the said Colffer to take upon him the
> said office and be sworne thereunto.

Contrariwise they did not always like him when they got him.
Acting on the principle that a poacher makes a good game-keeper,
the parishioners of Wells, Norfolk, appointed one Robert Jarye
in hope 'to have somewhat restrained him from his former un-
rulynes in gaming and using alehouses'; but, alas, he merely
employed his newly acquired authority 'to bolster out both his
owne loose behaviour and alsoe the ill demeanour of others'. They
therefore asked Sir Nicholas Bacon, J.P. to remove him 'by what
meanes your W.'s discresion shall think most meet. . . . And wee
have chosen Willm Holman for that office'. The people of Wells
were not the only ones to make this mistake. Ralph Josselin, Vicar
of Earls Colne in Essex, wrote in his diary on 8 January 1644:
'This day Court kept in Towne; ye Jury of Colne Comit. chose
for cunstables 2 men very unfitt to order ye alehouse and loose
people of ye Towne'.

Constables certainly did not always behave as they should have
done. In Cromer at the beginning of the seventeenth century there
were at least nine disorderly alehouses, which had been 'sett upp
by meanes of some of the constables and others'. Normally they
would have fetched a rent of no more than twenty shillings, but
'by this meanes letten for £3 or £4'. They could also behave in the
most cruel and callous manner, like the Bumbles of a later age,
towards the sick and poor in their charge. There was a notorious
case at Warham in 1603, where a sick lad of ten or eleven years,
'a wanderer', was removed to his place of settlement by the constable, Riplingham. Riplingham, who had already been refused
a certificate by the parson of Warham because of the boy's serious
illness, secured instead a warrant from a Justice by pretending
that 'his sickness was rather frowardnes then weaknes'; and
carried him away in a cart. 'He died upon the waie'; but Riplingham none the less 'brought him to Bynham and ther laide him
downe deade at the constables gate and so departed.' It is pleasant,
however, to learn that he was at least severely reprimanded as
being, 'void of human pittie'. On the other hand Adam Eyre,
petty Constable of Penistone in the West Riding of Yorkshire, was
constantly organising ales in aid of his poorer neighbours. As

always it was not the office, but the individual who held it that really counted in the life of the community.

Like churchwardens Constables were expected to keep accounts and produce them at the annual audit, when they had to justify their expense sheet before it was met. Occasionally, however, they were also paid a regular yearly wage, which at South Newington ammounted to 6s. 8d. Here we have preserved a full statement of the accounts for 1635 made up by the then Constable, John Taylor, whose expenses, apart from his salary, amounted to £9 16s. 4d. Items included a good many quite small sums paid out to the deserving poor, 18d. for presentments, some largish amounts expended on replenishing or repairing the parish armour and laying in a store of 'goenpouder', and £1 6s. 8d. for 'the King's carriage', i.e. this particular parish's share of the cost of the royal household whilst on progress in that part of the country. There is mention of the trained band, lost property, weights and measures, and 'item. layd out for the pound . . . 18d.'

A heavy expense item in most early seventeenth-century Constables' account books was the relief doled out to vagrants with passes, who were on their way to their native abode or place of settlement. The Constable of Stathern for 1630 recorded the following entries for the month of May alone:

Paide for a passe making ye ith of May . . . 2d.
Geven to tow poore men ye vith of May . . . 2d.
Geven to one poore man ye viith of May . . . 1d.
Geven to a poore man that had a passe ye xvth of May . . .1d.
Payd for a passe making ye 18th of May . . . 2d.
Geven tow men and there wifes and one child ye 24th of May . . . 6d.
Geven to one man & tow children ye 25th of May . . . 2d.
Geven to tow women & one child ye 26th of May . . . 2d.
Geven to one man & a child that had pa. yer 27th May . . . id.
Geven to one man & and his wife & two children ye 29th May . . . 2d.
Geven to thre men 31st of May that had a passe . . . 2d.

The Upton-by-Southwell accounts contain very similar doles:

Given to a poore man and his wife and five children which lay a day and a night in James Bloomer barne . . . is 8d.

> Given to a cripple woman being sent from constable to constable in a cart being very weake and feeble, she being releifed with meat and money . . . 8d.

Pregnant women in particular were hastened out of the parish lest they should give birth there and so claim a settlement for their children. The same harsh principle was applied to the very sick, in case they might need a grave in an over-full churchyard: At Wimeswold in 1608 'a Bygg belly woman' was given 2d. 'to goe forth of the towne'; while on 25 June 1631 the Upton Constable noted: 'Given to a woman that was great with child to gett her away . . . 2d. Given to a poor man, his wife and three small children. One child being very sore sicke for fear the child should die in this towne I gave them to be gone . . . 8d.'

Rogues and vagabonds were of course dealt with even more harshly. For them each parish provided its stocks and whipping post. 'Yron for the stocks and whipping post . . . 9s. 10d.', runs an entry for 1655 in the books of Cowden, Kent; 'geven to Robert Moodee', declared the Melton Mowbray Constable in 1602, 'for wippin' tow pore folkes . . . iid'. But he then added more charitably: 'And gave them when they were wipped . . . iid'. Gypsies had been banished from the land in the reign of Henry VIII; and some pretty savage penal laws were passed against them and any one who helped or harboured them. None the less many Constables seem to have tempered the wind to these luckless remnants of the wandering 'Egyptians'. The Upton accounts, for example, record:

> Given to six gieptians . . . 6d.
> Payd to Smith wife for candles the Egyptians had that lay in William Gill lath [barn].

The motive was usually not so much pity as a desire to get rid as quickly and cheaply as possible of an alien, thieving, community. In 1613 Melton Mowbray, 'to ride the towne of them', paid out xiid; so did Repton some years earlier, 'to avoyde ye towne'.

Besides the gypsies there were the Irish refugees fleeing before the Rebellion of 1641, to whom the Upton Constables used to give a shilling; the many maimed, sick and discharged soldiers, returning to their native homes from service overseas; and a vast number of unfortunate people of all types, who had been uprooted and ruined by the Great Civil War in England itself. All expected some kind of charity.

The Constable was responsible for maintaining the parish armoury, which was normally lodged in the church, and for seeing that the local militia was fully recruited and equipped. Expenses were met out of a parish rate; but it was the Constable who made the necessary purchases and rendered an account of them to the Vestry. The Upton Constable, charged with finding the necessary men and arms for the muster at Nottingham at the beginning of the Great Rebellion, made the following entries in his ledger:

payde to James Parkes of Southwell for ffurniture for ye horses . . . £1 3s.
payde to William Foster for a case of pistolles . . . 13s. 4d.
payde to William Gaskin for a sword . . . 8s. 6d.
payde to John Saddifer for the sword hilt that was broke at the muster . . . 13s. 6d.

Other tasks that fell to their lot were to enforce the excise duties imposed by the Long Parliament in 1643 on beer, cider and ale brewed and sold in the local ale-house; to collect payments due on postal packages; and to be ready at all times to act as the village policeman. Indeed the most familiar picture of the ancient Constable that has come down to us is the one of him engaged in the hue and cry. In 1577 the Essex high Constables reported a case of 'two rogues, a man and a woman' who 'were sent by warrant by Master Appeltone from constable to constable being brought to the constable of Heybridge and they setting them into the stocks fast locked and each of them a lock on his feet, and they breaking out of the stocks in the night and went their ways and the aforesaid constables made hue and cry after them with speed and could not find them'.

When there was a murder done or a theft committed, an affray started or some other disturbance of the peace, which the Constable was unable successfully to tackle single-handed, he had the right and indeed the duty to raise a great shout of 'out, out' and blow upon his horn. Whereupon every able-bodied male in the village must turn out on foot or horse-back, armed with the knives, bows and arrows that they kept ready for this very purpose, and pursue furiously after the miscreants. Failure to do so and to lend horses, when called upon, for others to ride could result in a heavy fine or even a term of imprisonment. Futhermore if a glaring robbery or affray took place and no township managed to apprehend the culprits, then each village in the immediate neighbourhood was liable to punishment. Usually, however, the offenders were caught and summary justice was executed upon them, either at the whipping post or on the ducking stool. Later their legs were incarcerated in the stocks on the village green, where they became the target for every kind of projectile and much coarse merriment and abuse. 'Given to the men', declared the Upton Constable with satisfaction after such a successful round up, 'that gathered for a robberie [to help apprehend the miscreants] . . . 1s.' Finally it was his duty to put his prisoners under lock and key, and watch them carefully until he could bring them under guard before the magistrates:

> Spent when Thomas Godfrey was watched all night and most parte of ye next day at George Cullin house by John Pettiford and Edward Graves . . . 1s. 6d.

> Spent when I did goe with Robert Tare and Thomas Godfrey and Samwell Sleaner before Mr Chude, and Edward Greaves to helpe to garde them there and backe againe . . . 1s. 6d.

It is scarcely surprsing that some Constables were reluctant or unable to render satisfactory accounts at the annual audit after their year of office. The Justices of Norwich in February 1585 were disturbed because: 'At this or meteing it apeareth unto us how unreadie and imperfecte many of or cheife Cunstables were to yeild there accomptes in sorte as they were chardged or required'. Certainly the Constable's lot, like that of the modern 'bobby', was not always a happy one. It was always arduous and rarely profitable; although each township was expected to raise 'a fifteenth', i.e. a rate of something like $1\frac{1}{2}$d. per beast and 6d. per score of sheep from each landowner, to meet his expenses.

By late Tudor and early Stuart times the lay Schoolmaster was beginning to come into his own, despite the fact that every school, whether private or public, was still subject to ecclesiastical control, and the clergy themselves continued to teach in very many of them. The threefold educational system of elementary or 'petty' school, secondary or grammar school, and the university was now in full swing. The damage done to learning by the destruction of the monastic and chantry schools had been more than made up by the out-pourings of benefactions from well-to-do individuals or public companies that endowed every type of school from humble village one-teacher foundations to already well-established and famous academies.

At the beginning of our period [writes Professor W. K. Jordan], Norfolk possessed almost no school resources. But by the close of the remarkable era under survey (1485-1660) there was an endowed school for every seventy-six square miles of the countryside. . . . A widespread and well-endowed system of education had been created within the reach of any poor and able boy who thirsted for knowledge and who aspired to escape the grip of poverty. No family in Norfolk in 1660 lived more than twelve miles from an endowed school of some sort.[8]

This was equally true of most other English counties; and such a rich educational harvest was primarily due to 'the new men', who had emerged from under the Tudor social revolution : the small Protestant gentry, the substantial yeoman, the well-to-do merchant, burgher, artisan or tradesman in the growing towns, a small but expanding professional class, and wealthy women of independent means, who either by direct giving in their life-time or benefactions under their Wills, established in their own immediate localities 'forever' entirely new schools or else sought to increase the size and importance of the places of learning where they themselves had studied.

Grammar schools were as a rule averse to providing elementary teaching, and sometimes even refused to admit pupils unless they could read and write reasonably well. 'It seemeth to mee an unreasonable thing', said John Brinsley, master of the grammar school at Ashby-de-la-Zouche in 1612, 'that tht Grammar Schooles should be troubled with teaching A.B.C. seeing it is so great a hindrance to those paines which wee should take with our Grammar Schollers, for whom wee are appointed'. Here the whole curriculum was based on Latin, whose grammar was to be taught and studied rather than its literature. 'Literature', declared F. Foster, in *The English Grammar School*, 'was, as it were, a concrete manisfestation, and a vast territory for illustration of grammatical rules'. So, in order to get their pupils grounded in its elements many such grammar schools established 'petty' acadamies of their own, or else relied on those already existing or rapidly coming into being both in towns and villages throughout the

[8] *The Charities of Rural England*, p. 165.

country. Alternatively, as far as the sons of the gentry were concerned, they could receive a preliminary education at the hands of a tutor or chaplain in their father's mansion.

Village schools, when they were not run by the clergy themselves, were either presided over by the Parish Clerk or possibly by some other literate layman, for which he would receive no more than a mere pittance of £4 or £5 a year. But according to Charles Hoole, another seventeenth-century grammar-school master, some of these were no more than dames' schools conducted 'by poor women or others, whose necessities compel them to undertake it, as a mere shelter from beggary.' Certainly, judging from Richard Baxter's description of his early schooling some of these lay pedagogues left much to be desired :

> In the village where I was born there were four readers successively in six years, ignorant men, and two of them immoral in their lives, who were all my schoolmasters . . .
> These were the schoolmasters of my youth (except two of them) who read Common Prayer on Sundays and holy days, and taught school and tipled on the week-days, and whipped the boys when they were drunk, so that we changed them very often.

His opinion of his later schoolmaster, Mr John Owen, who ran the free-school at Wroxeter, was very different. To him he attributed 'the chiefest help I had for all my learning in the country schools'.

These 'petty' schools would normally teach reading, writing, arithmetic, the casting of accounts, and of course both Scripture and the Church Catechism free of all charge; but might well demand small fees for 'extra' subjects. Much naturally depended upon the terms of the original endowment under which the school had first been established. These sometimes laid down how many children could be admitted and from what localities and homes they might come, together with the stipend payable to its Schoolmaster. It was, in fact, often difficult to distinguish between endowed charity schools where the master was allowed to take in extra paying pupils, and unendowed foundations where the profit motive alone operated. At a visitation of Bishop Neile's in Leicestershire during 1614 some twenty-five schoolmasters are mentioned, of whom about sixteen were laymen, but most of whose schools were very small and some of them catered for no more than half-a-dozen boys. This was equally true of other counties. At Appleton in Berkshire, for example, a charity bequest of Sir Richard Fettiplace, knight, Lord of the Manor there, by a deed dated 15 December 1604 gave a parcel of land situated in the Great Green and also a close, called the Common Close, to trustees for 'the maintenance and sustentation of one honest and sufficient learned scholar to teach and instruct as well in manners and learning the children and youth of the town of Appleton and Besselsleigh'. This school was still functioning in 1686, when an Archidiaconal return recorded : 'In Appleton a free school for wrighting . . . boys, a small class of 3 . . . given by Esq. ffettisplace'. The endowment was then producing about £5 per annum.

The hours of schooling were very long, commencing at 5 or 6 a.m. in the summer and 6 or 7 a.m. in the winter; and carrying on, with short breaks, for a ten hour day. Holidays amounted to no more than twelve days at Christmas and Easter, together with a few others scattered throughout the year and usually coinciding with traditional festivals. Apart from his meagre stipend an enterprising pedagogue could earn a little on the side by organising cock-fights on Shrove-Tuesday or, in certain circumstances, making house-to-house collections. Punishments were very severe; and most masters wielded the rod or birch both frequently and vigorously. At Louth school in Lincolnshire 22s. 4d. was paid 'for drawing and graving the common seale of the said scole', which depicted :

. . . a stalwart pedagogue seated with his legs apart, and on his left knee a boy; the pedagogue's left hand is holding up the boy's garment and baring the parts below the middle, on which a mighty birch erect in the pedagogue's right hand is about to fall. The boy's hands are clasped in a vain appeal for mercy.

This was the work of the then Schoolmaster, Mr Goodall, who flourished during the fifteen-seventies, and was certainly a believer in Solomon's precept. His salary was £20 and he also employed an usher. Other punishments included making a delinquent 'sit in the midst of the school alone . . . where his fellows may finger and point at him; or to keep him in school when others do play.'

The endowment usually provided for a Schoolmaster's House, which together with the stipend and perquisites made a not unreasonable living. This also carried with it a position of considerable general authority, and of almost complete power over the actual children entrusted to his care that could be used either for good or ill. Sir John Bramston of Screens, who went to school in the early seventeenth century, experienced both types. He was first under Andrew Walmsley 'a very meane superficiall scholler', who flogged incessantly, once giving a boy '50 blowes with a great rod' for a quite trivial offence; and then sent to the learned Thomas Farnaby, of whom he later wrote in his diary :

> I boarded with him. . . . The first day I came he tooke me into his studie; and after he had inquired what bookes I learnt, he gave me pen, ink, and paper, and bid me make a theme on *'Ex argilla quidvis imitaberis uda'*. I sayd I used to have a weekes tyme to make a theame. I do not desire much, sayes he, but let me see what thou canst doe. I sett myself to it, and did as well as I could. He came at xi of the clock to see what I had done; and reading it, cryed out, 'Oh Heavens ! where hast thou binn bred?' Soe in the afternoon he placed me in a forme under those that read Virgil, which was yet too high for me, but I thincke he was unwillinge to discourage me too much. With him I stayed more than two, nay, full three yeares. At partinge he shewed me my first and last theames, and sayd, 'Thus you came, and thus you goe; God speed you !'

The Ordinary claimed the ultimate jurisdiction over all schools within his diocese. No one, in fact, might start a school or teach any subject without his licence under penalty of trial in the spiritual courts. The Henrician Injunctions of 1538, supplemented by those of Elizabeth in 1559, decreed that the bishop must be well satisfied that each Schoolmaster should not only be a man of learning, but a person of humility who was well seasoned and grounded in true religion. He must, moreover, be a man of integrity and irreproachable morals. Should he be found to be 'a drunkard, quarreller or profanely curse or swear or use any unlawful games as cards, dice, table quoits, laggetts etc, or frequent suspected houses', then his parson must first severely admonish him; but if this failed to have the desired effect, present him at the next Archdeacon's visitation and get his licence taken away. Bishop Wickham of Lincoln's visitation articles in 1585 inquired :

> Whether the schoolmasters which teach within your parish either openly or privately in any nobleman or gentleman's

house or in any other place . . . be of good and sincere religion
and conversation; and be diligent in teaching and bringing
up of youth; and whether they be examined, allowed and
licensed, by the Ordinary; and whether they teach the grammar set forth by king Henry the Eighth . . . whether they
teach their scholars the catechism in latin lately set forth,
and such sentences of scripture as shall be most expedient
and meet to move them to the love and reverence of God's
true religion now truly set forth by the Queen's Majesty's
authority . . . and what be the names and surnames of all
such schoolmasters and teachers of youth within your parish
as well as such as teach publicly as those that hath in the
houses of gentlemen and other private men.

He repeated this article in 1588; and his successor, Bishop Chader-
ton, issued another in almost identical terms ten years later. The
episcopate and their clergy were fully determined that every type
of education should remain under their strict and vigilant eyes;
daily prayers were always to be said, the Catechism taught, and
the children brought regularly into the church itself when and as
required. Many village schools were often constructed in the
churchyard; and sometimes they were actually held in one of the
side aisles of the church. Every Schoolmaster, 'ludimagister' or
'pedagogue' was cited to attend the Easter visitation of the archdeacon, where he had to exhibit his licence, and, if a layman, pay
a fee of sixpence. Clerks in holy orders on the other hand were
normally charged half-a-crown. In accordance with the 1559
Injunctions, quite apart from the exhortations of individual
bishops and parsons, all teachers of youth were expected to 'stir
and move them to the true love and due reverence of God's true
Religion' as it had been 'set forth by publick Authority'. Consequently the Schoolmaster of Great Hadham in Hertfordshire,
who during the year 1639 refused to bow at the name of Jesus . . .
affirming it to be 'unlawful, neither will he do it', was immediately
suspended from his office; and William Glaze, a man of Presbyterian sympathies who kept a school at Neithrop near Banbury
and firmly declined 'to bring his schollers to church on sundaies
and holidaies', was cited before the Consistory Court and discharged from his post for 'so illegal and pernicious a Practice'.
    According to the 78th Canon a parish priest was always to be
preferred to a lay Schoolmaster, partly apparently 'for the better

increase of his living', i.e. his stipend, but also because he was presumably more adequately equipped for 'training up of children in principles of true religion'. None the less lay competition was strong, even among the ladies. At Horton, Oxfordshire, in 1620 the churchwardens reported : 'concerning Scholemaysters we have note any besyde the ministre, but one poor woman that teacheth petys'.

Evidently she was no serious rival to the incumbent. But it was far otherwise at King's Sutton a year earlier where the parson was forced entirely out of the teaching business by some enterprising schoolmarms. These blue-stockings, or so the churchwardens complained to the archdeacon, 'will cause our minister to give up teaching children, their teaching being an hindrance to him that his pay is not halfe worth his labours'. One of them, a certain Jane Toms, refused to give way to the vicar even after an ecclesiastical admonition, so she was again presented the following September on the grounds that she possessed neither 'licence, ability or fittness to teach so long as the minister will'. The same arguments were applied to Margaret Shipden of Sutton, Sussex, in 1624 'for teachinge of a schoole, whereas our curate who is allowed by my lord Bishop is willing and desirous for to doe the same for the more increasinge of his living'; and to Nicholas Cole and his daughter of West Wittering, who likewise, unlicensed, were taking the children away from yet another clergyman, 'being licensed to teach and doth gladly take paynes to teach children and to bring them up in good letters and for the better mayntenance of himself'. Undoubtedly the parson was still inclined to regard this profession as essentially his own, and to put as many stumbling blocks as possible in the path of lay competition. Consequently the Archdeacon and his Official were continually bombarded with letters from both sides asking for their support. On 26 November 1641 John Keate, curate of Great Milton in Oxfordshire wrote :

> Mr Holloway, my best respects to you remembered Sir.
> I John Keate Curate of Milton doe present one Richard Milles gent who keepeth a schoole in the parish of Milton contrary to Mr Dr Tookers Command.

But some thirty-odd years earlier in February 1606 a persecuted Schoolmaster, William Osborne of Banbury, penned the following pathetic petition to the same Authority :

Good Mr Dr : necessity moveth mee to trouble you; as I hear Mr Hollton hath moved the churchwardens to present mee for not catachising on the Sabaothes, where hee never requested mee herin, being neyther sicke, nor from home, nor himself otherwise troubled with preaching, neyther hath the schoolmaster ever been put to Catachise on the Sabaoths. All this ariseth on ill will because they dislike mee . . . I beseech your Worship let them not presse mee doune, nor impose farther burdens upon mee then belonges to my place; for their drift is to expell mee.

No, the schoolmaster's lot too was certainly not always a happy one.

Writing of the early seventeenth century Maurice Ashley comments in his *Stuart England* :

'It is doubtful whether primary education was widespread. . . . There is no reason to suppose that the majority of villagers were literate.'

But the charitable zeal of well-to-do people up and down the country was providing schools everywhere, of all types, and in ever increasing numbers. Financially and geographically education was within the reach of all; and parents were expected to have their children educated if it were at all possible. A love of learning and a burning desire for new knowledge were two of the outstanding features of Elizabethan and Stuart England; and it has even been suggested that in some places at any rate education had been made practically compulsory. It was reported to the Archdeacon from Bradenham in 1664 : 'That there are only 2 or 3 poore families who by reason of their poverty have not bred up children to reading and therefore our Minister knows not what to do with them. We have warned them to send their children to him but they have not.'

Schoolmasters, like the curates they often were, were sometimes jacks-of-all-trades : not averse to earning an honest, or not so honest, penny on the side, by such means as keeping an ale-house or dabbling in medicine, if they could hope to get away with it. The churchwardens of Cropredy in 1619 declared smugly : 'we have no scholemaster practisinge eny phisycke or surgery to our knowledge'; but those of North Lopham in Norfolk were not so fortunate (or were they?), admitting of their pedagogue, Thomas Rud : 'He practizeth phisycke and surgerye'.

It was an unhealthy age, where sanitation and hygene were almost completely unknown, and plague, small-pox, tuberculosis and other diseases were accepted philosophically as visitations from the Almighty. Doctors were still more than half quacks, although in some of the larger towns fully-qualified medical men, with an Oxford or even a Padua degree, were at work on scientific lines. After all William Harvey, physician extraordinary to Charles I, had discovered the circulation of the blood; and others, like Sir Theodore Mayerne, were aware of the importance of chemistry. But too many medical men still looked back to the Middle Ages or to Classical times for their inspiration and practice, with an avid insistence upon the letting of blood, mostly by leeches, and the enforced vomit as the only possible remedies for all ills, thereby keeping the so-called 'four humours' of the human body in balance. Fashionable physicians and surgeons could and did charge high fees; but in the small country towns and villages there were few qualified men, and the art of the apothecary or surgeon too often became a side-line to be taken up by other professional men like schoolmasters, barbers or parsons to help eke out their slender stipends. Here flourished such unorthodox persons as 'wise-women' and 'white-witches', who combined a knowledge of herbs and simples with a rudimentary understanding of the human frame handed down to them by their predecessors : trading upon the credulity or necessity of simple folk. Nicholas Breton, in *The Good and the Badde*, published during 1616, wrote of the medical profession of his day :

> A worthy physician is an enemy of sickness, in purging nature of corruption. His action is most in the feeling of pulses, and his discourses chiefly of diseases. He is a great searcher out of simples, and accordingly makes his composition. He persuades abstinence and patience, for the benefit of health, while purging and bleeding are the chief courses of his counsel. The apothecary and the chirurgeon are his two chief attendants, with whom conferring upon time, he grows temperate in his cures.

When, after her own physicians had failed to give satisfaction, Dr Frires of London was called into Yorkshire to attend Lady Slingsby, he diagnosed trouble with 'ye spleen' and recommended her to take : '2 or 3 steel pils for 4 or 5 mornings and drink after ym a dish of thin broath with cream of tartar in it'. Sir Henry

Slingsby commented in his diary : 'This man is of great fame for his skill and cures, wch he doth not a little brag off, who tell you of his £50 or £100 cures'. None the less Frires or Fryar failed completely to cure his wife, causing the baronet to add wryly :

The physitian commonly favours himself more yn ye patient and is more sure to find yt wch will do him good from the patient he undertakes yn can ye patient be sure to find any good from him; therefore it concerns him to extoll his skill above any experience he hath. He professeth to cure all manner of diseases and his practise is but a tryall, he never attains it; and if his practise were upon himself I should ye rather venture; but he would not pay for his skill at so dear a rate, tho' he fools us to venture on him.

The Church continued to keep a strict control over all who practised either surgery or medicine. In the Middle Ages she had been the mother of hospitals, and almost the sole dispenser of healing; and this position the new national state Church, that emerged from the Reformation, sought to maintain at all costs. By the Act, 3 Hen. VIII. c. II, every medical practitioner was required to obtain a licence from his bishop, for which he had to produce not only testimonials from two established members of his own profession as to his ability to perform his craft; but also from his incumbent as to his orthodoxy, morals and general fitness of character.[9] This did not, of course, prevent plenty of quacks and unauthorised interlopers setting themselves up in the same way of business, who at a time when illness and disease of every type abounded did very well for themselves; particularly when properly qualified and licensed doctors were often few and far between. In their visitation articles Elizabethan and Stuart bishops were always asking questions like the following : 'whether there be any in your parish or commonly going abroad in the country that practice physic and surgery without he be first examined of the ordinary and by him admitted and licensed.' These licences had regularly to be exhibited and renewed at the Easter visitation. In 1597, for instance, 46 and 18 were shown in Norfolk and Suffolk respectively, comprising 36 surgeons, 18 physicians, 6 who claimed to be both, and 4 bone-setters. Not very many for so large an area. No

[9] However a further Act, 14-15 Hen. VIII. c.5., permitted properly qualified physicians to practise simply after an examination by the President and three members of the London Society of Physicians.

wonder Bishop Redman's article dealing with the subject of un-licensed practitioners on this occasion was answered by parish after parish in the affirmative : Bridget, the wife of Edmund Dick of South Creake, practised 'bone-setting and not licensed'; Cecily Cobb, 'surgery and bone-setting'; the Schoolmaster at Halesworth, Phineas Reeve, was likewise indulging in a little un-authorised 'bonesettinge'; and at Swaffham a Mr Nicholls 'practyzeth physicke, but whether lycensed or no they knowe not'.

Certainly the women, whether as surgeons, apothecaries or both appear to have entered the East Anglican medical field at this date in a big way. For apart from those already mentioned there was the wife of Maurice Clun of Swaffham, 'the wife of Bastarde' at Wells, and the 'wife of Henry Becket' of Great Yarmouth, to name a few at random, all of whom had to be admonished and inhibited from further practice by the Consistory Court. On the other hand it was generally recognised that charity was a religious duty, and how far those 'wise-women', who compounded lotions and dabbled in the curative properties of herbs and simples were allowed to shelter under its umbrella, as defined in the Act, 34/35 Hen : VIII. c. 8., depended upon how this law was interpreted in the different dioceses. Becket's wife, for instance, had pleaded in her own defence that 'she onelie helpeth women when they can-not be delyvered of child byrthe with herbes and not otherwaies.' As regards the men : Nicholas Harmon, John Bonner and Richard Noble of Banbury were cited in 1610 and again in 1616 before the Archdeacon's court for the offence of unlicensed doctoring; and most Diocesan Courts dealt with similar culprits.

A particularly interesting case was that of Tristram Lyde, a surgeon, who appeared before the Rochester Assizes in 1601 charged with 'killing divers women by annoyntinge them with quicksylver. Evidence given that he would have caused the women to have stript themselves naked in his presence, and himselfe would have annoynted them; that he tooke upon him the cure, and departed because they would not give him more than their first agreement'. Lyde, who claimed that he practised under the authority of no less a person than the Archbishop of Canterbury himself, defended his action on the grounds that 'theire diseases were such as required that kinde of medicine, that it was there owne negligence by takinge cold, by going abroade sooner than he prescribed'. He was acquitted.

Among the more prominent of the pews in any Tudor or Stuart

parish church would be the 'churching pew'. Therein sat the mother who came to give thanks to Almighty God for her safe deliverance 'from the great pain and peril of child birth'. And, whenever possible, by her side sat the attendant midwife, ever anxious to advertise yet another proof of her medical skill. Still regarded in many quarters as more than half a witch, who could if she wished injure or destroy mother and child as easily as succour them, in Elizabethan times she was required to swear an oath, before receiving her licence, that she would not employ : 'any kind of sorcery or incantation in the travail of any woman'. It was further demanded of her in later years that she swear on the Bible :

> You will faithfully and truly execute the office of midwife in those places where you shall be licensed and authorised, you shall afford your help as well to the poor for charity as to the rich for reward, you shall not deliver any privately or clandestinely to conceal the birth of the child. If you deliver any whom you suspect to be unmaryed you shall acquaint the Ecclestiasticall Court of this Jurisdiction therewith and before you yield your assistance or helpe you shall perswade and by all lawfull means labour with them to declare who is the father of the said child, this you shall doe ffaithfully and truly. Soe help you God and the contents of this Booke'.

Consequently midwives sometimes witheld their assistance until the unmarried mother had been forced into disclosing the name of her lover :

> Uppon the Satterday before Michaelmas last [runs a grim minute in the Oxfordshire Archidiaconal records] the articulate Mary Blye being then delivered of a childe wch was unlawfully begotten and at the tyme of the extremitye of her travayle being charged by diverse of the women then present to confesse truly the ffather of the sayde childe, she the said Mary did ernestly affirme that the said Wm Smith was the father.

But before condemning these women for their cruelty, it must be borne in mind that the penalty for concealment was either a most unpleasant penance or at best a severe admonition. In December 1565 the Act Books of Southwell referred to such a penance performed by two midwives, who, in the case of an adulteress, 'did conceale and kepe secrett her evill and naughtie doinges from the knowledge of all her neighbours'.

So the midwife, too, had to walk circumspectly, and maintain the correct balance between her duty towards her patient and her obligations to her employer, the State Church.

CHAPTER V

The Congregation

BY the 1559 Act of Uniformity all parishioners were expected to attend divine service of a Sunday morning and again in the afternoon; to come on holy days; and, if over sixteen years of age, to make regular communions on the three or four 'sacrament' Sundays in the year. How far this Act was strictly enforced in every parish is, of course, impossible to say. It has been suggested that the very poor did not attend church at all. Filthy vagabonds and other undesirables would hardly have been welcomed there; and if every one had really come, would there have been room for them all? Many churches were very small. Besides how could such people pay the shilling fine, which might be stepped up to £20 a month for a persistent and wilful refusal to worship according to law? Obviously these penalties applied only to heads of households and those for whom they were responsible, i.e. their families, servants, journeymen and apprentices.

During the Laudian era, when communion was frequently increased to once a month, it was still customary for all those over sixteen to receive the bread and wine, whether they had been confirmed or not. Bishops were few and far between, spent much of the year in London, where they were engrossed in Parliamentary or other secular business, and visited their dioceses only during the summer months. Consequently Confirmation services were usually only held in the larger towns, to which many villagers were unable to penetrate. The country clergy on the whole were careful to instruct and examine their children in the Catechism; but did not always press very hard for their confirmation, especially in the more puritanically minded parishes, where they rested simply on their obligation to administer the sacrament to everyone who had been so instructed and was of the canonical age. In view of the manner in which Confirmation services were frequently conducted, this attitude was perhaps understandable, if regrettable :

Those who sought confirmation would scarcely have been edified by the spectacle, for multitudes flocked to the great and rare event, lest they might be too old or incapable of walking when next the bishop visited the neighbourhood. Hence there were throngs of disorderly persons crowding in from the surrounding parishes, jostling and pushing to get near him, tumults, banging of doors, and people leaving before the bishop gave his blessing; and the bishop himself who usually began the laying on of hands some hours before noon would be most eager to depart after the meal on the next stage of his tour with as many hours of daylight before him as possible.[1]

Nearly always some candidates emerged from the church still unconfirmed, since they had been unable to find a way through the press that surrounded his lordship. The rubric in the Prayer Book instructing would-be communicants to notify the curate well in advance of their intention to receive communion on a particular Sunday was even then more honoured in the breach than in the observance. But in an age where in a small country village like Upton-on-Severn as many as 206 communicants might appear at any one time, and in a country-town such as Tewkesbury 2,600, it certainly behoved the minister and churchwardens to make ample provision for bread and wine, as most parochial account books fully endorse. On non-sacrament Sundays the lengthy morning service, consisting of Mattins, Litany, Anti-Communion, and a homily or sermon would last from 9 a.m. until dinner-time; while in the winter one must be back at church for Evening Prayer at 3 p.m. and thus save any unnecessary expenditure on candle-power. Most of the clergy were unlicensed to preach, and the repetitive reading of the homilies from the 1562 Collection was an incentive either to slumber, restlessness or irreverence. Puritans, who demanded nothing short of the pure waters of 'The Word', Roman Catholic recusants, and those profitably engaged in buying, selling, husbandry, industry or commerce, were often conspicuous by their absence, fine or no fine; and this particularly applied to the more irksome weekday services on holy days, Wednesdays and Fridays. As always the local ale-house provided a formidable rival to the spiritual ministrations of the Church, by supplying tempting bodily refreshments, secular amusements and

[1] W. A. Pemberton, *Studies in the Ecclesiastical Court*, p. 446.

A MOST
Certain, Strange, and true Diſcovery of a

VVITCH.

Being taken by ſome of the Parliament Forces, as ſhe was
ſtanding on a ſmall planck-board and ſayling on
it over the River of *Newbury*:

Together with the ſtrange and true manner of her death, with
the propheticall words and ſpeeches ſhe vſed at the ſame time.

Printed by John Hammond, 1643.

BROADSHEET RELATING
THE DISCOVERY OF A WITCH, 1643

a hearty human fellowship that contrasted strangely and most favourably with the bitter cold, the stern discipline, the wearysome stereotyped worship and rigid class distinctions encountered at divine service. 'The lure of the game of chance, jovial companions, a lively fire in a snug room on a frosty day, were loud inviting voices of the world that drowned many a whisper of conscience at the hour of public worship'.

The authorities in Church and State were, of course, only too aware of such material allurements; and the ale-houses were accordingly strictly regulated. The following licence issued in 1609 at Fakenham Quarter Sessions to Richard Dunne of Holt, a husbandman, is typical of most. Its terms demanded :

1. That you suffer no neighbours children or servantes nor anie dwellinge in the same towne to typple in yor house.
2. That you suffer none to typple in yor house in one daie above one houre.
3. That you suffer none to typple in yor house upon Sabaoth or festivall daies in the tyme of the sermon or devine service, nor at any tyme after nyne of the clock at night.
4. That if anie vagabondes or suspicious persons come to yor house, you shall acquainte the officers wth it, and so allso if anie goodes be offered in yor house by anie to be sould.
5. That you suffer no dicinge cardinge or other unlawfull games in yor house.
6. That you suffer no dronkeness or dissolute order in yor house, but if anie happen to be, to acquainte the constables of the towne wth it that the offenders maie be punished.
7. That you brew not in yor house but take yor drinke from the Brewers (if it maie be had) and the best to be but at vis the barrell, and the worst at iiis the barrell.
8. That you drawe out yor drinke by the Ale-quarte or pinte, and not by Jugges or Cupps and sell the best after the rate of iiiid the Ale gallon and the worse at iid the Ale gallon.

Whether parishioners resorted to the ale-house or not, most parishes contained a substantial number of absentees from church, some of whom had not been inside it for many years. Many of these were Non-Conformists of one type or another, whose consciences forbade them to take part in Anglican worship; but there were always plenty of other reasons : Richard Clowes of Yoxford in 1597 ascribed his habitual non-attendance to the deficiencies of his rector : 'Mr Barlow, then rector', he declared, 'was not suffycient, neyther could he understand the saide Mr Barlowe'; while William Smyth of Twyford was frankly of the opinion that an appearance in church once a month was as much as a reasonable parson could possibly expect of any man. Others pleaded ill-health, fear of arrest, or even that they were already in prison and so incapable of attendance. But it was left to Henry Daynes of Redenhall to make a mock of the whole compulsory system of church-going : 'He hath not repayred to his church this half-year', it was alleged, 'and maketh a jest of it saying he shall save Cth mile going in the yeare, bycause the church is a mile from his howse'. Neither was the shilling fine always a deterrent. William Gosden of Sidlesham, Sussex, who was discovered drunk on a Sunday in 1622 during the time of divine service, 'scoffed at the authority of churchwardens for reforming such offences, as but a twelvepeny mulct to answere it'.

Freedom to attend the place of worship of your own choice was not encouraged, for whatever reason, since as a parishioner you were expected to go only to your parish church. John More and his wife, who went to Great Yarmouth rather than their native Gorleston, were ordered to return despite the pathetic plea 'that he is Corpolent and fatt and dwelleth nearer Yarmouth than Gorleston church, and by reason thereof he repayreth to Yarmouthe churche, he and his wife, and there have and doe comonlie heare dyvine prayers redd.'[2] A stock excuse of many recusants for not receiving the holy communion was that they were not in love and charity with their neighbours; but an indifferent Anglican was not averse to a similar plea. Henry Watson of Heath, for example, refused to communicate because he declared 'he is not in love and charitie wth the parson of Heathe'; and John Whytington of All Saints', Oxford, admitted in 1584

---

[2] Occasionally people were issued with special licences enabling them to go elsewhere. Such a licence, for example, was granted to aged folk of Waddesdon, Buckinghamshire, who lived more than two miles from their parish church, but within a quarter of a mile of Fleet Marsdon church. But it was conditional upon their attending Waddesdon three times a year for Holy Communion, and also upon their paying all their just dues, tithes and other ecclesiastical charges to the churchwardens and parson of Waddesdon.—See, *The Laudian Church in Buckinghamshire*, p. 49.

that he did 'not receave at Easter Last', because one of his neighbours John Clarke had maligned his wife, maliciously reporting
'that there weare xxtie as honest as this respondentes wyffc
whipped at a cartes ars'. Thomas South of Hempton, on the other
hand, who was discovered in an ale-house during the hours of
divine service, justified himself somewhat lamely on the grounds
that 'the butcher owed this respondent somme monie' and so he
'went to the ale-house with him, thincking to receave his monie',
totally forgetful of the day and hour. John Collie was more honest
and forthright, admitting the offence but excusing it on the plea
of necessity :

> He is a brewer by his occupation [he told the court] and is
> forman to foure houses so that he cannot come to the churche
> so ofte as he woolde because of his charge that he hath in
> hande, for when he doeth beginne to putt fyre under the
> furnes he cannot departe from yt neither by day nor night
> until his burden be forther, nor anie other of the companie
> that are wth him and by that means is sumwhat slacke in
> coming to the churche as all others of that trade are, but
> deniethe that he doeth absent himself in contempte of the
> Quene's laws . . . and saithe ffurther that he doeth receave
> orderlie at the leaste twyse in the yeare.

The Act Book of the Archdeacon of Taunton for 1623 records
the names of fifty-eight persons from some twenty-seven parishes,
who had been presented for non-attendance at divine service and
fined, including that of a man from Langford Budville who
pleaded unsuccessfully that he had come into church during the
reading of the first lesson. It is of interest to note in passing that
a similar attempt about the same date at Chesham Magna, Buckinghamshire, to claim church attendance simply by standing in
the churchyard was likewise disallowed.[3]

The Canons of 1571 had instructed the churchwardens to
present 'all those which rudely behave themselves in church . . .

---

[3] People were expected to attend the whole service. In 1634 Henry Stephen-
son of Walton, Buckinghamshire, was presented with his wife, because while
he stayed at home altogether in order to look after their four small children,
she only put in an appearance after the first lesson. At the same time Henry
Reeve of Hawbridge was charged with arriving only when the sermon was
due to commence; and William Cocke of Chesham Magna for leaving before
the Blessing.—See, *The Laudian Church in Buckinghamshire*, p. 49.

or by walking, by talking or noise shall let the minister or preacher'. Misbehaviour, irreverence and sometimes down-right brawling were no uncommon features of a Sunday or weekday service. This is very understandable when we remember that a large proportion of the congregation was there by compulsion rather than choice; that the services were very long; most sermons exceedingly dreary; and all except the very largest churches would be crowded to suffocation point. This last could be most unpleasant on a hot summer's day, with so many recently buried, uncoffined corpses, exhaling a pestilential odour. Then there were the rigid conventions and stern disciplines that decreed the separation of the sexes, the allocation of pews according to social status or the habitation of certain houses, and above all the herding together of the less desirable elements in the community, particularly youths from the labouring or pauper classes, on hard narrow forms or benches at the west end of the church. This last invited and provoked trouble of many kinds. At Kingston Ferring in 1625 some 'boyes and servants' were presented 'for striving and iustling and pinching one another for want of seats . . . to the offence of the congregation and the disturbance of divine service.' On 17 August 1656 Ralph Josselin wrote in his diary : 'This day Sam Burton and lame Byat, while I was reading the chapter, were sittinge in the maids seate and made a disturbance; the justice commanded the Constable to take them forth to the cage; the mother went out of the churche and took her son from the Constable, and said her husband paid scott and lott in the towne, and her son should sit anywhere.' The inevitable 'prank' at the back of the church during the sermon could no doubt usually be ignored, as when one youth broke 'an addled egg' on the shoulder of his next-door-neighbour, or another bitterly complained that 'he sitteth under the loft in the church and some persons above did spitt on his head'. It was a different matter, however, should such misbehaviour take a destructive turn as it did in Kings Sutton church on 1 December 1609, where John Clements and George Toms broke the church windows 'in sermon time'. The breaking of church windows, whether out of pure devilry or for doctrinal reasons, appeared to have been a popular pastime among the young. The churchwardens of Mursley in Buckinghamshire were obliged to request the Vestry that 'a great glasse windowe at the west-end of the steeple . . . maybe made up with stone so high that it may be out of the Boys reaching who do continually break it'; and those of Holy Trinity, York, were actually presented in 1613 because they had carelessly allowed cobbles, used for the repair of the fabric, to 'lie up to the church windows by means divers children have climbed up and broken the glasse windows of the church with stones'.[4]

Far worse than window-breaking were the deliberate attempts made by many parishioners to disrupt the service itself, as when William Hills of Holton St Mary, Suffolk, in 1597 'used in the tyme of devine service open and lowde speeches to the disturbance of the minister'; and two men at South Petherton, Somerset, during 1623 were excommunicated for 'abusing themselves in Church by brawling'. Less disturbing from the congregation's point of view, but just as heinous in the eyes of the Church Authorities, was the case of Richard Wood of Sampford Arundel, who persistently broke the 18th Canon of 1604 by 'using himself very unreverently in church i.e., that he doth not kneel all the time of prayer'. Others were even more 'unreverent': men talked, laughed, swore, kept their hats on, put their hands in their pockets, went to sleep, refused to stand up for the Creed or the Gospel, to turn to the east or to bow at the name of Jesus. Many noisily left the building before the service was concluded.

Some of the worst offenders were women, especially when they believed themselves to have been defrauded of their rights and privileges or wished to revenge themselves for real or suspected slights. Here are a few examples taken at random from the end of Elizabeth's reign: Margaret, wife of John Coates of Shropham, Norfolk, 'interrupted the minister by speaking to him in tyme of devine service, vi or vii weekes'; at Blythburgh in Suffolk Mary Knights 'do bringe maistifes to church into the stoole with her wherebie the parishioners cannot have ther seats, and also she useth to chide and braule in the churche'; the wife of Thomas Wynter of South Walsham, 'came into Halvergate church about a fortnight before Michallmas last and made an uprore'; and Jane, wife of Francis Hayword from New Buckenham, entered church one Sunday when the service was well advanced and abused the parson 'callinge him blacke sutty mowthed knave, to the greate disgrace of his callinge'. They were also, as we have already seen, very tenacious about their right to sit in certain seats and made a great deal of trouble should they be disturbed in

---

[4] Moulsloe church windows in Buckinghamshire were frequently broken by children 'that play at catt and stoole ball in the churchyard Sundaies and holidays usualy'.

them. Alicia Maynard, for instance, was presented 'for thrusting Anne Parratt up and downe a seate in the Church of Wing [Buckinghamshire] and for pulling of her hat from her head, and throwing it into the end of the other seate in tyme of Divine service upon a Sabeth day'; and the Southwell Act Books recorded on 6 February 1587 that a certain Nottinghamshire woman, Joan Halome, had alleged : 'that the . . . said Luce Wentworth did give the first occasion of making the disturbance in the churches, for that she would not kepe her place, where she was first sett; but came over her backe and marred her apparell in the stall where she was sett. Wherappon the saide Johanne Halome did pricke the said Lucie with a pynne'.[5]

It was not easy to prevent people working on a Sunday, and especially on a holy day; when, particularly in harvest time, their very livelihood depended upon it. Moreover the pleasant warmth and relaxation of the ale-house was an inviting alternative to a cold and crowded church, where the eagle eye of the church-warden was ever upon one to see that each was in his rightful place, worshipping and behaving in a reverent and seemly fashion. Certainly the laws on this matter were strict and unequivocal : shopkeepers might not display their wares with intent to sell; carriers, waggoners, and drovers of cattle, could not make any journeys; the butcher must not slaughter his beasts; the crafts-man should not ply his trade nor the husbandman go forth to plough, sow or reap. Even the housewife was expected to refrain from such unnecessary tasks as washing or baking. All, in fact, were directed to keep the 13th Canon which directed them to hear 'the Word of God read and taught, in private and public prayers, in acknowledging their offence to God and amendment of the same, in reconciling themselves charitably to their neighbours . . . in often times receiving the Communion . . . in visiting the poor and sick; and using all godly and sober conversation'.

But the Ecclesiastical Authorities did not always take into account the necessities of the husbandman when preventing him from working either on a Sunday or a holy day. Much sympathy could be felt for Robert Hogsflesh of Upmarden, Sussex, who in August 1622 was detected 'turning of pease in his field upon a sabbath day . . . betweene morning and evening prayers', for which he was presented by an over zealous churchwarden, despite the fact that he had also attended church twice on that day.

[5] For even more violent assaults *see* Appendix I.

Equally hard were the cases of Romulus Rolf and John Long of Otterburne in Hampshire, who had been 'mowing oates on the Sabbath before Morning Prayer', but 'left work before sunrise and came to Church'. None the less they were ordered to pay two shillings to the poor and acknowledge their fault before the minister and parishioners. When Richard Moreton of Whitney was accused in 1584 of 'workinge on the Saboth daye', he replied : 'that on St Markes last he fett in a loade of wood into his yard because he was afrayed yt woulde have beene stolen yf yt had leyne in the streetes, he is sorrie for his offence'; and Alicia Hen of Launton on a similar charge put up the defence 'that on Sundaye last being desired bye Joane Milman shee did healpe her to swill iii or 4 peeres of linen clothes, but doeth not use to doe enie woorck on the Sabaothe daye, nor ever did the like before'.

Such incidents helped to breed an anti-clericalism among ordinary people; and none more so than the manner in which the parishioners of Selsey were treated by their unsatisfactory rector, Robert Johnson, who ordered his whole congregation to attend church on a certain Wednesday promising them a sermon, but then himself failed to put in an appearance or even send an apology : 'whereby', we are told, 'the parrishioners, having a long tyme expected him at the church, were at length inforced to depart home without any service or sermon, to theire great griefe and discontent, it being in the middest of harvest'. On a totally different footing was the sly excuse of shopkeeper George Smith of St Peter's-in-the-East, Oxford, who 'confessethe that he doeth sumetyme upon the Sondayes and holidays sett his windowe a littell ashore because he hathe no other light into his house, but not purposelie to the intent to sell anie wares, yet sum he selleth to cuntrie folkes'; or the brazen attitude of Richard Pebworth, who frankly admitted : 'upon Sondaye in the morning abowte a fortinght agoe he did hunte and divers other holidayes and sumtymes at service tyme'. But perhaps the most curious case of all was that of Edith Clarke of Marsh, Buckinghamshire, who was presented in 1634 for 'charming Joan Mayes of Thornton's teeth on the Sabbath day'; and was excommunicated for contumacy.

Considering the many secular temptations, strong religious differences, and considerable physical handicaps such as sickness, bitter winters and bad roads, church attendance was on an average extremely high. In the Archdeaconry of Buckinghamshire, for instance, the total number of absentees recorded during the years

1633 to 1636 were respectively: 40, 42, 104, and 94. Young people were the chief offenders. Lads and lasses, being but human, not infrequently played truant when they saw the opportunity for a little fun and games. At Yapton in 1623 they spent the best part of one Sunday dancing to the tunes of a fiddler from Boxgrove; while the churchwardens of Havant in 1607 discovered another 'playing on sabbath day in open assembly' and duly presented him for so doing. Cricket was another temptation; a game which was not uncommonly played in the churchyard itself, where it could and did cause a good deal of damage both to property and the person. During 1622 a number of parishioners at Boxgrove, after repeated warnings, were presented for this offence, which, or so declared the churchwardens, was not only contrary to the 7th of their book of articles, but 'they use to breake the church-win-dowes with the ball', and 'a little child had like to have her braynes beaten out with the ball'. In this particular instance the case was made more difficult by the attitude of the previous wardens, who during their year of office had 'defended and mayn-tayned' these budding athletes.[6]

Catechising on a Sunday afternoon, whether before or during the afternoon service, was not on the whole popular with the clergy, who often neglected to undertake it; or with the laity, who all too frequently failed to send their children, apprentices and servants to be instructed as the 59th Canon directed. None the less a persistent refusal to compel them to attend could and often did result in the excommunication both of parents and employers. William Hilles of Holton St Mary, 'who doeth not cause his children and servants to come to be catechised' was so punished in 1597. But when as at Sydenham, Oxfordshire, in the latter half of Elizabeth's reign the curate did not catechise for ten years, there appears to have been no protest from his parishioners; and in other churches the task was willy-nilly delegated to the school-master. So much so in fact that as no more such help was forth-coming at Amersham the rector, instead of shouldering the task himself, blandly declared. 'In respect their was no schoolmaster and the schollers were dispersed . . . none of the rest of the parish-

<hr>

[6] Not all clergymen were opposed to Sunday sport. Thomas Lawrence, rector of Fugglestone with Bemerton, who was also Master of Balliol and Lady Margaret Professor of Divinity at Oxford, set up a Maypole at his rectory door, allowed his parishioners to use the churchyard as a bowling green and skittle alley and gave a 'fiddler who played for dancers sixpence and his dinner'.

ioners either children or servants would come to it'. Neither would they come if the parson himself was too long-winded or dull. The churchwardens of King's Sutton, replying to the items 8 and 9 in the Archdeacon's Book of Articles in 1619, wrote : 'our minister did catechise so long as could have any to come and when no more came then he left; and therefore desire your worships advice what to do herin for if we present any we must present all the parish'. The problem of getting children to come to Sunday School is then by no means a modern one !

One of the more exciting events at Morning Prayer, to which, alas, a heartless generation looked forward with undisguised glee, was a public penance. Actually there were several types of penance, of which the 'public' one was the most severe and degrading. The lightest was the 'acknowledgment', which was usually awarded for persistent absence from church, working on Sundays and holy days, brawling in church or churchyard, and a clandestine marriage. This must be performed in front of the minister and churchwardens in church, but not publicly in service time and once only. Then there was the 'Confession', decreed for either abusing the minister or churchwardens, harbouring an unmarried mother, incontinence between a couple who were subsequently married, drunkenness, the holding of conventicles, and for a churchwarden who either did not present offences or failed to carry out repairs that had been ordered. This, too, was performed before the minister and wardens out of service time, but with a certain number of substantial parishioners, probably vestrymen, also in attendance at the church; and more than once.

But it was 'Public Penance', reserved for incontinence of all kinds, excepting that preceeding marriage, that attracted the greatest attention. Some poor wretched girl, who had proved herself to be no better than she should be, and had been caught red-handed in the act, must parade herself, bare-headed, bare-legged and bare-foot, robed in a white sheet from the neck and shoulders downward, and carrying a white wand in her hand, at Morning Prayer. There she knelt

> . . . in the sight of the congregation till ye gospell is to be read and then standing upon a step a two high near the ministers deske the better to be heard and seene of the congregation there present shall in a penitent manner and with an audible voyce say after the minister as folloeth : I, A.M.,

spinster of this parish, not having the fear of God before mine eyes nor regarding my owne soule health to the displeasure of Almighty God, the danger of my soule and the evill example of others committed the vile and heinous sinne of ffornication.

The penance was then certified by the parson and churchwardens and returned into the Archdeacon's Court. Sometimes such a penance had also to be held in the market place, a much more trying ordeal, since here unlike the sedate congregation in church, the mob was free to jeer and cat-call, to throw garbage and to press with their stinking bodies close to the luckless penitent, gloating over her shameful garb and pitiful distress of mind and body.

It was perhaps through the 'occasional offices' that individual parishioners came most closely into contact with their parson and church. The birth rate everywhere was very high, seven or eight children to each family; and although many of these never survived infancy, all those who lived long enough were to be brought to the font and baptised with the sign of the Cross, after their mothers had first been 'churched'. The puritans objected to both as 'superstitious' and 'unscriptural' and sought to escape them whenever possible by having their children secretly christened in their own homes. The wardens of Burcot, for instance, presented Thomas Bond and his wife 'for not frequenting there parish church and receiving ye sacrament in Ester also that for ought we know or can learne their children are not baptized'; and their colleagues at Benson cited William Martin and his wife into court for a similar offence. In Hampshire in 1607 the wife of William Powlewheele of St Maurice Winton, and those of Leonard Bruning and John Hellier of Hambledon were all excommunicated for obstinately refusing to be churched; while at Kingston Ferring, Sussex, it was reported : 'wee have divers greene women that yet have not given thanks.' On the whole, however, most mothers regarded their 'churching' as an important public service and insisted on the midwife being present at their side in the special pew provided for the ceremony. So jealous indeed were they of their rights that at Abingdon it was put forward as an excuse for their non-appearance that : 'woemen refuse to be churched because they have not their right place, and midwives are excluded'. A certain 'wife of William Barnes Taylor' was actually presented 'for intruding into the pew appropriated for churching women', when she had no legitimate cause to do so.

Most parents, too, were only too pleased to bring their children to church for their christening; unless the child happened to be born out of wedlock, when not unnaturally they were reluctant to advertise its existence. Roger Brown of Benson, for instance, was accused 'of not baptizing a bastard child which hee had by a whore whom he keeps in his house as his wife'. After the Long Parliament had established itself and the Puritan Revolution began, many parsons found themselves openly challenged on the question of signing with the Cross. At Radwinter in March 1641/2 John Smith the blacksmith asked the curate to christen his child whilst omitting this particular ceremony. The curate refused; whereupon Smith retired in a rage. 'But', we are told, 'upon second thoughts, bringing the child, as soon as it was christened, he violently snatched the child out of the curate's arms, before he had signed it with the Cross; to the general offence of the sober-minded and the encouragement of others in disorder; for at another christening in the afternoon a woman attempted the like'. A similar scene occurred in the same church a few weeks later on 8 April at the baptism of Richard Clark's daughter, Alice, when one of the congregation, John Traps: 'confronting the curate by coming up close and standing in a daring manner by him, told him that he should not have her out of the godmother's arms, nor sign her with the sign of the cross; and to that end flung the cloth over the face of the child, keeping his hand upon it and saying, "It is the mark of the Beast".' About the same date Thomas Newcomen, Rector of Holy Trinity, Colchester, finding himself compelled by *force major* to give up making the sign of the Cross in baptism, used boldly to parody the Prayer Book words of admission and say : 'We do not receive this child into the congregation of Christ's Church flock, neither do we signe it with the signe of the crosse, in token that hereafter it shal be ashamed to confesse the faith of Christ crucified'. Public baptism went out of fashion during the period of the Commonwealth and Protectorate, so much so in fact that Josselin wrote on 5 October 1656 : 'Sacrament of baptisme administered this day in publiqu, which was not for a long time before in Colne'; and children were entered in the Register as 'borne' instead of 'baptised'.

Marriages could not be solemnised, according to the 62nd Canon, except by a licence granted by a surrogate or after the publication of banns on three successive Sundays or holy days during divine service.[7] The ceremony itself had to be performed between 8 a.m. and 12 noon in the parish church of either bride or bridegroom. A solemn betrothal, *consensus facit matrimonum*, whether in fact it was either *sponsalia per verba de futuro* or *sponsalia per verba de presenti*, and made publicly, with witnesses present and tokens exchanged before a clergyman or layman in similar form to the promises of the marriage service, constituted a marriage in *practice*, although later, of course, it had to be solemnly celebrated in church. Such a betrothal, as in the famous case of King Edward IV, could even be used as grounds for nullifying marriage with another person, or in bringing a breach of promise action. None the less until the actual marriage ceremony in church the union remained incomplete, since it still lacked God's and the Church's official sanction and blessing. For instance it was admitted before the Archdeacon's Court in 1584 in the case of John Stacie and Jane Banister of Sandford-by-Thames 'that theare hath beene good will and motion of marriage betweene this respondent and Jane Banister but noe perfett contract because the frendes of this respondent and the same Jane have not yet concluded'; and intimacy between them was strongly denied. This, alas, was not so with Edward Saul and Alice Capon of Adderbury, who confessed 'that theare was a promise of marriage betwene them after they had knowledge one of another'.

A good example of a case of a contract *per verba de presenti* is to be found at Tadmarton where, after Whitsuntide, Alice Butler and John Saman

. . . plighted theire faith and trothe together using theis wordes . . . I doe take thee to my wiffe and doe promise never

---

[7] According to ancient canon law there were certain 'close seasons' of the year when it might not be celebrated at all. These consisted of the three periods between Advent Sunday and St Hilary's Day (January 13th), Septuagesima to Low Sunday, and Rogation Sunday to Trinity Sunday. The 1604 Canons simply forbade marriage 'at unseasonable times'; but these, generally speaking, were taken to refer to the same days as before; although attempts were made, unsuccessfully, both in Parliament and Convocation to make marriage lawful at all seasons of the year.

On the fly-leaves of old parish registers were sometimes found the lines:

Advent marriage doth thee deny
But Hilary gives thee liberty.
Septuagesima says thee nay,
Eight days from Easter says you may.
Rogation bids thee to contain,
But Trinity sets thee free again.

to marie wth any other, and thereupon [she] used the verie same wordes to him againe wch wordes were spoken in the presence of one Elizabeth Standishe and James Whitley, and immediatelye after the faith and trothe was given betwene them cam in Mr Thurston Standishe [Rector of Tadmerton] to whom the said Saman did acknowledge the contracte and promised never to go from it.

Richard Freland, a gentleman of Greatham in Hampshire, described on 29 April 1567 how such a solemn betrothal had taken place before him in the house of John Hodges, uncle to the girl, Christian Hodges. Freland asked her and her intended husband, William Coles, 'whether they were agreed and free from all other in the way of marriage, and they answered him both yea they were so. And then this deponent bid him the said William take her the said Christian by the hand and so did. And then the said William spake these words as followeth holding her still by the hand, viz.

'I William take thee Christian to my wedded wife for better for worse for richer for poorer in sickness and in health till death us depart and thereto I plight thee my troth.' [Christian herself then made a similar declaration; and, according to Freland, about fifteen days later] agnised and acknowledged herself to be the wife of the said Coles.

If one partner to such a contract later broke it by marrying some one else he or she laid themselves open to a charge of adultery. This actually happened to Joan Farmer, originally engaged on 19 September 1580 to Laurence Banks of Dranfield in Derbyshire, who became the wife of Richard Claye of Gotham. Eventually the matter was amicably settled out of court, when Laurence and Joan mutually agreed to release each other from their betrothal. In these cases the tokens given to one another as pledges of the contract were solemnly returned. They were usually of nominal value. In 1584 Robert Lynne gave Bridget Mychaell a groat 'and she gave him a pennye in token of goodwyll in full promyse of the same'.

Clandestine marriages, whether within the prohibited degrees, in private houses, out of hours, or for a variety of other reasons, were all too frequently performed either by the laxer clergy for pecun-

iary purposes or by puritanical ministers for doctrinal reasons :
often without licence or the calling of banns. At Rising in Norfolk
during 1613 Eleanor Clarke, who was under sixteen years of age,
was married to James Flawes after only half an hour's notice, and
when a licence was neither asked for nor produced : 'And sone
after xi thei were married by the minister of the said church who
had xiid for marieng them and the Clerk iid'. In that case the
fees were moderate enough; but when Daniel Hallame was wedded illegally in Skegby parish church by the Revd. Anthony Beret,
the latter 'plundered him (the bridegroom) of six shillings and eight
pence'. The penalty, however, to the clergyman performing such a
clandestine wedding, if caught, could be severe. Thomas Lan-
caster, curate of Dorchester, married William Innes and Elizabeth
Chirrell in a private house, with only one witness, Joan Price,
present; for which offence he was suspended from office, although
he was able to produce the licence, had faithfully used the full
Prayer Book service, and had kept within the prescribed hours.
Many of these clandestine marriages were performed in the night
or very early morning : John Cole was united to Jane Grant at
Exbury in Hampshire 'at break of day by candle light . . . without
banns or licence'; and the curate of Sydenham married a certain
Robert Coney Clarke 'one Whyte monday at nighte'. Another
couple John Prowting and Margaret Edsall were actually wedded
outside the back door of Bishop's Sutton Vicarage, where they
arrived one autumn morning in 1575 and demanded to see the
vicar. 'Mr Vicar', said John, 'so it is there hath been love and
good will between this maid Margaret Edsall and me a long time,
and we are come to you to contract us'. The vicar, after closely
questioning Margaret concerning a rumour that she was already
betrothed to one, Roger Ryng, which she flatly denied, affirming
'she would only marry the said John Prowting and none other',
eventually agreed to their request, produced his Prayer Book, and
although no banns had been called or licence produced, married
them then and there, but without a ring.

Undoubtedly one of the dangers inherent in such secret weddings was that one of the parties to it already had a lawful spouse
still living. On 14 January 1569/70 John Bradshaw appeared in
court at Nottingham charged with having two wives, viz. Katherine Burdocke and Joan Godbeheare. It then transpired that he
had married Katherine secretly 'in the house of a certain John
Harryson in Ilkeston . . . by Cuthbert Bee, clerk, curate of Dale-

abbey'. For this crime he had to perform the following humiliating public penance :

> . . . shall go from the parishe churche of St Maryes this saterdaye with a sheete about his myddell and a white wand in his hand after the manner of a penytent rounde aboute the markett place and a paper uppon his backe which shall declare wherefore hee ys enjoined this pennaunce, and the said Katherine Burdocke and Jone Godbeheare shall folowe him in lyke manner and in the same araye as penytentes and so shall retorne agayne to the sayde parishe churche.

The joke of it was that two months later John was able to produce letters testimonial from the Official of Derby that he had never been married to Katherine after all, since Cuthbert Bee was not in holy orders. Consequently the Judge on 8 April dismissed John commanding him 'not to consort with her (Katherine) but to live with the said Joan Godbeare as his wife'.

The clergy had certainly to be careful and make some pretty searching inquiries before joining a man and woman together as husband and wife. At the Archdeacon of Oxford's Court in 1584 William Pickering of Burford was prosecuted for 'reviling' his parson. His defence was that the latter had refused to call his banns; so he told him, apparently in no uncertain terms, 'that he used not this respondent well in stayeing of the banes betwene this respondent and Suzane Brayne alias George'. But after the whole matter had been thoroughly investigated it became very clear that the banns had not been called because of a strong suspicion, ammounting almost to a certainty, 'whether he weare not contracted to another in London'.

On the other hand some parsons could be willing accessories : William Proctor, Rector of Stradishall in Somerset was accused during 1623 of marrying a woman in her own house; '4 days later she had child, he churched her and gave her sacrament without public confession'. Later he tried, unsuccessfully, to persuade the Justices of the Peace not to punish her. Some parishes, indeed, got the name of 'lawless churches' because of the number of clandestine marriages performed there : little English Gretna Greens, to which, when their own incumbent stood upon the letter of the law, couples could slip away, be happily united, and no awkward questions asked. Biddlesden in Buckinghamshire during the Laudian regime was a notorious centre, to which people resorted from far and wide to be married by the curate, Thomas Taylor. Banbury was another, of which Thomas Holloway informed the Archdeacon by letter, dated 23 February 1606 :

> I doubte not but Mr houghton at Banbury yf he kepeth a registery of those he marrieth without banes as also at tymes inhibyted by law but that he will be accomptable unto you for good score of money : the church by a curious proverbe (bothe in respecte of the gyvinge and ministrations of the sacraments as also for nomber of mariages without banes) is called a lawless churche.

Most shires also possessed their hedge or wandering ministers, who were only too pleased to perform this ceremony behind a hedge in return for a small fee.[8]

In an age when the average male did not normally marry before he was twenty-six and the female twenty-two, there was inevitably a good deal of incontinency in most parishes, where in the closely packed houses there were innumerable cases of incest, of female servants being seduced by their employers and even daughters or sisters-in-law by their male in-laws. If sexual immorality was proved, and irrefutable proof took the form of a bastard child, then a public penance had to be performed by the unhappy girl, while the churchwardens made vigorous efforts to discover the father, lest his illegitimate off-spring be left a burden on the parish. This was by no means easy, since the mothers often refused to tell even in the pains of child-birth, and the fathers themselves either 'ran away' or became adept at concealing their identity. Neither were they always to blame; for in all too many instances it was the woman who proved the temptress. John Neighbour of Sydenham alleged in May 1609 that a certain Annis Monday : 'came to his bed over nighte this year he beinge first in bed and that she huckled close to him as yt were to tempte him, and as he affermeth he thrust her owt of his bed, and byd her begone for shame'. Arthur Charman of Southnewton likewise

---

[8] Many counties swarme with a number of mynisters going from county to county to offer their services, who having once obtained a general licence of any Bishop or Chauncelor to serve in that diocese, under color to seeke service thereby, going from place to place in miserable sorte, breede a sclaunder and contempt of their callinge and are made a common pointing and jesting stocke to the scornfull adversarie of religion and atheist—*The Seconde Parte of a Register*, ed. A. Peele, I, p. 166, 1584.

declared, 'that diverse and sundrie times by the space of twelve moneth the wife of one William Spratley viz. Anne Spratleye, hath cume unto this respondent divers tymes to his bedd syde lying in the mill and there hathe provoked him verie mutche to have carnallie to doe with her'; but strenuously denied that 'ever he had anie carnall knowledge of her bodie'.

Contrariwise the lady could be equally resourceful in getting rid of an unwanted suitor. For example Joan Stayer of Bishops Waltham in Hampshire testified on 20 March 1584 in the case of *Barfote* v. *Barfote*: 'She did see the said Gilbert Comber in the morning in the said close lying upon the ground by the said Christian Braffote as she was milking and . . . did see the said Christian spring out milk forth of the cows teats upon the said Comber which caused him to tumble away.'

Mothers of illegitimate children were, of course, well aware that once their 'crime' was discovered they would immediately be hauled before the Justices of the Peace and the house of correction awaited them. They and their lovers therefore were naturally anxious to keep the birth a secret; and in this they often found willing helpers, although it was a penal offence to shelter such unfortunates which could result either in a penance or a heavy fine. On 9 March 1584 William Cooke of Sandford was convicted of harbouring an unmarried mother, who had added to her shame by getting into trouble with the curate of Bampton. William admitted:

> that abowt Candlemas last one Robert Hiat, curate of Bampton, did bring into this respondentes howse the articulate Jane Pusie beinge great wth child and promised that this respondent should have xs for a moneth, and that they would discharge him this respondent againste the courte, and saith further that he kepith the child still and that he should have of the said Mr Hiatt xiid a weeke for keepinge the said child.

Another such kind-hearted soul was Isabel Gathy of Thame, who was presented on 16 October 1609 'for entertaining a woman that was with child in her house and ther she is brought to bed of a bastard.' The penance exacted from these good Samaritans, when apprehended, was certainly no light one. For when William Phillipe was convicted at Risborough on 28 May 1606 'for keeping in his house a woman great with child and for suffering her to depart unexamined and without punishment', he had himself to perform a public penance at Morning Prayer in his parish church on 7 July, where with :

> . . . a white sheete wound about him from ye shoulders to ye anckles, and a white rod in his hand, bare legged and bare footed, and open faced, shall kneele in the sight of the congregation untill the gospell be read, and then standing uppe in some open place where he maie well be seene of the congregation shall saie after the minister as followeth viz. Good people whereas I not haveing the feare of god before my eies nor regarding my soules health, gods holy commandments, nor the wholesome lawes established in this Realme, have kept in my howse one Katherin Adams great with child whome I suffered to depart unexamined and without punishment, to the evil example of others : I am nowe come hither to acknowledge such my fault, and am right hartely sorie for the same, beseeching god and you all whome I have offended not only to forgive mee but also to take example by this my punishment that neyther you or I offend in the like sort againe, saieing as our savior christ hath taught us. Our father which art in heaven etc.

The performance of this penance was then certified by the parson and churchwardens concerned, who duly notified the Archdeacon accordingly 'at the next court daie following'.

Since Protestants did not regard marriage as a sacrament, they were not theoretically opposed to divorce and remarriage; although in practice this rarely happened, even where adultery could be proven. The Medieval Church, whilst rejecting divorce, had made so many annulments possible on the grounds of far-reaching degrees of prohibited relationships or former betrothals, that remarriage had been rendered relatively easy. But the high Anglican, whilst reducing the number of prohibited degrees and insisting that all contracts, whether espousal or wedding, were equally binding, would allow no more than a separation *a mensa et thoro*, from bed and board : a position legalised by the 1604 Canons. There was, of course, always the odd exception; and in 1605 Laud of all people found himself obliged to marry the adulterous Penelope Devereux to her paramour the Earl of Devonshire. It was not until the end of the seventeenth century that formal divorce became legally possible; and that only after every case had been scrutinised by Parliament and a special Act passed for the dissolution of each particular marriage.

In days when there were few other entertainments or amusements that of malicious gossip could be rated high on the list, and one had to be something more than Caesar's wife to escape scatheless in a tiny, isolated village community. For people were certainly not mealy mouthed, and slander and scandal were freely voiced and circulated very rapidly; although the innocent victim had his or her remedy, and an uncontrolled tongue had sometimes to be paid dearly for in the Ecclesiastical Courts. Innumerable are the cases that dealt with the 'common curser and swearer' 'common scold', 'sower of sedition among her neighbours', and those good ladies, who used to refer, rightly or wrongly, to some member of their sex as 'a drunken queane', 'an old whore', 'a base whore', 'a barren bitch' or by any other such uncomplimentary titles. There is the amusing tale of Anna Wrigglesworth, who was accused of repeating a rhyme that she had picked up in the Oxford market at Christmas from one, Robert Newell

> . . . who did sing it by the way, and the ryme is this viz., 'Yf I had as faire a face as John Williams his daughter Elizabeth hass then wold I were a taudrie lace as goodman Boltes daughter Marie dosse, and if I had as much money in my pursse as Cadman's daughter Margarett hasse then wold I have a bastard less then Butlers mayde Helen hasse.'

No wonder the conditions under which marriages took place were scrupulously examined by the clergy and their churchwardens; and any couple that produced a child within nine months of that marriage were hard put to it to escape detection, censure and punishment.

After a wedding the breakfast was usually held in the Church House, to which also sorrowing relations and friends resorted for the baked meats of a funeral repast. Parishioners who could afford to do so—and all had this right—were interred within the church, and costly monuments were raised in their honour, some of which were never paid for. Widow Bloom of Cromer, or so it was reported to Bishop Redman in 1597, 'gave a legacy of xs uppon condicion he [Walter Johnson] should be buried in the church of Cromer; which was done. She also promised to give xs more uppon condicion he might be buried under a stone; which was done, but the money yet unpaid'.

A funeral could sometimes be turned into a demonstration against an unpopular clergyman, especially in the turbulent years that succeeded the calling of the Long Parliament, as Sir John Bramston noted in his diary for the year 1641/2 : 'He [John Michaelson, Rector of Chelmsford] was one day at the grave burying a corpse, with a Book of Common Prayer in his hand; the rabble threw him into the grave and had buried him and the book doubtless, for they began to throw earth on him, had not some of the wiser townsmen rescued him'.

Drake, Rector of Radwinter, recorded about much the same date in his Autobiography :

> After a burial in the churchyard widow Seaman and the wives of Richard Smith, Henry Smith, Samuel and Henry Reef and Josias Ward, coming impudently upon the curate as he was passing from the grave, laid violent hands upon him, drew their knives and . . . cut and rent off his surplice and hood in a barbarous manner before the whole congregation; and so carried away their spoils, triumphing in their victory.

These were the concerted and deliberate actions of a number of parishioners hostile to their own particular parson; but equally distressing, if not so dangerous, could be the irresponsible behaviour of individuals. At King's Sutton in May 1617 Anne Chapman, 'a scolde', while the committal prayers were being read, contemptuously raginge, blasphemouslye swearing . . . to his [the parson's] great greafe and the congregations, disturbed him as he was reading divine service at the grave'. Two years later Humphrey Justice was cited into court for an even worse offence, since : 'the grave being made and the corpse being coming neare the church stile the said Justice came like a madman to the grave and scrabled in the earth with his hands and feet into the grave and filled the grave half full of mould'.

But when the parson tried to intervene Justice first abused and then assaulted him with such ferocity that the Clerk had to come to his assistance. At Sproughton in Suffolk towards the end of Elizabeth's reign there is a curious story of a man who buried members of his own family himself although there is no suggestion that he was in holy orders or even possessed a lay-reader's licence to do so. His name was Bradshawe, and he was presented in 1597 'for haveing his children buried in another parishe and burieth

K

them himselfe. He hath buried three of his children in Burstone'.
A more excusable case occurred during the Laudian period at
Ackworth, Yorkshire, when a Mr Bannister, gent. was cited into
court 'for reading prayers at the buriall of an infante childe, he
being a layman', and successfully defended himself on the grounds
'that there was noe minister to bury the child in regard that the
nowe [new] minister was not come to reside, soe least the corpse
should have stunk he did adventure (in charity) to bury it'.

Those who were unbaptised, under the greater excommunication, or had taken their own lives, could not, of course, be granted
a funeral service or interred in consecrated ground. 'To the minister and churchwardens of Banbury', wrote Dr Oliver Lloyd
'Commissarye', on 18 April 1610, 'I have ordered Robert Har-
wood amongst other things already done, that he shall acknowledge before you that he is sorrie for offending the law in inter-
ring his wife in the churchyard contrarye unto the Law being excommunicate'. Subsequently the wardens of that peculiar kept a
sharper look-out in the future; as also did those of Cropredy, who
were able to report to Dr Lloyd in July 1619 : 'We have had
dyvers excommunycated persons by your decree . . . and none such
are buryed with us in church or churchyard.' None the less it
was no uncommon occurrence for unwanted bodies in many
parishes 'to be buryed at night in our church yard', but by whom
'we knowe not.'

Archbishop Laud in the 12th article addressed to churchwardens prior to his famous Metropolitical Visitation, which
covered the years 1633-6, had asked : 'Doth your minister in the
Rogation Days go in perambulation of the circuit of the parish
saying and using the prayers and suffages and thanksgiving to
God appointed by Law'? These annual Rogationtide processions
were kept up in most parishes, which looked forward to them as
one of the high-lights of village life. They originated in A.D. 480
when Bishop Mamertus of Vienne ordered Litanies to be sung out
of doors in time of earthquake. Soon they became associated with
the blessing of the growing crops; and medieval England became
accustomed to the sight of the local priest and his congregation in
the Springtime meandering in procession through the fields chant-
ing Psalms and Litanies. Despite puritanical dislike of such things
Rogation processions survived the Reformation, but changed in
character; for they came to serve a useful secular rather than their
former religious purpose : namely, the scrutinising of the parish

boundaries, lest they had been encroached upon by neighbouring villages; and the setting up or renewal of boundary markings. When a stream formed a barrier some of the younger members of the congregation, after a little good-humoured horse-play, would be ducked in it; if a prickly hedge, pushed well into its interior; and if a line of trees or a grassy bank, given a sound spanking— in order to impress their youthful minds with the location of their village bounds and where and how it marched with its neighbours. At the end of it all, after a walk of anything from ten to twenty miles, hoarse from singing, with aching feet and legs, and some with sore bottoms, scratched arms or wet and touselled hair, the whole party would sit down to a sumptuous repast, provided free and for nothing by the Church, where a copious supply of wine and ale would set tongues wagging freely and reminiscences of 'the good old days' came rosily to mind.

The churchwardens of Upton-by-Southwell recorded in their accounts :

1604. for breade and ale in rogation week 1s. 8d.
1615. Paide for breade and drynke in Procession weeke 5s.
1616. for breade and drinke at the perambulation about ye feides 6d.

The strong anti-clericalism of this period stemmed not so much from puritanical objections to vestments, ceremonies, the Book of Common Prayer and episcopally ordained clergymen, although these of course all had their important part to play; but only too frequently they were used as no more than a stick to attack a parson who was obnoxious to his parishioners for quite other and more fundamental reasons : particularly during the stormy years that followed the break-down of Archbishop Laud's High Church Anglicanism in 1640. It was, in fact, an assertion of the sturdy independence of the ordinary villager against the rigid disciplines imposed by Church and State alike on the life of the tiny community in which he lived; an expression of his rebellion against their iron grip on every activity of his daily life; and their brazen and constant prying and intrusion into his private affairs. In imposing such a discipline and carrying through such an inquisition the parson was necessarily a key-figure and incurred much of the corresponding odium. When, for instance, a Yorkshire labourer in 1616 and a blacksmith some seventeen years later exclaimed respectively and impulsively : 'I care not for the constable or the

King', and 'The Devil go with the King and all the proud pack of them', they were voicing the feelings of very many simple people, which were sometimes expressed in even less polite language concerning their minister. Mr Shepperd, vicar of Nettlebed was told by the wife of Thomas Eyres in 1620, 'that he was a divell and not a minister, and that when he should die, he was such a troublesome man none should be troubled to bury him for the divell would fetch him away'. Neither were clergy-wives and their off-spring any the more popular in a conservative countryside that regarded clerical marriage with the gravest suspicion. Richard Fox of Grinley-on-the-Hill, Nottinghamshire was heard to remark on 3 August 1584 : 'that it was never a good world synce prestes were maryed, and called the vickers wyfe of Grinley paynted stocke. Also he said that preestes calves and byshoppes calves would over rone the Realme.' Robert Cunney, Vicar of Sydenham, wrote on 16 October 1616 : 'I the minister of Sydnam doe present Robert Sule for his common contempte of mee his minister boeth at home and abroade usinge at all tymes and in all places so abuseively odious and intollerable skoffinge and chestinge on mee; when he is most in company, most given to abuse mee. I never givinge him any occasion soe to doe.

Abusive words sometimes gave place to blows, as when in 1584 the curate of Bampton was beaten on his back with a cudgel, after he had administered a sharp reproof to a parishioner; or Thomas Seamer was arrested 'for irreverently useing Mr Carville, Parson of Catton, at the time of catechisme in this chapell', i.e. at Stamford Bridge. In the belfry of Wickham church, Hampshire, John Dashe junior, 'being forbidden to ring the bells, flung the rope at the minister'; and at Coldwaltham in Sussex during 1622 Roger Eager was presented by his minister 'for laying violent hands upon mee, in saying a turd in my teeth, calling of mee rogue, slave, knave etc, in violently plucking and tearing my coate off from my backe'.

But as long as Crown and Church maintained their iron grip on the country as a whole, such offenders were swiftly dealt with either in the Church Courts or by the Justices at Quarter Sessions. It was another matter, however, after Anglican Ecclesiastical Authority began to crumble from 1640 onwards. Then, indeed, some old scores were paid in full. John Webb, Vicar of Halstead, speaking of his parishioners on 10 May 1643 said : 'I never knew like inhumanity where religion is so professed. Did not the butcher, baker and brewer trust me, my wife and six children should have neither meat nor drink.' The notorious High Church Rector of Chelmsford, John Michaelson, was actually assaulted during Morning Prayer by a group of young hooligans led by a clothier, who seized him by the throat, tore off his surplice, and would undoubtedly have done him grievous bodily harm, except that some members of the congregation came to his rescue and beat off his assailants. Richard Drake of Radwinter suffered even greater indignities and dangers, where the ruder and rougher element in the parish, egged on by a puritanical churchwarden, and no longer afraid of the Consistory Court, got completely out of hand. They stole service books from the chancel and tore them up, came into church with their hats on, interrupted the service, and abused and threatened the officiating minister. The women and children of the parish also took full advantage of the situation to get their own back on an hitherto strong disciplinarian. On March 8, 1642/3 some forty or fifty boys and girls rushed into church during a service, shouting abuse and drowning the curate's voice, while others 'jangled the bells'. Two days later the wives of John Montford and Thomas Cormel entered the chancel and 'cut the surplice about a foot deep before and behind'. This persecution culminated on the following 15 January, when Drake who was officiating, was attacked in his desk by men with cudgels, led by the self-styled 'parish lecturer', William Voyle. A tremendous struggle then ensued. Drake fought his way into the pulpit; was pulled out of it; but recovered himself 'taking hold with both hands on the pulpit door and rail'. Superior numbers, however, in the end prevailed : the rector,

> . . . was again pulled down by the said William Voyle, John Smith, Matthew Spicer and Stephen Sellon, and thrown down in the desk, and from thence haled on his back on the church floor, and getting on his legs again was punched on his back, tugged by his gown, and violently thrust out of the church by Matthew Spicer, Richard Smith and John Hawkins, a stranger . . . Augustine Hawkins of Sampford Magna said : 'Let us have him out of the church and knock out his brains'. John Smith and Richard stamped and trod on him being thrown on the ground in the middle alley.

Drake himself admitted later : 'I was so violently driven forward that had not some charitable hand, by God's providence upheld me, my brains had been dashed out against the church door.'

The parson's wife and children were equally liable to similar persecution and even violence. At Pebmarsh in Essex, after Mr Wiborow the incumbent had himself fled the parish, an attack was launched against the parsonage on 10 June 1643, which was still occupied by Mrs Wiborow. She and her children were seized, dragged down stairs and thrust out into the stable yard. Here they found Meriton, Simpson and Cooke, the sequestrators, who with their friends had assembled to witness :

> . . . this joyful spectacle, a poor oppressed gentlewoman and her small children cruelly cast out of their own habitation by rebels and traitors. . . . When she perceived that all her entreaties and her childrens' tears prevailed nothing, she entreated the sequestrators that, in case she might not be permitted to dwell in her own house, yet she might have some other place of accommodation provided, to receive her and her children. Meriton insolently replied, that he would provide his tumbrill, that is, his dung-cart, to carry her and her children from constable to constable, till she came to her husband. They refused to allow her to enter the house to bring out provision for her children's supper.

They then proceeded to seize upon all Mr Wilborow's possessions, including the corn in his barn and the cattle on his glebe, and drove his wife forth with what she and her children stood up in to take refuge with kind neighbours. For if the anti-clerical spirit of the times was given full rein during these troublous years, so too did the parson's friends and supporters rally to his side; and sometimes completely turned the tables on their adversaries. It is noteworthy for example that most of these savage attacks on the clergy were mitigated or at least prevented from taking a final and tragic turn by the intervention of 'some wiser parishioners' or 'some charitable friends', who later, often at considerable risk to themselves, sheltered and fed the ejected clergy and their dependents until they were able to shift for themselves. Occasionally this was the squire who welcomed him into his manor house, but more frequently it was some humble churchwarden, Clerk or sexton, who came to his assistance.[9]

[9] Viscount Scudmore helped more than seventy ejected clergy, including Thomas Fuller and Robert Herrik and left them small legacies in his will.

In some parishes the war was carried into the enemies' camp, when parishioners refused to pay tithes to intruded ministers. This happened at Tempsford and Potton in Bedfordshire, where the sequestrated incumbents, Giles King and George Sheeres, continued to enjoy them. In the latter village Sheeres, accompanied by armed members of his erstwhile congregation, actually forced his way back into his vicarage and assaulted his successor's wife and servants. Nor was this an isolated case; at Aston in Derbyshire the rector's wife, Mrs Clark, 'with the help of divers turbulent persons forcibly occupied the house, seized corn in the rectory barn and threshed it for her own use'. The population of Soham in Cambridgeshire rose up in their wrath on behalf of their vicar, Roger Hechstetter, prevented the intruder, J. Fenton, from entering the church, drove him and his servants out of the vicarage, threw their goods after them, and then triumphantly re-instated their true incumbent. After John Watson, rector of Woolpit in Somerset, had been ejected, he refused to accept the situation. He, his wife and nine parishioners went into the church on 28 February 1643/4, which was a fast day, read prayers and preached. When the intruded minister, aided by his supporters, attempted to evict him, Mrs Watson and her friends went to her husband's assistance, 'and kept out a godly minister, who was to have preached'.

Another perpetual source of friction betwen a parson and his people was the matter of his tithes, which, ruthlessly enforced by the all-powerful Medieval Church under the pain of excommunication, were not so easily secured after the Elizabethan Settlement; and particularly in the early seventeenth century, when an unholy alliance between Parliament, the Common Law Courts and the Puritans sought to reduce his claims to the minimum. Dr D. M. Barratt has pointed out that contrary to general belief the majority of tithes had not been commuted by 1600,[10] and a large number of incumbents were still fiercely contending to maintain or even extend their tithing; while their parishioners with equal ardour and obstinacy sought to deny or reduce their demands in this respect. Undoubtedly at certain seasons of the year much of a parson's weekday time was taken up with their attempted collection; and even more in fighting for his rights in the Ecclesiastical or Common law Courts. The ordinary parishioner still took for

[10] D. M. Barratt, *The Condition of the Parish Clergy between the Reformamation and 1660*, 1949.

granted that he had to pay tithes, just as he had to pay his manorial dues; so it was over the exact amount demanded or the interpretation of the customs of the parish that the fiercest disputes took place. It was in the parishioner's interest to maintain custom, in that of the clergy to ignore or revise it. Tithepayers indeed often banded together in opposing their parson, and maintaining custom. For this purpose they would whip round amongst themselves to help one another raise the necessary cash in order to engage, if need be, in a long and obstinately contested lawsuit, the success of which too often depended upon who possessed the longest purse and was prepared to use it to the limit. In 1605, for instance, when Joseph Nixon, Vicar of Steeple Barton, sued Paul Hurst for his tithe, we are told : 'William Hannell and divers of his neighbours have agreed together to defray some part of the charges in this suite for Paul Hurst to maintaine their custom'. Maintenance of custom incidentally not only limited an avaricious clergyman's demands, but compelled a rector to fulfil his side of the bargain : by repairing his chancel, keeping a bull or boar for the use of the parish, and providing refreshments, 'drinkings', on tithing days.

The easiest and most profitable tithe to collect was corn. The statute of 1548, reinforced by custom, obliged the farmer to allow the parson or his deputy access to his land, to 'view' his tithe, which must be bound into sheaves and stooked. It was then the latter's job to cart it away. Unfortunately such 'access' sometimes entailed passing across another farmer's land, who either out of pure cussedness or perhaps because he was in league with his tithed colleague, would refuse his permission. This could lead to serious trouble. In 1634 Nathanial Barker, Rector of Stoke Talmage, was thus denied entrance to a certain Christopher Dodd's fields, over which he had to pass in order to reach, 'view' and carry away his tithe from another farm. The rector, however, was determined to do so; and on being informed :

> . . . his cart should not pass that way . . . told him [Dodd] hee would goe that way with his said Cart. . . . Then the said Dod layed hold on the head of the foremost horse of the said Cart wth an intent to stopp theire goinge further but the said Mr Barker drove on the horses eyther by himselfe or at least commaunded his servantes to doe soe, wch the said Dod seeing, hee came to the said Mr Barker and laying hold on him

tooke him about the middle violently withstanding him to
passe yt way. And . . . a peece of the said Mr Barkers band
about his necke was torne in the said opposicion. . . . Mrs
Barker seeing the said Mr Barker her husband layed hold on
by the said Christopher Dodd did thrust at the said Dodd
wth a pichforke wch shee had then in her hand bidding him
let her husband goe or else shee would runn him through'

The tithe on hay and wood was less profitable, as under the
open field system that still prevailed in the greater part of the
country, cultivated meadow land was owned in very small quantities and scattered thinly over wide areas; while only non-timber
trees, i.e. those of less than twenty years' growth, were titheable.
In most parishes, too, where wood was cut either for firewood or
fencing this also by ancient custom was exempt from tax. Its levy,
however, was no more popular for that, or less conducive to
violence. Thomas Pushill, a yeoman and Constable of Dodderhill
in Worcestershire, giving evidence in the course of one such tithe-
dispute during 1575, said :

In the beginninge of hey harviste laste past . . . he was present
at Copies wood cawled Elmebrige where and when the said
vicars servauntes were there to take awaye the tythe wood
thereof, and that Wm Dethicke in this article came to fetche
away the same tythe woode, and soe then and there the said
Wm Dethicke dyd quarrell wth the said vicar and his servauntes likely to feight wth them, and that this deponent
then and there beinge Cunstable did require the said Dethicke
to keape the quenes pease, and that there within the sighte of
this deponent the said William Dethicke did strike the said
vicars servante upon the head wth a staffe, and after that
dyd carry away the whole tythe there left.

But it was in the tithing of the young of animals that some of the
greatest trouble and bitterest controversies arose; since only rarely
were the right number forthcoming at any one time. In 1588, for
instance, William Underhill, Rector of Barton-on-the-Heath in
Warwickshire, claimed a tithe calf from William Berry, who
refused to yield it on the grounds that in 1587 he had six calves
and in 1588 another one, but that no tax was due, 'when they
fall in divers years'. Then, where there was a litter of ten pigs and
one died the farmer was sure to declare that this was the animal

marked for the tithe, and so nothing further could be claimed from that source.

Many disputes were over sheep, which had been deliberately moved out of the parish before shearing-time and then back again, or fictitiously sold in their wool in order to deprive the rector of his tithe of their fleeces.[11] By such practices and evasions parishioners sought to compel him to accept an unwanted *modus decimandi* or a cash payment in lieu of the wool to which he was legally entitled.

But perhaps the most irritating tithes of all were those claimed on such perishable domestic or garden products as milk, eggs, fruit and even garden herbs, that somehow seemed an unwarrantable intrusion into one's private life. By custom these were only due in the season of plenty, and eggs were usually taken in place of hens or ducks; but some greedy rectors would claim them all the year round, together with chickens and cheese, and so provoke an endless litigation, which must in the long run have cost them far more than they could ever hope to recover in tithe. At Kingsclere in Hampshire during the court case of Philpot v. Atfield, John Willyes, an eighty year old native of the village, said on 11 November 1592 : 'The ancient use and custom there hath been that the occupiers of any herb garden or ancient gardens in that parish have only paid tithe out of the said gardens for pears and apples, and tithe for bees and not for any other commodity whatsoever growing or increasing yearly in such gardens, but only a garden penny always at Easter'.

Not only then were most incumbents regarded by their parishioners as hard and grasping; but to many a go-a-head farmer, who was in business for profit rather than mere subsistence, the titheowner must have appeared as no more than a sleeping partner, who regularly took a tenth of his out-put, yet none of the risks, and was involved in no capital outlay whatsoever. This was par-

---

[11] In the parish of North Stoneham, Hampshire, it was the custom for the incumbent to choose one from ten lambs, or, if necessary, one from seven, 'saving the parson then alloweth a half penny for each lamb that wanteth between 7 and 10'.

The clergy were not always Shylocks. Elizeus Hewes, Vicar of Sparsholt, when he learnt in Octobeh 1580 that two of his parishioners, John Wayte and Thomas Symes had unbeknownst to himself sold twenty sheep in their wool between St Edward's Day and All Hallows Day 1579 declined to take any tithe of them, since, he said, he was 'naither accustomed to receive any such tithe for so short a time, neither would demand anything of them'. The culprits, however, insisted upon giving him 'sixpence for the said tithe'.

ticularly true of the rector, who refused to commute even his smaller tithes for a fixed money payment. On the other hand the parson very well knew that to do so at a time of galloping inflation would all too quickly lose him a considerable part of their value. Giles Moore, Rector of Horsted Keynes in Sussex, indeed, warned his successors : 'never compound with any parishioner till you have first viewed your lande and seen what corn they have upon it that year and may have the next'.

The spirit of anti-clericalism bred from these disputes waxed mightily after the barriers were down from 1640 onwards, when every advantage was taken of a chaotic situation to pay as little tithe as possible either to the legal incumbent or, if he had been evicted, to the intruded minister who had taken his place. Even a well-liked and doctrinally acceptable vicar, such as Ralph Josselin of Earls Colne, was more than once nearly starved out of his parish. 'Being as it were forsaken and neglected by the inhabitants of Earles Colne', he wrote in his diary on 12 September 1648, 'and destitute of competent maintenance to live upon, I sett this morning apart to seeke unto God for direction in this matter'; and added a month later : 'Dec. II. I was hard putt to it for money receiving none from my people'. Whereupon his friend and squire, Richard Harlakenden, came to his rescue and collected it for him, with gratifying results, since even in those days a squire's little finger was often a good deal thicker than his parson's loins. Josselin recorded with joy : 'December 21. This day Mr Harlakenden and Mr Ellison went about to gather my money yt was much in arreare; they brought me in £3 6s. 0d., and a good report generally of a willingness in the people to doe something towards my maintenance.'

Such a 'willingness' was not so apparent in the case of the more Anglican and royalist clergy. John Mow, curate of Great Bardfield, not far from Earls Colne, was quite unable to collect much tithe in 1644 although he boldly attempted to do so. Foolishly, if not unnaturally, he lost his temper completely with some of his more hostile parishioners, and said things about them, which were afterwards quoted against him in an attempt to secure his eviction. In one collision with a certain Mary Scott over her tithe of pigs and apples, he was reported to have told her : 'he wished she might live in want untill his pig was restored again. And because the said Mary Scott did not give him so much for her tithe apples as he required, he wished she might perish, and this he wished several times'. The more pacific meekly bowed to the storm. John Kellond, Rector of Pyworthy in Devon, it was said: 'being a very meek and lowly person . . . having received some affronts from the disaffected mob . . . did in the midst of harvest [1651], whether by force or his own action I know not, leave his place and tythes he had gathered to the mercy of his enemies'.

Sir Henry Mildmay was only voicing the disquiet felt by all thoughtful men and women, when on 12 August 1643 he wrote to Sir Thomas Barrington M.P. suggesting that he should try and persuade the House of Commons to pass an ordinance

> . . . that good ministers may be paid their just tithes or else we shall endanger the losing of a great part. For Mr Wharton (Felsted) and Mr Collins (Braintree), with divers other godly ministers, do grievously bemoan themselves that they cannot get bread for their families and abundance of them intend to come up with a petition to the House.

Both Wharton and Collins were doctrinally acceptable to their people; how much worse then those must have suffered who were not.

Prior to the great Rebellion and Commonwealth the puritanical House of Commons was inclined to condemn the compulsory payment of tithes to the clergy; but when in power they quickly found that some such system was indispensable in order to maintain any sort of ministry at all. So as far as possible, particularly under the rule of Oliver Cromwell and his Major-Generals, tithing was strictly enforced; while at the same time, through the Trustees for Maintenance, poorer livings were augmented by direct state grants. The aim was to bring all benefices up to a minimum income of £100 per annum; although this proved impossible except by uniting some of the smaller ones: a policy completely at variance with the puritan's previously declared hostility to plurality in all its forms.

The somewhat unpleasing picture of the average country congregation that emerges from this study is a reflection of the social-religious system that established itself at the Reformation and continued well into the eighteenth century. It was based upon the conception that Church and State were one, ruled over by the Godly Prince, assisted by the lords temporal and spiritual and his faithful Commons, whose laws must be ruthlessly applied by a host of minor officials throughout the country, including such indispensable figures as the parish priest, the churchwardens, the Constable and the Overseers of the Poor; and enforced through the machinery of the Ecclesiastical and Common Law Courts, Quarter and Petty Sessions.

The Medieval Church had exercised a fearful power over mens' minds and hearts; but it had been a personal and religious power radiating from the aura of the priesthood, not a State compulsion of which the minister was the mere representative. Attendance at mass was in theory at any rate a purely voluntary matter for the individual conscience; a man was not driven there by fear of heavy fines and punishments; and once mass was over he was free to spend the rest of Sunday as he pleased. Now in every aspect of his life, both public and private, he was subjected to an intolerable discipline, a prying and a spying; pushed hither and thither, badgered and bullied and brow-beaten, until he was almost afraid to call his soul his own. Inevitably, when one recalls the sturdy independence of the English character, there grew up everywhere a permanently passive resistance, a smoulder that from time to time, in one place or another, broke into flame and never more so than during the chaotic years of the great Rebellion. Non-conformity was by no means all puritan or Catholic, for the discipline of the Kirk was no better liked than that of Archbishop Laud; but was rooted in a deep-seated instinct, which found expression in the proliferation of independent sects, for an individual freedom of choice. Discipline, of course, was restored at the Restoration; but the whole system quickly began to decay and eventually broke down altogether towards the end of the eighteenth century. Officially at any rate the nineteenth-century parson ceased to be the moral policeman of his parish, and the Ecclesiastical Courts no longer concerned themselves with the manners and misdeeds of the laity.

It is highly improbable [writes Arthur Warne] that this discipline endeared either the Church or the clergy to those who were required to submit to it. The rôle of corrector of public morals is never popular with the public. One suspects that here was one reason for the later spread of Methodism, for the doctrine of Free Grace, preached so consistently by the Methodists, must have had a particular attraction to those who had suffered the humiliation of public penance.[12]

[12] *The Church and Society in 18th Century Devon*, p. 127.

The modern conception of the parish priest as the friend, servant and pastor of his flock was the product not of the sixteenth- and seventeenth-century Reformation, but of the Evangelical Revival and the Oxford Movement.

THE LUDDENHAM CHAPEL RIOT

'High Commission Court : 28 August 1634. Office against John Murgatroyde, James Murgatroyde Jnr., Henry Murgatroyde, Thomas Bradley and Susan Helliwell alias Bradley his wife, of the Chapellry of Luddenham. At Bishopthorpe.

'Upon which day houres and place the said parties being publiquely called in Courte, they all appeared personally except onely the said Susan Helliwell alias Bradley; for whom the said Thomas Bradley her husband offered to make fayth that she was then bigge with child, and neare the tyme of her delivery of child birth.

'And then the breefe of the cause being read in open Courte; the Counsell for the office did recapitulate and urge the proofs which made for the party, and behalfe of the office; And likewise the counsell for the deffendants, did in publique Court reinforce and open those points which made for the party, and behalfe of the deffendants.

'And then upon a mature and deliberate hearing of the cause, and of that which had been pleaded on both sides. Forasmuch that it appeared unto the Courte upon proofe made by testimonie of witnesses, that the said deffendants had committed divers misdemeanors prophanacions and outrages within the Chappell and Chappell porch and Chappell yeard of Luddingden aforesaid upon the xvth day of August *1632°*. As namely that the said John Murgatroyde with others the day aforesaid; had laid violent handes upon the bodie of one John Tilletson within the Chappell porch of Luddingden aforesaid, the said John Murgatroyde then cryeinge alowde kill Jack Tilletson, kill Jack Tilletson, and pulled and tore his breeches in the said Chappell porch. And that the said Henerie Murgatroyde the day aforesaid, had alsoe laid violent handes upon the bodie of one Richard Oxnard within the Chappell yard of Luddingden afforesaid, and by his violent blowes upon the face and mouth of the said Oxnard caused much effusion of bloud from him the said Richard Oxnard. And that James Murgatroyde the younger upon the aforesaid xvth day of August *1632°* did take one Ellen Waterhouse in his armes, and violently threwe her against the Wall or doore of the said Chappell of Luddingden, and made her face bleede in two or three places. And that the said Susan Helliwell alias Bradley the day afforesaid, threwe downe one Grace Helliwell in the Chappell of Luddingden afforesaid, saying shalt thou goe before the Murgatroydes. And that the said Thomas Bradley in unciveill manner trode upon the necke of the said Grace Helliwell alias Bradley in the middle alley of the Chappell of Luddingden afforesaid, the day afforesaid.

'Upon which the said deffendants misdemeanors, prophanacions and outrages, his Majesties Commissioners afforesaid proceeding to the giveing of their fynall and definitive sentence in this cause; did order and decree as followeth viz. First that the said deffendants and every of them for their misdemeanors, prophanacions and outrages afforesaid should stand excommunicate for the space of two yeares; Secondly that they and every of them should perform publique pennance *habitu penitentiali* in the Chappell of Luddingden afforesaid, and in the parish Church of Hallifax upon two severall sondays according to an order or forme of a schedule to be delivered unto them in *concepis verbis;* under the handes of three or more of his Majesties Commissioners. Thirdly the Courte did impose a fyne of CCCC li. upon the said John Murgatroyde to his Majesties use. And upon Thomas Bradley and Susan Helliwell alias Bradley his wife a fyne of xx li. a peece to the like use. Fourthly the said deffendants were condemned in charges and costs of the suite which are to be taxed. And the said John Murgatroyde standing formerly committed (for some other misdemeanors) to the Castle of Yorke, the Courte did order that he should remayne in the said Castle of Yorke untill he had entered bond with good and sufficient suerties to performe the order of the Courte. And did likewise committ the said James Murgatroyde, Henerie Murgatroyde and Thomas Bradley to the custody of Roger Blanchard his Majesesties Messenger untill they and every of them shall likewise enter bond with good and sufficient suerties to perform the order of the Courte afforesaid.'

In the year 1587 a certain John Wilkinson of Egglescliffe, County Durham, admitted in Bishop Barnes's Consistory Court : 'that in the churche yarde he smote off the said Jaxson's cap . . . he caused the said Jaxson . . . bleid . . . with his naile'.

CHAPTER VI

The Nonconformist

'A PURITAN', wrote John Manningham in 1602, a shrewd observer of people and events, 'is a curious corrector of things indifferent'; or as Bishop Curle put it more rudely: 'such an one as loves God with all his soul but hates his neighbour with all his heart.'

But to the puritans themselves these 'indifferent things' were matters of principle and indispensable to the reformation of the Church as a whole. For the majority, from the beginning of Elizabeth's reign down at least to the rise of Independency on the shoulders of Oliver Cromwell and his New Model Army, were conformist puritans, i.e. those Presbyterians who were anxious to capture the Church of England from within for their Calvinistic system, and not to separate from her and form their own churches like the Brownists or Baptists. It was in fact a struggle waged between the divine right of a theocratic presbytery and the divine right of kings and bishops. Under leaders like Thomas Cartwright and Walter Travers a form of church government and ecclesiastical discipline was hammered out which demanded that ministers, through their classes and synods and in conjunction with a lay eldership, should wield an autocratic power over their parishioners; enforcing it by the weapon of excommunication and calling upon the civil magistrate, 'to see their decrees executed and to punish the contamners of them'. Other religious bodies, whether Roman, Anglican, or Sectarian, must of course be ruthlessly suppressed; and heresy should be punishable by death.

The chief breeding grounds of Presbyterianism lay in Yorkshire, the Midlands and South Eastern counties, where they were supported by many influential members of the rising class of gentry, whose patronage supplied their ministers with livings, private chaplaincies and lectureships.

Puritanism was also strongly represented in the House of Commons; and during the fifteen-eighties a determined attempt was made in certain well-entrenched Protestant areas, such as Northamptonshire, Suffolk and Cambridge, to substitute Travers's *Book of Discipline* for the Prayer Book, and ignoring the bishops, archdeacons and their courts, to govern solely through the presbytery. The Church Courts in particular were regarded with abhorrence by the puritan, since they were largely in the hands of laymen, who in the opinion of Presbyterians, unless they also happened to be elders, had no right to intermeddle with ecclesiastical government. The fact then that, on the information of a lay apparitor, men and women could be cited into court, and there tried, condemned and sentenced by the lay officers of the bishop or archdeacon, added substantially to their grievances. It is actually recorded at Bishop's Stortford in 1634 that the churchwardens voted 5s. to be paid to the bell-ringers *not* to ring the bells when the bishop's Chancellor arrived there, and a further 2s. 6d. *for* ringing them on the day he went away. For to the presbyterian,

> . . . all ecclesiastical government in the parishes was vested in pastors, elders, deacons and widows. The ministers of twelve parishes combined to form a classis to handle matters common to the parish. Delegates from the ministers and elders of twenty-four classes formed a provincial synod or council and the delegates from these synods formed the national synod or general assembly.[1]

This movement, *imperium in imperio*, was decisively crushed by the determined opposition of Elizabeth herself and her 'little black husband', Archbishop Whitgift, during the 'nineties; while in the next century his successors, Bancroft and Laud, strongly supported by the first two Stuart monarchs, James I and Charles I, completed the apparent discomfiture of Presbyterianism, drove it underground, and prepared the way for the great Rebellion. At the Hampton Court Conference in 1604 James, replying to Dr Reynolds's puritanical demands, said : 'If this be all your party hath to say, I will make them conform at once themselves, or else

---

[1] *Presbyterian Movement in the Reign of Queen Elizabeth as Illustrated by the Minute Book of the Dedham Classis*, ed. R. C. Usher, p. xvii.

I will harry them out of the land or else do worse.' The instruments for this policy were provided by the 1604 Canons and the subscription required from all ministers to the three Articles, declaring their acceptance of the Royal Supremacy, that the Prayer Book of 1604 contained 'nothing contrary to the Word of God', and that the 39 Articles of 1562 were 'agreeable to the Word of God'. Inevitably there was resistance, leading to the deprivation of some of the more obstinate clergymen and the harrying of the puritan laity. But just as the Tyburn executions of 1593 drove the separatists overseas, so the Hampton Court Conference and the 1604 Canons turned conformists into Nonconformists, provided for the day when in 1640 the exiles both on the Continent and in the New World would be welcomed back to this country, and ensured the initial triumph and ultimate permanency of Independency.

Meanwhile in most parishes in England, whether urban or rural, Nonconformity to a greater or lesser extent, in a passive or more active rôle, not only existed, but persisted and in many places flourished; proving itself a perpetual and growing thorn in the side of episcopacy, and a continuing nuisance to the orthodox Anglican, incumbent : tares growing up amongst the wheat which must be rooted out at all costs. Puritan grievances were many and varied, but were either ruthlessly condemned or studiously ignored by the new Canons, which although sanctioned by Convocation and given royal confirmation, were never passed by Parliament. Consequently the puritans declared them to be illegal, since in their opinion they were contrary to statute law. 'The free men of the realme', it was alleged, 'are not bound to obey any canons or ordinaries, made by the Clergie of the realme, in any of their convocations, unlesse afterwardes the said Canons be confirmed by authoritie of Parliament'. None the less they were enforced by the bishops as the law of the Church.

Puritans were anxious to return to the pure worship of the Primitive Church as portrayed in the New Testament, with its ministerial orders of presbyters and prophets, supported by the lay officials : elders and deacons. They insisted that the two sacraments of Baptism and the Lord's Supper should be copied closely from scripture; and that the Church should be stripped bare of the complicated and idolatrous rites, vestments, ornaments and superstitions, which she had accumulated down the ages. Consequently a puritan attending his parish church would try and keep his hat on, stand or sit to receive the Holy Communion, and refuse to stand for the Creed or bow at the name of Jesus, because he wished to show his hatred and contempt of idolatry. Furthermore he would try and prevent the parson from signing his children with the Cross at their baptism, fitting a ring on to his daughter's finger at her wedding, or churching his wife. His concern for the need of a learned ministry that could preach the pure Word of God without fear or favour, would compel him if necessary to forsake his own parish church, where only homilies were delivered, in order to attend another and more 'profitable' one in the neighbourhood, and even communicate and have his children baptised there : since 'the sign without the word is dumb'. Here also he could probably escape the unbiblical but none the less legal obligation to produce godparents other than the child's own parents. As a strict sabbatarian he objected to weekday and holy-day services, and whenever possible attended puritanical prophesy-ings, conventicles and meetings of the faithful in private chapels or houses. The surplice—the sole vestment worn by the parochial clergy at this date—was to him like a red rag to a bull; and he likewise objected to the wearing of the cassock and the university hood. Ministers, he felt strongly, should either officiate in a black Geneva gown or else simply in lay attire.

Each and all of these practices were condemned by the 1604 Canons : Canon 30, although admitting that 'the sign of the cross in baptism is no part of the substance of that sacrament', then went on to affirm that it was the duty of 'both minister and other, reverently to retain the true use of it prescribed by public authority'; and Canon 29 demanded that 'no parent shall be admitted to answer as godfather for his own child'. Furthermore it declared a baptism was equally valid whether it 'be administered by a minister that is no preacher, or by one that is a preacher', an assertion which the puritan vigorously denied.

Canon 28 discouraged people from deliberately migrating from one parish to another to sit under a so-called more profitable ministry, and ordered the churchwardens to keep a weather-eye open for strangers, who 'come often and commonly from other parishes to their own church', and 'to remit such home to their own parish-churches and ministers, there to receive the communion with the rest of their neighbours'. Other Canons prohibited the practice of the Geneva discipline, the setting up of separatist conventicles, and meetings or services in private houses.

As regards the surplice: 'Every minister shall wear a decent and comely surplice with sleeves, to be provided at the charge of the parish'; and kneeling was made compulsory for all communicants, despite the fact that the black rubric had been omitted from the new Prayer Book. Preaching was to be strictly controlled. Canon 50 proclaimed in unmistakable terms: 'Neither the minister, churchwardens, nor any other officers of the Church, shall suffer any man to preach within their churches or chapels, but such as, by showing their license to preach, shall appear unto them to be sufficiently authorised thereunto'. Every preacher had to inscribe his name in a book, together with that of the bishop who had licensed him.

The placing of the holy table was to follow the directions of the 1559 Injunctions—although in practice the Laudian Church was to insist upon its location at the east end of the chancel with a rail about it—and puritans who scrupled to receive the sacrament from their own parson were to be first censured and then, if remaining obdurate, excommunicated. Finally the Canons defined a true member of the Anglican Church as

> . . . one who confesses that the King's supremacy over the Church in causes ecclesiastical is legitimate; that the Church of England is a true and apostolic Church; that the Articles of Religion are scriptural and true; that the rights and ceremonies are such as can be used with a good conscience; and that the government of the Church by archbishops, bishops and other clergy is agreeable to the Word of God.

No true-blue puritan was likely to accept such a statement, since he stoutly maintained that Anglican worship as defined in the Canons and written into the Prayer Book was corrupt, superstitious, illegal, unscriptural and repugnant to the law of God. So it could not be obeyed; and as most parishes contained at least a small minority of people prepared to put this principle of disobedience into practice, orthodox parsons and their wardens often had some difficulty in enforcing uniformity in their churches. Let us, then, look at what was happening in some of them and how such 'lawlessness' was dealt with.

At Brampton in Suffolk in 1597 the wife of John Snellinge was presented because 'she hath dyverse tymes this yeare lefte her owne parishe church uppon Sabaoth and holidayes and go to Holton to heare a sermonde, and neglecteth diverse Sondayes and holidays to come to church'; and at the self-same visitation it was reported of Thomas Sugar of Barncy, Norfolk, 'he obstinatlye refuseth to come to his parishe church to hear prayers redd and to receave the Communion and that he refuseth to come to heare prayers unlesse there be a sermond.'

During the year 1606 the curate of Banbury declined to administer the sacrament of Holy Communion to those who persistently refused to kneel at or near the altar rails, but remained seated in their pews or, at best, stood up in them. This action led to a considerable exodus of parishioners from his church, who, when cited into court, pleaded unsuccessfully 'that ther departure from their parishe churche was not subject to any punishment intended by the rule of the canon'. Robert Wood of Sampford Arundel in Somerset was presented during November 1623 : 'for using himselfe very unreverently in church i.e. that he doth not kneele all time of prayer'. He was ordered to 'admit the offence before the minister wardens and 6 others after evening prayer'; he did so, and later the Archdeacon's Court was duly notified that this penance had been performed. A similar penance was performed by John Gill of Adderbury, who was told :

> . . . to coome into the churche on Sundaye senight next and theare tarrie the whole eavening prayer and after eavening prayer in sooome convenient place of ye churche before Mr Ralins [Vicar of Adderbury 1554-89] ye vicare the 2 churchmen [churchwardens] and iiii honest paroshioners to confesse his faute and theyre deliver vis viiid to Mr Ralins to the use of the pore and undertake to paye vis viiid moare to ye same use at the feaste of St Michael next.

As has already been seen baptism with the sign of the Cross could lead to unseemly scenes in church. When in 1602 Elizabeth Hearne tried to prevent such a christening at Great Berkhampsted by 'disturbing the Menester in baptising of a child in saieing that the child should not be signed with the sign of the crosse', she was presented, cited into court, and on failing to appear was excommunicated. Another Nonconformist excommunicated for the same offence was absolved by her incumbent in 1605/6, Dr Robert Chaloner, who wrote to the Archdeacon's official : 'Sir I have received from your court an order to absolve one Mrs Iris of Chessham upon her private acknowledgement of her fault before me, our churchwardens and six more with hir oathe to obey the lawes of the Churche heareafter' and, apparently, expressed sorrow for 'withdrawing the child from the crosse'.

It was, of course, an even more heinous offence not to bring a child to be christened at all in church. A baby born in the house of Elizabeth Alderman of Milverton, Somerset, a widow, during 1623 was successfully kept hidden there for a time, 'was never brought to be baptised; whoe were the parents and what is become of the child it is unknowne'. Elizabeth herself had 'not been at the parishe Church to heare Divine service since the last Visitation'. She was excommunicated.

From the Protestant strongholds of Yorkshire and Nottinghamshire come a similar stream of prosecutions of puritans after they had been presented by their churchwardens at the visitations. For those thus presented were almost invariably summoned before the Ecclesiastical Court as it went on its Circuit and summarily dealt with by its Judge, who charged them directly with their offences and to whom they had to answer immediately. Most of the accused frankly admitted, indeed gloried in their guilt; although they were also quick to show plausible reasons for their alleged misdemeanours. The defendant was then either dismissed after an admonition to keep the law, and later obtained a certificate from his incumbent and churchwardens to this effect; fined or ordered to perform a penance. Failure to appear before the court or an obstinate refusal to carry out its dictates could result either in the greater or lesser excommunication. 'In serious cases, or where the judge deemed it appropriate, the accusation was remitted for formal prosecution, and the offender was referred directly to the archbishop'.[2]

The churchwardens were obviously the linch-pin in this procedure, since until they or their incumbent presented, the Nonconformists were likely to escape scot free; unless, as sometimes happened, the Judge received private information from some informer or other. But, alas, wardens were only human and were inclined to turn a blind eye on many of their neighbours' misdemeanours; so that 'when the visitation comes they are locked up with an omnia bene'. Puritanically minded churchwardens were liable to take advantage of the detailed instructions supplied to them by William Prynne from prison on how to evade or circumvent the Laudian regulations; and some were even prepared,

[2] R. Marchant, *The Puritans and the Church Courts*, p. 5.

judging from the following lines in Wither's *Juvenilia*, to perjure themselves in a righteous cause :

> There are churchwardens, too, I shame to see
> How they run into wilful perjury;
>   Partly in favour, and in part for fear,
>   They wink at much disorder in a year.

So, as at Birstall in June 1635, they were sternly commanded to keep their eyes open and not flinch from doing their duty : 'They are to walk in the alleys after the second lessons at morning and evening prayer upon sundaies and holy dayes and take notice who are absent or who doe behave themselves unreverently and to the end that better order may be kept, they are to present their names.' For the greater convenience of such snoopers pews could be legally reduced in height, and the old-fashioned box-pews, that often faced in different directions, demolished altogether. By this means the congregation could both see and be seen of the minister and his lay officials. Even so churchwardens could not always be relied upon to fulfil their obligations; and in 1635, for example, both sets, the out-going as well as the in-coming wardens from Sheffield, were summoned before the Consistory Court and fined £13 for turning a blind eye on puritanical practices. But behind the churchwardens were sometimes men of greater substance, whom it was not so easy to discipline. Alderman Thomas Hoyle of York, for instance, later to be a member of the Long Parliament, regarded the incumbent of St Martin's Micklegate as little more than his private chaplain : so under his auspices and those of his fellow alderman, Matthew Topham, puritanism grew apace in the parish. Members of the congregation sat with their hats on, did not kneel for the prayers, refused to stand for the Creed or bow at the name of Jesus. Some of them kept their shops open on holy days and received the sacrament squatting in their pews. Preachers were invited to use the pulpit, who were not licensed to do so; and an afternoon lecture took the place of catechising. Women were churched and the sacrament of baptism administered in private houses. The matter came to a head in the Spring of 1632/3, when the churchwardens were prosecuted for the non-presentment of offenders. Whereupon one of them glibly affirmed that he suffered from an eye ailment that prevented him from seeing properly; and the other pleaded that he was absent for many months of the year on business. Hoyle, for his part, frankly confessed that 'on holy days being faire and market days' he had opened his shop. Eventually they all made a formal submission and proceedings against them were stopped. For a time the puritans kept quiet; then the rector, John Birchall, no doubt incited by Hoyle, held a meeting in the latter's farm house in the parish of Bolton Percy at the very hour that Morning Prayer was being said in the parish church. This was not only an affront to the rector, Henry Wickham, but was nothing more or less than a conventicle, where extempore prayer was offered up. As such it was a flagrant violation of the Canons and Prayer Book. Subsequently Birchall found himself in the Chancery Court, which sat from March to April 1634/5, but Hoyle was not interfered with. When some five years later in 1639 his co-patron, Henry Barker, was cited into court for refusing to go to church except to hear sermons, and refused to attend, he, too, was not excommunicated, unlike the plebian Thomas Boucher and his wife, who were accused of a similar offence. There was, in fact, one law for the rich and another for the poor.

In the countryside, especially in the East and West Ridings and the Plain of York, there were many puritanical squires who supported the Nonconformists for political as well as religious reasons against Archbishops Laud and Neile, and Charles I. Here the power to nominate clergy to livings lay very largely in the hands of lay patrons, whose social prestige as much as their religious fervour compelled the farmers and peasants of their villages to follow where they led. Sir Matthew Boynton of Barmston was responsible for puritan practices and pressures in that district. He was described as 'being a Religious Gentleman that gave much countenance and shelter to the puritans, and scrupling conformity to the Injunctions imposed on those times, was so troubled and prosecuted that he was forced some years before the War to fly to Holland'.

At Buttercrambe Sir Richard Darley and his son Henry played a similar role, employing as their private chaplain Thomas Shepperd, an extreme puritan, who had already been silenced by Laud, and allowing him to preach unlicensed in the parish church. Both he and his successor, Francis Pecke, were presented, cited into court, and on their failure to appear were excommunicated. Richard Darley, the younger, who had purchased the manor of Sand Hutton in 1630, also employed a Nonconformist minister, Thomas Lowry, to preach. The latter was inhibited in March

1636/7, and two years later fled to Scotland to escape arrest by the High Commission. This type of encouragement and protection of Nonconformity by the rural squirearchy had been going on ever since Elizabethan times. Sir Thomas Hoby of Hackness had been a tower of puritan strength from the late sixteenth century onwards. 'It was Hoby practice', we are told, 'to maintain two ministers at Hackness, one acting as his chaplain, one as the curate of the parish'. Both were puritans, and frequently in hot water with the Ecclesiastical Authorities; but Hoby's influence usually got them out of it. In 1633, when his wife died, he built himself a private chapel in a remote part of the parish, endowed it with the tithes from the townships it served, persuaded the Bishop of Sodor and Man to consecrate it in 1636, and secured a licensed curate to serve there. This was a remarkable achievement on the part of such a well-known puritan as Hoby, since Archbishop Neile normally refused either to consecrate that type of chapel or to allow curates to be appointed to them, lest they became—as they usually did—places for conventiclea. Even so loyal a squire as Sir Henry Slingsby of Scriven was refused this privilege; which none the less did not prevent him from occasionally holding services and listening to sermons in his unconsecrated and unlicensed chapel: 'Although', as he frankly admitted, 'we incurr some danger if it were complained off, it being contrary to the orders of the church'—a striking illustration of the power and independence of the gentry *vis à vis* the Church. In fact Neile's only remedy against such gentlemen was to keep a strict eye on the churchwardens, discipline them when need be, and to insist that their pulpits were closed to unlicensed preachers. Part of the trouble was caused by the Government's decision to exercise local government not through the local squirearchy, its natural leaders, but the Council of the North, a bureaucracy directed from London, where the Scarlet Woman reigned in the person of Henrietta Maria. Consequently Neile's attempts to coerce Nonconformity were regarded with suspicion even by loyalists like Slingsby. 'We do', he wrote in his diary, 'draw near to the superstitions of the Church of Rome'.

Conscious of this substantial and growing support for their cause in town and country alike, the average puritan layman, far from hiding his light under a bushel or walking delicately like King Agag, was all too often aggressive, truculent and abusive. On 25 June 1574 Thomas Cooke and William Ryshton, both of

Mansfield, were cited into court for contempt of their vicar; but when charged, did not hesitate to attack the Archdeacon himself, John Lowth, declaring that his preaching did more harm than good, as it disagreed with the Word of God, and that he 'knoweth no more what a puritane is than his oulde hors'. Three men from Arnold in 1579 openly scoffed at the Catechism, saying 'that yt ys nothinge but the old sh-st the popes', and 'ys nothing but the old christ in the popes tyme'. There are innumerable cases of parents cited into court : 'for not sending his familie to be catechised having had lawfull warning'; and even 'for keepinge his child unbaptised a moneth or more in his house without anie lawfull cause showed'. At Littleborough in May 1584 the churchwardens themselves were charged 'for not being at the catechisme at evening prayer the last sonday'; who insolently replied : 'that they did not heare the belles ryng to service which was the cause'.

Jane Ireton, the mother of Cromwell's future son-in-law, refused in January 1606/7 'to be churched accordinge to the rites and ceremonies of the Church of England'. The same year on Easter day Ellen Denham of East Retford forced her way into Babworth church 'and did disturbe the minister for the time beinge from the exequucion of divine service and also did impugne the rite and ceremonie of the crosse in the sacrament of Baptisme by force and violence contrarie to the booke of common prayer'. For this she had to perform a penance; and another was enjoined upon John Owle of Sneiton because he declined to go to church as long as the curate wore a surplice. Thomas Jessop of Mattersby a year later informed the Judge who was trying his case : 'it is to dishonour Christe to saye that a man must receave the communion kneelinge'; and when three men and some women were fined a shilling each for absenting themselves from church for a month, they flatly declined to pay : 'because the Word was not preached there'. At Mansfield in 1619 the churchwardens presented Emund Bee and his wife, 'the husband for staying at home on All Saints' Day to make a pig-sty, but the wife for going to Sutton—a noted puritan stronghold—for Evening Prayer on Sundays and receiving communion there'; for which she was excommunicated.

When the Anglican Oliver Bray took over the living of Worksop from the precision, James Collie, he quickly found himself at odds with members of his congregation. One of them, John Owen, said to him : 'You have made manie men of Worksop to goe to the devill'; and his own Clerk, Christopher Carlile, openly defied him. 'If you be priest', he told the vicar, 'I will not obey you. You are a preemptorie man not fit to governe in the churche'. During a funeral Bray asked Carlile for a spade with some 'moulds' on it 'to cast into the grave', whereupon the latter promptly threw his spade away. In church he refused to co-operate with the vicar in reading the Psalms and canticles, because he was a non-preacher; and even went so far as to call him a liar to his face.

Particular hotbeds of puritanism in the early seventeenth century were the parishes of North and South Collingham, Marnham and North Clifton in Nottinghamshire. Thomas Parry of North Collingham actually had the audacity to 'mainteyne by publique disputation that whosoever cometh into the Church in time of divine service and shall kneel down to pray . . . offereth the sacrifice of fooles and his prayer is abominable'. Richard Ash, Vicar of Marnham, held private religious exercises at his vicarage, which were attended not only by members of his own family, but also by many of his parishioners. To this practice his churchwardens turned a conveniently blind eye. Such conventicles were not uncommon elsewhere : in Buckinghamshire, for example, where at Long Crendon meetings were held in the house of a shepherd, John Freeman, 'almost 20 persons comeing thither upon Sunday between prayers and stay there many times all prayer time'. The 'repetitions of sermons' in laymen's houses to sizable gatherings of their friends were further reported from Chenies, Woburn, Sheringham and Wendover. Ivinghoe, Clifton Reynes and Newport, on the other hand, were so strongly Brownist in character that the wardens, who were friendly, deliberately shut their eyes to their large, undisguised gatherings.

Puritans were especially opposed to the removal of the holy table from the nave to the east end of the chancel, to its fencing in by a rail, and to the adoption by the celebrant of an 'eastward' instead of the 'north-end' position, which, or so they declared, rendered the words largely inaudible; while the crush of people going in and out of the chancel disturbed their devotions. As one man said : 'he could not have any meditacion'. Between the years 1635 and 1639 some 45 people were before the courts in the Archdeaconry of Nottingham for the offence of refusing to communicate under these conditions; and in 1638 43 puritans declined to come up to the altar rails of St Peter's, Nottingham, on Easter day.

As Charles I's eleven years of personal rule drew to their close, and the rumbles of the forthcoming storm were to be heard ever more loudly, it became increasingly difficult even to discipline puritanical churchwardens. In 1638 and 1639 some of them refused to be sworn in at the Easter visitation, to answer questions concerning the repairs of their churches, to make altar rails or even sign their presentment bills. At Stanton-in-the-Wolds a man actually removed the table by force from behind its rails. Presentments dwindled alarmingly; until on 28 September when the Registrar went to St Peter's, Nottingham to hold his usual Michaelmas visitation, he found the doors locked against him by the churchwardens. That was the end of the Laudian ecclesiastical discipline in the Midlands and the North. In other parts of the country, notably in Lincolnshire, East Anglia and some of the Home Counties, the puritan Nonconformists were equally active at the beginning of the seventeenth century; causing a great deal of trouble in their parish churches. John Ellis of Great Bentley in Essex pulled his 'Childe awaye at the tyme of Baptizinge thereof when the minister cam to signe yt with the signe of the Crosse'; while his wife 'irreligiously covered her face with her hands to thentente she might not see the Crosse used in Baptisme'. Agnes Wallen of Thurlaston and John Ware of Thornton actually left their own parishes, the former 'to bee delivered of child' lest 'it should be baptized with the signe of the crosse', and she herself 'bee churched after the booke of common prayer', and the latter to go by boat to Stanton, where he knew his baby would 'bee christened without the signe of the crosse by Robert Hargrave [a notorious puritan minister] there'. Indeed where a strongly puritanical ministry prevailed as at Ashby-de-la-Zouche, the conformist Anglican layman in his turn was likely to get short shrift. Richard Spencer, a parishioner, had requested the curate there to give out a notice in church asking for the return of some money which had been stolen from his house after it had been burnt to the ground. He received the dusty answer: 'nay, nay, the crosse hath lighte on the, and a worse judgement hangeth over thy head. Thow wilte have thy children baptized with the crosse'. Spencer retorted that this was the law and 'yf he had anie more children he would have them baptized with the signe of the crosse according to his Majestes lawes'. He added for good measure: 'his Majesties lawes was godes lawes'. Not unnaturally the curate was upheld by his equally puritanical rector, Arthur Hildersham, and his wife. The last told a woman, who had suffered equally with Spencer in the same fire : 'Jone be of good comfort £iiii will build up thy howse againe, and as for Spencer the crosse hath lighte on him, let him beware the surplesse'. It was, in fact, war to the knife.

The surplice, of course, remained a stumbling block to many. Churchwardens who failed to provide one for their incumbent were admonished, told to produce it within a fortnight, and then certify to the Consistory Court that it was being worn. At Hareby in Lincolnshire during 1604 they were ordered 'to tender it to their minister' and inform the court at Lincoln accordingly; which they apparently did since a marginal note in the Act books records : 'he weareth it'. But they were not always so obliging. The Vicar of Gosport in Hampshire, for instance, complained in 1607 that his warden had 'conveyed away the surplice' and presumably destroyed it, since he was later ordered by the Winchester consistory court 'to pay what the surplice was worth'. On the other hand the Thurlaston wardens reported of their rector, Richard Sherwood, 'two surplisses have beene tendered him, which he reteyneth at his howse, sayeing he tooke them thither to see what condicion they were of'; and officiated without them, while continuing his leisurely inspection.

A refusal to kneel for the sacrament or stand for the Creed, the wearing of hats in church, abuse of Anglican rites, and prayer meetings in private houses were equally prevalent in the South and East as in the Midlands and the North. The wife of Robert Barnard was presented in 1607 by the churchwardens of Holy Trinity, Colchester, 'for that she affirmeth that she never will receive the Communion except at the hands of suche a minister as will suffer her to receive yt sitting'; and Abraham Hubberd of Brandiston : 'for receavinge the communion settinge and not knelinge'. Five men of Hinckley refused point blank 'to stand, kneele or put their hatts off in the time of divine service'; while Roger Carter of Edlington was cited into Stamford 'for having his hat on in the tyme of the devine service', compelled to apologise and promise reformation. Clementine Tallmage of Hindlesham, Norfolk, denied 'the Church of England to be the trew Church of Christe', and attacked its rights and ceremonies 'saying they be not lawfull'. John Brown of Coggeshall and William Lambe of Salcott in Essex were even more violent in their language. The former 'did saye that he wold not putt off his hatt when the book of Common prayer was in reading and that the Bishops ought not to be prayed for at service and sermon and that the book of Common prayer was nothing but mingell mangell'. The latter declared 'that the booke of Comon prayer was but trumperye and came from the divell and was made by the divell'. Abuse was all too commonly accompanied by violent actions against the incumbent. Robert Burbedge of Market Harborough called Thomas Gower, Vicar of Great Bowden : 'Lowsy Rogue, cogginge companion, and scurvey Rascall and did challenge him to the feild and did lay waite for him for usinge the rites and ceremonies of the churche . . . and further hee said hee would incense the parishioners of great Bowdon against their minister, which hee did indeede. . . . And alsoe did call his minister puppye'. Francis Bunyge of Barholme in Lincolnshire, 'layeing violent hands upon John Ball, minister' called him 'paltrie priest'.

When Susan Cook of Little Baddow, Essex, was charged 'with laying her linen in the church to dry';[3] she replied insolently : 'she might lay her rags there as well as the surplice', and bid the incumbent, Mr Newton, do his worst. She was suspended from entering the church; whereupon her daughter, Ann, said : 'It were a good turn if he [Newton] were hanged up there.' The Sharpe family, who returned to Essex in 1636 from New England, must have been an exceptionally sharp thorn in the side of their parson, the Rector of Sandon. They consisted of Thomas Sharpe, his wife Tabitha and son, Thomas the younger.

> They nor any of them [the wardens reported at the autumn visitation] have been at Divine Service on any holiday, Wednesday or Friday since Whitsuntide last. . . . They do all refuse to bow at the blessed name of Jesus or to stand up at the Creed according to the Canon, but do scoff at the minister and others who do. The said Tabitha did not come to be churched in a veil nor did kneel by the Communion table according to the rubric. The said Thomas Sharpe is a common depraver of the government ecclesiastical and of the rites and ceremonies of the church since his coming from

---

[3] Churches in the early seventeenth century were frequently treated with little reverence either by Anglican or Puritan. In 1612 the Woburn curate baited a bear in church; and at Knottingley on three successive Shrove Tuesdays in the 'thirties there was cock-fighting round the communion table, with the minister and wardens looking on. People smoked, spat, and used the altar for putting their hats on or for writing up accounts. The fact then that Cromwell's troopers stabled their horses in churches and cathedrals might well have aroused no undue comment at the time.

New England. He is a common sower of discord and conten-
tion in the parish that no neighbour can live quietly by him
and threateneth the churchwardens and sidesmen that they
dare not perform their office.

In 1632 some doggerel verses by one Feeth John were aimed
'A Gaynst the parson or priest of St Nicholasses in Colchester',
the Revd. Theophilus Roberts, who was accused of all the usual
Laudian practices and failings. Of the altar rails which he had
had erected it was said :

> And built a pound, yea out of hand
>   For to fulfil his will;
> And some time like an ass he stands
>   Therein against our will.

> And now all those who will not pay
>   To building of the same
> Then unto Doctor Aylett's court
>   He will return their name.

On the other hand he was scoffed at for his lack of preaching
ability :

> For why he is an idle drone
>   'Tis pity he is not cast out;
> Yea a dumb dog and but once a month
>   A little he then barks out.

> And then, alas, to no effect
>   He doth not please me well;
> For much ado he has even then
>   His hour glass to fill.

The average Anglican parson, therefore, had much to put up
with from his Nonconformist parishioners; and never more so
than when after 1640 the Church's discipline broke down altogether and the puritans were no longer afraid of being hauled up
before and punished by the Ecclesiastical Courts. In particular
the soldiery billeted in Anglican parishes made themselves objec-
tionable. Those sent to fight against the Scots in July 1640 were
accused by Lord Maynard of breaking into churches 'even in the
time of divine service to pull down the rails about the Communion

table'. At Icklingham in Cambridgeshire they compelled the parson to swim the river for his very life; and when Dr Barkham, Rector of Bocking, supplied them with drink as a conciliatory gesture, it so inflamed them that they broke into his church, 'pulled up the rails of the communion table in the chancel and brought them before their captains' lodging and burnt them'. Richard Drake of Radwinter, who was in Cambridge at the time, recorded in his autobiography how incited by his own parishioners the troops tore down a statue of Christ, together with a number of cherubim and seraphim, carried them to Saffron Walden, where they made a bonfire of them; while at King's Walden in Hertfordshire they actually profaned the church under the very eyes of the congregation at Morning Prayer. Perhaps the worst outrages took place in Chelmsford parish church. This possessed a remarkably fine medieval stained-glass window at the east end, which had escaped the Elizabethan iconoclasts. But, after the Long Parliament had passed an ordinance for the removal of superstitious pictures, the churchwardens took it upon themselves, without consulting the rector, to replace the pictures of the Virgin Mary and Christ on the Cross with plain glass. This, however, failed to satisfy the more extreme puritanical element among the parishioners, who 'very ill satisfied with this partial and imperfect reformation', were determined to 'make a thorough Reformation'. This they achieved on the not inappropriate occasion of the anniversary of the Gunpowder Plot : 'On the fifth of November in the evening all the Sectaries assembled together in a riotious manner with long poles and stones beat down and defaced the whole window.'

The arrival of the soldiery from Colchester and Ipswich, who were billeted in the town, led to further trouble. They sat in church with their hats on, made loud noises to drown the curate's voice, and called upon him 'to come out of his Calves Coop and make an end of his Pottage'. In despair the service was brought to an abrupt conclusion. The Rector, John Michaelson, was an especial target for their attacks : someone fired a carbine at the window of his study; and when the news of the abolition of episcopacy arrived in the town the troops marched to the rectory, made a bonfire of its woodyard in order to celebrate the occasion, and attempted to throw Michaelson into it. They also took the Book of Common Prayer out of the Church 'carried it into the street and tore it up; some of the leaves they trod under foot, cast

M

others into the gutter, and fixed some on the end of their clubs and cudgels and in a triumphant manner marched with them up and down the town'.

On 18 February 1641/2 Abraham Chapman, a cobbler of Radwinter, entered the chancel of his parish church with a club in his hand and demanded of Richard Drake his surplice and hood. Drake kept him engaged in argument, whilst the curate hid them safely away; and Chapman had to content himself with stealing two service books, which he later 'threw behind the church'. The next June the following disgraceful scene took place in Radwinter church:

> The curate entering the desk to say evening prayer was told by Edward Montford that if he went to prayers he and his companions would go to ringing. The curate replied they would answer it then to authority. However in the middle of the Confession, Montford, Crowland, Chapman and one Wait, a stranger, all animated by Montford who would bear them out, began to jangle. That done, in the Psalm and Lesson Montford especially derided the words which were read, with blasphemous answers, impious mockeries, unseasonable Amens; crying out, 'Hold your peace, Hob; down on your knees, Hob' with much laughter; scornfully pulling off his hat and clapping it on again; bending the knee and bidding others to do so in derision while the Lessons and Hymn were reading: then went they again to chime and jangle, with incredible performances as words and gestures, and so went out of the church. But when they came at the church gate they returned again, with what intent God knows; Montford, Crowland and Waite came immediately up to the reading-pew, told the curate they must pray with him, opened the door, came in, thrust him out; whereupon he departed with silence, 'Now I like your obedience', quoth Montford; Crowland told him he had been well enough served to have been taken by the heels and had his brains beaten out.

Drake prosecuted the ring-leaders at the Chelmsford Assizes in July, where they were found guilty; but no further action was taken against them.

Such scenes only terminated with the forcible eviction of the Laudian clergy and the sequestration of their livings; but the more puritanically-minded incumbents who survived, and the Presbyterian ministers intruded into the vacant parishes, quickly found that once the floodgates had been opened and parishioners given their heads, it was not easy to close them again or re-impose the old disciplines. Nonconformity flourished as vigorously as ever in the shape of the Independent Sectaries, notably the Quakers, Baptists, Fifth Monarchy Men, Ranters, Familists, Seekers and Muggletonians.

Perhaps Quakerism was the most difficult to deal with. Its chief feature was the founding of a fellowship of 'friends', who were under a continual necessity to express their feelings publicly and to bear witness to their beliefs in market place or church regardless of the consequences. They plunged recklessly into controversial debates; flooded the country with violently-worded pamphlets; opposed all rites and ceremonies; kept their hats on in all circumstances as a sign of defiance; refused to take oaths, engage in war or countenance capital punishment; addressed all classes without fear or favour in the plainest of language; rejected the need for an officiating minister at baptisms, marriages or burials; and often went naked 'as a sign'. They felt themselves to be prophets of a new religious era, and like the prophets of old they must demonstrate their 'apartness' : a society within a society, an *imperium in imperio*, the children of light, the seekers and the finders of the indwelling Christ. They carried, in fact, to its logical conclusion what many other of the Sectaries, such as Ranters, Familists and Seekers had set in motion.

Cromwell was no Quaker, yet he wrote of his favourite daughter, Lady Claypole, in 1646 : 'she sees her own vanity and carnal mind; bewailing it, she seeks after (as I hope also) what will satisfy. And thus to be a Seeker is to be of the best Sect next to a Finder, and such shall every faithful, humble Seeker be at the end'. Certainly they suffered their persecutions; as well as proving themselves an almost intolerable nuisance to more sober Christians, both Anglican and Puritan. Ralph Josselin had many a brush with the Quakers at Colne, but he always treated them with consideration, and usually emerged from the encounter with credit. On 31 October, 1665, he recorded in his diary : 'In ye lane sett upon by one called a quaker, the Lord was with my heart that I was not dismayed; I had some discourse with him, the Lord bee my helpe'. Again on 21 August 1659, he wrote : 'A Quaker wench came boisterously into ye church up almost to the deske, I perceived persons expecting some disturbance, but she staid ye end and then went out quietly, blessed bee God.' Others were not so charitable or forbearing. When, for instance, in 1654 Richard Sale walked barefoot and bare-legged, dressed in sack-cloth, with ashes on his head, carrying flowers in one hand and weeds in the other, through the streets of Derby, the people set their dogs on him. He was then thrust into a hole in the wall of Northgate prison, known as 'little Ease', where he was crushed to death. Some three years later another Quaker, Ellis Hookes, was subjected to third degree methods in Stanton Harcourt House by Lady Waller, who was endeavouring to convert him :

> She had him into her chamber. She took the hat off his head, locked the door and rated him soundly. He remained silent until she cried out that now his hat was gone his religion was gone, and he could not speak, but only hum. Then he angered her still more by saying unceremoniously, 'Woman, shew thyself a sober woman'. She fell to beating him about the head and pulling his hair, saying she was never called Woman before. When she had wearied herself, the young man spoke a second time, 'Woman, I deny thy religion that cannot bridle thy tongue nor thy hands', a speech that only added fuel to her passion. She commanded her man and her son to stand before Hookes and keep him up in a corner of the room, where she continued to beat him, and called for a stick, as her fists were sore. After a time he said : 'Instead of showing thyself a sober woman thou hast showed thyself more like a beast'. Then Sir William Waller struck him down with a blow on the head, he was turned out of doors, bare-headed and deafened, and his father ordered to turn him out of doors, which he did.

But the Establishment, whether Anglican or Presbyterian, did not by any means always have its own way; particularly after the final dissolution of the Long Parliament. Ralph Josselin argued all one day with Oates the Anabaptist that 'they had no ministry, and yt particular Christians out of office had no power to send ministers out to preach'. It was in fact 'contrarie to Scripture'. He might just as well have saved his breath. 'For the man boldly continued in Town till Wednesday, exercising all three days'; and Josselin, apparently, was powerless to stop him. The orthodox Presbyterian minister of Henley-in-Arden argued heatedly in his church with five self-styled preachers, a nailer, a baker, a plough-wright, a weaver and a baker's boy on the highly controversial subject of 'preaching without a call'; but with little success. And at Kendal a Baptist preacher, Thomas Taylor, to the great joy of his supporters, disputed with three Presbyterian divines in the parish church and got the better of them all on the subject of infant baptism. Whereupon his followers ran up Kendal high street crying out : 'Mr Taylor hath got the day! Mr Taylor hath got the day!' Religious liberty, if not licence, certainly flourished in the latter days of the Protectorate; never to be entirely obliter-ated again even under the Clarendon Code. Yet there was one form of Nonconformity in the seventeenth century that found little favour in the eyes of authority anywhere or at anytime, even in the eyes of Cromwell himself—Roman Catholicism.

Probably the majority of people in Elizabeth's reign, at least up to the Armada when Spain and the papacy became the official and national enemies, clung secretly to the Old Faith; hoping, and no doubt expecting, since Mary Stuart was still the heiress presumptive, for yet another swing of the pendulum. Certainly as late as 1586 Philip II was given to understand that their numbers were very large, particularly in the North, where in Yorkshire and Durham the mass continued to be celebrated in secret in many places.

This faith and hope was kept green and vigorous by the invasion of England first by the seminary priests from Douai and later by the Jesuits. Sandys, Archbishop of York, writing of the recusants in his own province in 1571, said : 'They will not say Amen to the prayer for the Queen, they glory in their ignorance of the Bible, they prefer prison to conference with the archbishop'. Here he was referring to the small defiant minority, who openly refused to conform even nominally. These were liable to savage penalties : fines, imprisonment, even death; although the first was the favourite form of punishment, since they were often men of sub-stance, whom it paid the State to keep under observation without necessarily enforcing the ruinous sums legally demanded. As regards the penalty of excommunication Bishop Overton of Coventry and Lichfield noted sadly in 1582 that it was a blessing to them in disguise, as they did not intend to come to church any-way; and this punishment saved them from having to pay the usual fine.

Others sought to wriggle out of having to take the sacrament, by pretending to be out of charity with their neighbours or the parson, particularly so, of course, as Easter drew near. Christopher Boreman of South Newington declared in 1584 : 'that he is not in love and charity with his neighbours'; Philip Wateridge of Newton Valence in Hampshire, who absented himself from the altar for over a year, affirmed in court that the incumbent 'Mr Stanlie . . . is his adversary'; and others expressed their willingness to receive, 'if ministered with wafer' : any excuse, in fact, in order 'to shift off the communion'. Sometimes they could get away with it for years on end. It was reported of John Downes, a gentleman of Babingley in 1597 : 'He is a notorious recusant and obstinately refuseth to be partaker with the Church of England. He hath not repayred to chuch this xx years'.

Women offenders usually far out-numbered the men, since it was often considered advisable for the head of the household to conform at least nominally as it was he and not his family who was liable to the full penalties of the law. Priests who celebrated mass and those who dared to teach popery were, of course, par-ticular targets of the Law. Anyone convicted of saying or even hearing mass was liable to a fine of 200 marks and a year's im-prisonment under the Act, 23 Eliz., c. I., sec. 4. Then all recusants over the age of sixteen years not attending their parish church could be fined up to £20; and in the case of a landowner, two thirds of his property held forfeited until such time as he should conform (23 Eliz., c. I., se. 5 and 3 Jac., c. 4. sec. 8.). They were also barred from practising either the legal or the medical profes-sions.

The Vicar of Lancing wrote to the Archdeacon's Official at Chichester in 1625 : 'I present Sir Richard Mullenor and his wife for not repayring to the church at all to heare divine service. I present one whome we suspect to be a popish priest, who abideth in her howse under the colour of teaching her children French, but repayreth not to the church at all'. The famous composer William Byrd and members of his family, who lived at Stondon Massey, Essex, were unrepentant recusants, frequently in trouble for try-ing to make proselytes to the Old Faith :

> The said William Byrd [it was stated in 1605] hath been the chief and principal seducer of John Wright, son and heir of John Wright of Kelvedon in Essex, gent, and one Anne daughter of John Wright the elder. And the said Ellen Byrd,

as it is reported, and as her servants have confessed, have appointed business on the Sabbath Day for her servants of purpose to keep them from church, and hath alsoe done her best endeavour to seduce Thoda Pigbone her now maidservant to draw her to Popery as the maid has confessed, and besides hath drawn her maidservant from time to time these seven years from coming to church. And the said Ellen refuseth conference, and the minister and churchwardens have not as yet spoke with the said William Byrd because he is from home. And they have been excommunicate these seven years.

Except in times of panic, as immediately before the Armada or after the Gunpowder Plot, the Ecclesiastical Courts tended to treat recusants with leniency and forbearing, seeking their conformity without imposing the maximum penalties. For unlike their puritan opposite numbers, they created little trouble in their parishes and, indeed, only asked to be left in peace. They were occasionally ordered to confer with their Anglican incumbent, but rarely did so; and even more rarely asked for absolution after excommunication. The local Justices of the Peace, churchwardens, and even the parson himself were reluctant to take action against good, quiet and friendly neighbours. So all too often the blind eye was turned on well-known Catholic practices or abstensions; and in an astonishingly large number of parishes throughout the country absurdly small numbers of recusants were officially presented. In the Oxford diocese at the beginning of the seventeeth century, for example, there were only 2 at Benson and Nettlebed, 3 at Pishill, 6 at Clifton, 16 at Warborough, 5 at Dorchester and 2 at Burcot. From places like Milton, Sydenham, Tetsworth, Towersey, King's Sutton, Banbury, Cropredy, Claydon and Wardingdon no returns were made at all. The Act Book of the Archdeacon of Taunton for 1623 records the names of only 54 people from some 20 parishes, who were charged with failure to receive Holy Communion in their parish churches; but only a very small proportion of these were well-known recusants. Again, the Act Book of the Archdeacon of Lincoln for 1603 tells us that there were 3,619 communicants in the 20 parishes of the Aveland deanery, but only one recusant. The Calcewaith deanery with 37 parishes and 4,484 communicants likewise only had one recusant. The majority of the Lincolnshire deaneries had none at all. On the other hand defiant, active papists, who harboured Catholic priests, had their children taught the Catholic Faith at home, or sought to make proselytes, could be and often were savagely dealt with, and sentenced to the greater excommunication. John Moore of Christchurch, or so it was said, 'keeps his children from church : allows recusant Rob. Crewe to see them'. He was promptly admonished and ordered 'not to harbour sd Crewe', who was evidently a papist teacher; so too was Jane Tompkins of Newton Longueville, Buckinghamshire, concerning whom the Clerk of the court was ordered to 'proceed against her speedily'. An even worse offence was to seek to persuade others from participating in Anglican rites. When Elizabeth, the wife of John Smythe of Winnall in Hampshire, who had been ill, expressed a desire to receive the Holy Communion, her recusant cousin, Richard Smythe, asked scornfully : 'Oh cousin, what will you receive?' The lady replied that she would receive the sacrament like other people. Then the said Richard Smythe said : 'Take heed what you receive, for there is no virtue therein and it is contrary to God's Word as it is now set forth'.

Under the greater excommunication recusants might not, of course, receive Christian burial in consecrated ground. Hence there is the curious story of Annis Tull of Burcot, who, along with her husband Roger, and Edward and Annis Filpot, had been presented for recusancy in July 1623 and excommunicated. The following May the Burcot churchwardens, replying to the articles of visitation, reported : 'It. upon 37 we present that Annis Tull was buried in the churchyard of Dorchester by Annis More widdow once the wife of Thomas More of Burcoate and by others more wth her whom we know not'. It looked as though William Winchester, the curate of Burcot, had refused to have her interred in his churchyard; whereupon the little local group of recusants had taken her body to Dorchester Abbey, at one time a famous medieval monastery, and buried it themselves secretly at night in consecrated ground. This was by no means the only case of its kind. Two years earlier the Dorchester churchwardens had made a very similar return : 'two from Warborrowe—May and Thomas Bullie—but knowe not who were with them at the buryall, were buried by night in our Churchyard.'

During the reign of James I official policy towards the papists varied from excessive tolerance, for political as much as humanitarian reasons, to savage persecution, especially after the discovery of the Gunpowder Plot. But when Charles I ascended the throne their lot on the whole was a good deal easier and their numbers increased. At Midhurst, Sussex, for example, the astonishingly large number of 46 recusants were named in the official returns, of whom John Phage was presented 'for practising phisicke without a licence', and William Dallam was excommunicated for instructing 'divers in popery'. During the lean years of the Great Interregnum, however, their numbers again fell away; and many of the more lukewarm and faint-hearted were weaned or dragooned into abandoning the Old Faith.

Nonconformity, then, during this period, whether it took the form of Presbyterianism, Independency or Roman Catholicism, could be and often was an ever-running sore in a parish : a source of much embarrassment and a good deal of friction. Sometimes, as we have seen, it even took the form of physical violence directed either towards the resident incumbent or his churchwardens.

CHAPTER VII

The Pious Englishman

THE late sixteenth and early seventeenth centuries produced the age par excellence of the God-fearing Englishman and the pious matron. 'They were not in a majority', wrote Canon Maynard Smith, 'but there were enough of them to establish a standard of life, which was well recognised and understood to be admirable, even by those who made no effort to maintain it'. It was a type of piety that concerned itself with practical good works rather than with mysticism; with living the good life through the microcosm of the family group, yet without cutting oneself adrift from the macrocosm of the community as a whole; and with endeavouring, consciously or unconsciously to leaven the ungodly lump of secular society with the sweet yeast of a sound religion, which was Calvinist in origin and based on the Scriptures, but also drew part of its inspiration from Catholic tradition and the dictates of conscience, reason and common sense.

On the face of it this was a very different conception of piety from that of the monastic ideal, which appeared to seek for spiritual perfection only within little, tightly-knit, closed groups of carefully selected monks or nuns, who, going out into the wilderness, deliberately abandoned an evil world, tried to find God simply for themselves alone, and to achieve a purely selfish salvation through the taking of vows, a regular round of work and worship, prayer and communion, the stern disciplining of body mind and spirit, and a steady contemplation of the divine mysteries. In the famous puritan tract, *The Arminian Nunnery*, which was aimed against the Ferrar family and their religious way of life in the early seventeenth century, the author took for granted that it was nothing more or less than an attempt to revive such

AN EDIFYING DEATHBED SCENE
from *The Roxburghe Ballads*

a monastic ideal. 'Oh the stupid and blind devotion of these people', he wrote, 'for Men and Women in health of able and active bodies and parts to have no particular callings, or to quit their callings and be-take themselves to I wot not what new forme of Fasting and prayer, and a contemplative idle life, a lip devotion'. This, of course, was a complete caricature of what the Ferrars were actually attempting in the manor house at Little Gidding, where they made a considerable contribution to the wellbeing of their immediate neighbourhood in terms of charity, education, medical service and other good works.

In the same way the pre-Reformation monasteries, right down to the Dissolution, played a very much more active part in the life of the Church and Society as a whole than has generally been supposed. As Archbishop Bramhall rightly surmised in *A Just Vindication of the Church of England*, their suppression had been carried through for far different reasons than the much publicised accusations of their selfish exclusiveness, corruption and idleness: 'We fear that covetousness had a great oar in the boat, and that sundry of the principal actors had a greater aim at the goods of the Church, than the good of the Church . . . I do not see why monasteries might not agree well enough with reformed devotion'.

All this was true enough up to a point; but none the less the new 'reformed devotion' was to be built up upon quite fresh foundations from those of the old: based on the household rather than the community; and geared to a new type of religious ideal, which was to be scriptural and ethical rather than mystical and sacramental.

Late sixteenth- and early seventeenth-century orthodox Anglican piety took as its motto: *Deus, Rex, Familia, Vincia* (God, King, Family, Neighbourhood); and shrank back from anything that seemed to savour too much of an unnatural asceticism or a fanatical enthusiasm.

Day by day the head of each family called its members together for morning and evening devotions; whilst on Sunday he and his household attended their parish church twice, clad in their best raiment, and taking the seats assigned to them by the churchwardens in accordance with their social status. 'He did not himself ask if the services were attractive or assess their spiritual value for himself. He was there not so much to receive a benefit as to offer his homage to the majesty of God.' At home he made it his chief business to see that his children and servants were brought up, under strict discipline, in the care and nurture of the Lord; and was particularly watchful to make sure that they were fully instructed both in the Prayer-Book Catechism and the Bible. Sermons were taken down in short-hand by sons who had learned that art at their grammar schools, and later repeated after dinner in the family circle. It was, indeed, said of Mary Rich, Countess of Warwick, that she 'heard her maids say their catechism, and, after church, heard the 'young ladies' repeat the sermon; and when my Lord could not go to church she read to him'.

'Fathers' were regarded with awful reverence by their offspring as prototypes of the 'Heavenly Father', whose all-seeing eye noted their slightest fault and punished it with the utmost rigour. Children therefore were constantly being whipped, even from the tenderest age. When Edmund Verney was only three years of age old Lady Denton felt compelled to intercede with his parents to try and modify his constant beatings. 'Let me begge of you and his mother', she wrote, 'that nobody whip him but Mr Parry [his tutor]; if you doe goe a violent way with him, you will be the first that will rue it, for I veryly believe he will reseve ingery by it, he is of a gentill sweet nature, sone corrected.' These corrections were not, of course, inflicted in any sort of sadistic or vindictive spirit, but in accordance with the Solomanic principle of sparing the rod and spoiling the child; since children must at all costs be saved from themselves, i.e. the old Adam, and brought up in Grace as the true sons and daughters of God.

This kind of Anglican holy household, of which the country parsonage and the manor house set the model, in addition to its regular round of worship and prayer, its Bible study and the reading of countless books of devotion, of which perhaps the favourites were Fox's *Book of Martyrs*, Lewis Bayly's *Practice of Piety*, Jeremy Taylor's *Holy Living and Holy Dying*, and *The Whole Duty of Man*, likewise impressed upon its members the need for industry and abstemiousness; and a benevolence towards the deserving poor, the old, the impotent and the sick, that, especially during the first half of the seventeenth century, gave rise to a multiplicity of charitable foundations, ranging from the setting up of schools, hospitals and almshouses, to the free distribution of clothes, food and money. Finally it inculcated the catechismal virtues of submission to authority, honestly, truthfulness, chastity, and the humble acceptance of that position in society which had been assigned to every individual by the Almighty himself.

One the other hand the vices of the age: drunkenness, immorality, gambling and fighting, were condemned in no uncertain terms; and although these holy households continued to drink wine and beer in moderation, since most water supplies were contaminated anyway, a very strict watch was kept on their consumption. Drunken sons were chastised, and drunken servants discharged without a character. Members of the family who failed to fit into such a godly pattern of living were, if all other means of persuasion or indoctrinisation failed, expelled from the group. Edward Ferrar, for example, was sent abroad; whilst Henry Newcome had his ne'er-do-well son, Daniel, deported on a trading vessel to Jamaica. Writing in his Autobiography on 25 April 1670, he recorded :

My best friends were positive in it, that the best way was to send him beyond seas. And when we were thus resolving in the general, and fixed on Jamaica as the fittest place, Mr Jonathan Ashurst, a merchant, going himself thither, and by the solicitation of friends, he was easily induced to take him

with him, a trading voyage, by Tangier, the Maderas, Bar-
badoes, and so to Jamaica : which all judged much to his
advantage. The poor child was gotten linked with vile knaves
that had made a prey of him : and he could not stir in any
place for them. So that to tarry in the city was no way fit,
unless we would seemingly undo him; and to send him in the
country he did not mind it himself; and besides I had no
employment for him, and so idleness would ruin him. And
therefore we took this course. About two on Monday morning, my dear child took a boat for Gravesend, and so I took
leave of him with a rueful heart; and the sad cries of his
mother I shall not quickly forget.

But in the case of Squire Bruen's cousin, Mr Done, who was suspected not to be observing the sabbath as he should and indulging
himself in unlawful pastimes, a concerted family pressure was in
itself sufficient to bring about his reformation.

Cards and dice were absolutely prohibited in these holy households; while incontinence, fornication and adultery were regarded
as deadly sins that fully merited the greater excommunication.
Blood-sports, particularly bear-baiting and cock-fighting, were
also roundly condemned by the more puritanically-minded; but
fishing was in quite a different category. It was regarded not only
as permissible but even praiseworthy by all. There was no more
pious layman than the saintly Isaak Walton, yet in his Introduction
to *The Complete Angler*, he wrote enthusiastically : 'And I am
the willinger to justify the pleasant part of it because though it is
known I can be serious at all seasonable times, yet the whole discourse is, or rather was, a picture of my own disposition, especially
in such days and times as I have laid aside business and gone a
fishing with honest Nat and R. Roe.'

This type of family, like those of the Evelyns at Long Ditton,
Godstone and Wotton, Sir Henry Slingsby at Scriven, Lord Falkland at Great Tew, the Laudian Mary Ferrar at Little Gidding
in Huntingdonshire or the puritanical Mary Rich, Countess of
Warwick, in her Essex home, spread their influence far and wide.
This they did not so much by active propaganda or missionary
endeavour as by the very fact of their existence; whose chief
characteristics were those of the faithfulness of husband and wife;
the stern but loving upbringing of their children; the kindly
interest shown in the lives of their domestic servants, estate

GODLY INSTRUCTION
from *The Roxburghe Ballads*

employees, and other dependants; their charity to the sick and poor; and in the case of the more robust Anglicans an unswerving loyalty to Church and King. This last became a fetish. The King could do no wrong. He was the Lord's Anointed, the Godly Prince ruling his people as God's vice-regent, the Supreme Governor of the Church of England established by law. As young Henry Vaughan wrote:

> To God, thy country, and thy friend be true :
>   If priest and people change, keep thou thy ground.
> Who sells religion is a Judas Jew
>   And oaths once broke, the soul can not be sound.

Loyalists such as Sir Henry Slingsby might heartily disagree with much of the 'Romish superstition' that Laud was busy introducing into the Church of England. He told Prebendary Thurscross of York that he disapproved of bowing in church, for 'I thought it came too near idolatry to adorn a place wth rich cloaths and other furniture and to command to use towards it bodily worship'; and later he noted in his diary : 'It is not amiss to have a place consecrated for Devotion, as our churches are, to separate ym for yt use; but we cannot stay ourselves here, but must attribute a sanctity to ye very walls and stones of ye church; and herein we do of late draw near to ye superstition of ye Church of Rome'. Others, like Lord Falkland and Sir Edmund Verney, found themselves violently at odds with Strafford's policy of 'Thorough'. Yet, when the call came, they were all prepared unreservedly to sacrifice everything they had—family, estates, life itself in defence of Church and King. During the few days of his reprieve before his execution on Tower Hill in 1658 Sir Henry Slingsby compiled what he called *A Father's Legacy to His Sons*, which expresses in general terms the kind of conduct expected from the children of these loyalist holy households : 'Fear God above all things. Be honest in your ways : spare in your words; plenteous in good works. Ever reflect on Him that made you : and make Devotion your constant Diary to direct you.' He exhorted them to be considerate and courteous to those of their own rank in life, but 'humble to all'; and be sure to learn 'how to obey, that you may know better how to command'. They were to be ever diligent 'in the vocation or employment you are called unto; and be ever doing some good work : that the devil may never find you unemployed'. 'Be not too curious in enquiring what you are to receive after this life; but so labour that you may receive your reward of glory after this life'. They should 'pray continually', keep their bodies 'undefiled', 'honour their mother', 'be charitable to all, but familiar to few'. Above all, he told them, make the service of God your 'anchor-hold' and 'let your whole life be a line of direction to yourselves and of instruction to others. Be more ready to hear than to teach; and let your fame be a living doctrine to your family'. Loyalty to King and Church was to be their motto, and they were to beware of 'Novellisme', i.e. strange doctrines, heresies, sects and schisms.

A good example of how such precepts were put into practice by a pious English country gentleman is to be found in the life of Squire Bruen of Bruen Stapelford in Cheshire, who succeeded to the family estate in 1587. He married thrice, had at least a dozen children, and also made himself responsible for the education and fortune of twelve younger brothers and sisters. 'In order to discharge his increased duties with fidelity', declared his biographer, 'he immediately disparked his park, relinquished hunting and hawking, dog-kennels, and cockpits, and having abridged all other unnecessary expenses, formed his plans and regulated his household according to the strict rules of religion'. Fortunately, being of a puritanical turn of mind, although a staunch upholder of Crown, bishops, Prayer Book and Creeds, he was inclined to regard hunting as the work of the devil. He took particular care of his family prayers, which he considered 'the very goads and spurs unto godliness, the life and sinews of grace and religion'. He himself rose very early every morning, at 3 a.m. or 4 a.m. in summer and 5 a.m. in winter, when he first made his own private devotions, read and meditated upon a portion of Scripture, and composed a fair copy of 'some part of such sermons as he had by a running hand taken from the mouth of the preacher'. He then rang a bell that summoned the household together for corporate worship. This consisted of an introductory prayer, which Bruen himself recited with hands upraised to heaven imploring the Blessing of the Almighty upon their religious exercise, followed by the singing of psalms, the reading and expounding of the Scriptures, and concluding with a prayer of thanksgiving. A repetition of the exercise took place in the evening. On Sundays the squire walked to Tarvin church, which was about a mile away, 'calling all his family about him, leaving neither cook nor butler behinde him, nor any of his servants, but two or three to makes the doores and tend the house untill their returne'. On his journey he picked up as many of his tenants and neighbours as possible, marching at the head of his little army 'with a joyful and cheerful heart' and leading them in the singing of the psalms. He was, however, always careful to arrive at the church in good time before the service commenced—

so he might more comfortably joyne with God's minister and people, in the confession of sins, in prayer and praise, reading and hearing of the word, singing of psalms and partaking of the sacrament; all of which hee did performe with such a reverent attention and gracious affection, with so holy a carriage, and so good a conscience, that hereby hee did much increase his owne comfort, so was his godly example a great encouragement to many others.

N

Between the services he remained in the church with as many of his neighbours as he could persuade to stay with him, occupying the time by repeating the sermon to them, which he had taken down in short-hand, in pious discourse and the singing of psalms. Later, on their way home, he repeated the evening sermon, sang more psalms, 'and if any amongst them was afflicted', comforted and prayed over them.

An ardent royalist and a conformist Anglican Bruen yet strongly sympathised with puritanism, regularly attended the public exercise in Manchester Collegiate Church during the latter years of Elizabeth's reign, and insisted on 'pulling down the painted puppets and superstitious images' in the windows of his family chapel at Tarvin church on the specious plea that 'they darkened the light of the church and obscured the brightness of the Gospel'.

Like his famous contemporary Bernard Gilpin of Houghton-le-Spring he acquired such a reputation for holiness in his immediate neighbourhood that a number of the gentry entrusted their children to his care and guidance. 'Severall families of distinction', recorded his brother-in-law, William Hinde, 'became inmates of his house, in order that they might profit by his religious counsels.' At one time he had as many as twenty-one boarders in residence, besides his own family and servants. His charity was an ever-flowing stream. Every week, we are told, the poor people of Chester and the surrounding neighbourhood, in addition to his own parishioners, flocked to the gates of Stapelford House to receive his bounty, which like that of William Law at Kingscliffe in the next century he bestowed without discrimination or checking up on the *bona fides* of the recipients. 'The fleeces of his flockes were entirely consumed in their clothing'; he gave away his corn with his own hands until none was left; and allowed anyone who so pleased to treat his house as an inn, but without having to foot the bill. Almost inevitably he went bankrupt and had to retire into obscurity at Chester for some five years in order to recuperate his fortune. The puritanical streak within him made Bruen at once furnish his house with 'faithfull, godly and gracious servants . . . that he hath now . . . a church in his house'; and have a horror of every form of gambling, excessive eating or drinking, and even such comparatively harmless festivities as church ales, wakes and 'rushbearings'. Members of his own family who indulged in these pleasures of the flesh were ceaselessly urged to abandon them.

A Three-fold Difcourfe betweene
three Neighbours, *Algate*, *Bifhopfgate*, and
John Heyden the late Cobler of
Hounfditch, a profeffed
Browniſt.

Whereunto is added a true Relation (by way of
Dittie) of a lamentable fire which happened at
Oxford two nights before *Chriſt-tide* laſt, in a
religious brothers fhop, knowne by the
name of *John* of *All-trades*.

LONDON,
Printed for *F. Cowles*, *T. Bates*, and *I. Wright*.
MDCXLII.

A Threefold Discourse, 1642

One cousin, Thomas Dutton, who piped and danced on Sundays, was continually harrassed by Bruen and his pet parson until 'he promised that all piping and dancing should cease on the sabbath day, both forenoone and afternoone . . . and do continue so until this day'. Another relation, Mr Done, who carelessly left his pack of playing cards in his bedroom, found to his chagrin that the four knaves had been removed and burnt, 'so for want of such knaves his gaming was marred, and never did he play in my house, for ought that I ever heard any more'. The squire also recorded with glee how he had destroyed a backgammon board that he found in his study : 'being in one of my studies, and seeing a paire of tables under my feet, I took them with the thirty men and the dice, and all the cards I found, and put them into a burning oven, which was then heating to bake pies'.

A good landlord, who charged only moderate rents, Bruen was always prepared to help his tenants in difficult times; while at home he treated his employees as his own children rather than servants, catechised them regularly, discussed their religious problems, doubts and fears, and encouraged them to hold prayer meetings in the servants' hall besides the regular gatherings of the whole household at the morning and evening exercise in the parlour. He himself strictly observed the text : 'seven times a day will I praise thee'. Two large Bibles were bought and placed on lecterns in his hall, so that any inmate of the house could consult them at any time. None the less the squire was no ascetic. His table groaned under its good things; and in order to keep it supplied he bred pigeons and rabbits, and kept large, well-stocked fish-ponds 'surpassing all about him.' For like the High Anglican, Isaac Walton, he too was a keen fisherman and caught in the gentle art of angling no whiff of brimstone or taint of evil. In his study he kept a store of Bibles, Catechisms and various devotional works to supply those requiring spiritual refreshment; and to others in material need he was prepared to give the very suit from his body or the food from his mouth. The squire never touched strong liquor, and on one occasion actually declined, royalist as he was, to drink the Prince's health. 'You', he said, 'may drink his health and I will pray for his health'. Wine, however, was served at his table, and he had no objection to relations or friends drinking in moderation.

We are accustomed to associate a melodramatic deathbed scene with the Victorian Age; but some seventeenth-century ones could be equally memorable. Bruen's end was particularly edifying; for despite growing physical weakness he refused to abate one jot or tittle of his religious exercises, while at the same time exerting himself to make his Will and put all his worldly affairs in apple-pie order. Finally we can picture him lying in his four-poster bed; too feeble now to do more than take his food from a spoon; while his family and relations and friends stood weeping around him. In a whisper he continued to instruct them : 'turne your tears into prayers . . . you are in the way, I am at my journey's end. Walke on still as you have begun.' When he could no longer speak he lifted up his hand if he wished to be prayed for, 'which he did very willingly and readily'; and he continued to pray for himself : 'silently and secretly, by the pulling of his armes out of the bed, and lifting up his hands and his eyes towards heaven.' Thus he quietly and happily passed away, 'meekly and graciously yielding up his pretious soul, into the hands of God the Father that gave it.'

Sir John Bramston of Skreens in Essex also described at length in his diary the edifying death of his father, an Anglican High Churchman, who 'after he had resolutely denied Crumwell lived at great quiet, spending his time very much in readinge the Bible, and good and holy tracts, and in devout meditations.' At the ripe old age of 78 he was suddenly and violently taken ill whilst on a visit to Lady Barrington at Tofts; and on returning home it soon became obvious that he had not long to live. His medical adviser, a certain Dr Leonard from London, therefore advised him : 'if you have anythinge to doe as to your estate, it were well if you did it'. The old man replied : 'I thancke you, doctor, with all my heart; I have nothinge to doe, but to dye, and I hope I am prepared well for my change'. The evicted Rector of Chelmsford, Dr John Michaelson, who was also present in the house—

> sayd prayers in his chamber, to which he gave, as ever he had done, great attention; and when all was ended he sayd to the doctor (repeatinge that expression 'and diligently to live after Thy commandments') 'What a word is that diligently!' and expressinge great satisfaction he had in the doctor, his companie, and comfort of his prayers. . . . The next morning he prayed with my father, after which he desired the doctor to give him the absolution of the Church (I think the doctor askt him the question) which the doctor

gave, and he devoutly and thankfully receaved; and within less than an hour after died, his senses continuinge to his last gasp.

Although outwardly the Nonconforming puritan might practice his piety in a very different form from that of his High Church Anglican contemporary, yet in their fundamental approach towards and conception of 'the good life' they possessed a great deal in common; notably their firm belief in the inspiration by God's Holy Spirit of every word of the canonical Scriptures, and a determination to live and die in accordance with its precepts. Most Englishmen at this time, too, accepted some form of predestination of their lives by God, which must be accepted with meekness and resignation whatever sorrows or sufferings it involved. They were swift to see the hand of God at work everywhere and in every thing, taking his 'signs' or warnings very seriously, and expecting his personal intervention in their everyday lives, either for good or ill. When at Gorton on 2 March 1658 Mr Rootes was catechising all those who wished to take the sacrament, 'a man and his wife and daughter came, and he began to catechise the daughter. What (says the man) will you catechise her? Ay (says he) and you too. He forthwith calls his wife and daughter away, and said he would never come there more; and before the next Lord's day he and his wife were both dead'. Henry Newcome, who related the incident, entered a more pleasant one into his journal the following 8 December :

. . . my son Daniel was in the College Court, and was about, in his play, to throw a snow ball, and a dog of Mr Greene's came upon him and pulled him down, and got hold of his leg. He frightened the child sadly. It was black with his teeth, and yet he had no hurt of it. Not long after, he fell in the school yard, and might have fallen down the rock to his utter spoiling, if the Lord had not prevented. Thus the child hath been saved by the Lord.

It behoved every Christian then to be constant in leading the 'good life' : regular in his prayers and worship, and in the practice of the great Biblical virtues of temperance, soberness, chastity and charity. But for the puritan there was also no distinction between serving your heavenly and your earthly master, your material and your spiritual interests.

A good man worked, and if he worked he might receive prosperity. . . . There was no suspicion of marriage or of the begetting of children. But he practised early rising, days of fasting, temperance at all times, austerity in dress, and he kept few personal comforts in his house. . . . His ideal was to keep his station in society, simply and modestly, and cut away the trivialities and decorations that diverted. The christian was to live in the world and use its gifts as God's steward.[1]

Like John Bruen the puritan regarded his household as 'a little church' : a household that included besides the ordinary members of the family and domestic servants, apprentices and sometimes journeymen. Richard Baxter indeed spoke of it as 'a society of Christians combined for the better worshipping and service of God'; and J. Mayne in *The English Explained* wrote : 'The parents and masters of families are in God's stead to their children and servants . . . every chief householder hath . . . the charge of the souls of his family'. Households were regarded in Reformation England as the basic unit of society, and their heads were at once the link between the Authorities in Church and State and their own servants and dependents; and a kind of lay-ministry, which was responsible for their proper relationship with the Almighty. Each householder, according to Thomas Taylor, must 'instruct every one of his family in the fear of God, to contain everyone of them under holy discipline, to pray with them and for them'. The specifically Anglican practices of the observance of night watches or the canonical hours, beloved of Nicholas Ferrar and John Cosin, together with the outward adornment of their churches and the Catholic vestments of their priests, were undoubtedly viewed with loathing and horror by the puritan, who condemned them as superstitious, unbiblical and unedifying; enhancing in his eyes the value of family worship as a salutory alternative to this type of church worship insisted upon by Archbishop Laud. Yet none the less the similarity between the rules advocated for puritan families by men like William Gouge, Richard Baxter, and Richard Greenham, and those adopted at Little Gidding or Bruen Stapelford are very striking. In each case the piety was more Biblical than sacramental, and was not in any sense monastic. Certainly most Laudians, although they must have

[1] Owen Chadwick, *The Reformation*, p. 183.

felt an awful reverence for the sacrament, partook of it but seldom; since they considered themselves unworthy of such an intimate approach to the divine majesty as the frequent celebration not merely allowed but invited.

One of the main features of puritan piety was, of course, its sabbatarianism. The first day of the week, which they now equated with the Jewish sabbath, was God's day that, apart from various weekday fasts and lectures, was to be the sole occasion of public worship, and must in all circumstances be kept holy unto the Lord. During its hours no form of recreation was to be permitted, work must be reduced to a minimum, and excessive eating and drinking forbidden. When the town of Tiverton was twice burnt down, Lewis Bayley went so far as to ascribe these calamities to the fact that the townspeople had prepared for their Monday market day on the Sunday. 'God grant them grace', he wrote, 'when next it is built to change their market day'. Travelling on the sabbath, studying books other than the Bible, Catechisms, or similar works of devotion, even talking about secular matters, were all strictly *verboten*; while as far as the women were concerned they had no right to engage in 'trimming, painting and pampering themselves' on a Sunday. The celebration of Christmas, Easter and Whitsuntide, let alone saints' and other holy days, was regarded as superfluous since, as Richard Greenham pointed out, Sunday was alone the appropriate day for thanksgiving when : 'we may meditate of all those benefits which our Saviour Christ by his nativitie, circumcision, passion, resurrection and ascension hath purchased for us'. The rest of the week should be devoted to the praise of God by their work in the world, which would at once redound to the glory of the Lord and promote their own material prosperity; but must be supplemented by the regular gatherings of family groups for corporate devotions, besides private prayer and Bible study.

Sunday, however, was like the glittering iceberg above the monotonous waters of every day life, which should be carefully and especially prepared for on the previous Saturday night by fasting and prayer. The following morning, after brief family devotions, the whole household walked silently to church meditating upon the Scriptures. The principal ingredient of puritan public worship was the sermon, the 'opening' of the Scriptures, to which the congregation must listen very intently indeed, since they were well aware that after the midday meal had been eaten the head of each family would closely examine them concerning its contents. He would then give a brief exposition on the main points, and catechise until it was time to return to church for the afternoon service. At dinner he welcomed poor men to his table, and sent out parcels of food 'to the poor who lie sick in the back lane'. The visitation of the sick in their homes or the houses of quarrelsome neighbours in an endeavour to reconcile their differences were further sabbatical tasks undertaken by the pious puritan; who would conclude as he had begun the day with family worship and his own private devotions.

Within the household its head was supreme. 'Most of the guides to godliness,' writes Christopher Hill, 'though they stress the duties of masters as well as servants, emphasize the over-riding importance of passive obedience on the part of the latter, however badly the former behaved : a king might be called to account by his subjects, but not a master by his servant'.[2] This authority was further increased when, after the breakdown of Anglican ecclesiastical discipline, the householder began to usurp ministerial functions and to preach as well as to catechise. That in its own turn led to a reaction against authority or discipline of any kind, and prepared the ground for the emergence of such independent sects as the Levellers, Diggers and Fifth-Monarchy Men. As one servant had already expressed it as early as 1646, on handing in his notice to quit, 'I would have the liberty of my conscience not to be catechised in the principles of religion'.

The puritans, whilst they admired celibacy in their ministers, were not averse to clerical marriage, and regarded it as indispensable for the layman. It was not, however, to be a union of equals. The wife was essentially the weaker vessel, who was legally subject to her husband, and might be beaten with a rod no thicker than his thumb. As Richard Greenham once told a bride, that although she possessed both grace and beauty 'yet if you wanted obedience to your husband I tell you true that you are nothing worth and you could have no part in Jesus Christ who denieth Himself to be governor of any that will not acknowledge their husband to be their head'. On the other hand the wife had her rights : she must not be made a drudge or ordered about like a servant; she should be loved and cherished—'Her cheeks are made for thy lips and not for thy fists'—and she was always to be second in

[2] C. Hill, *Society and Puritanism in Pre-Revolutionary England.*

command in the household. The main end of marriage was the propagation of children, who must be brought up strictly, if not harshly. 'The Birch', it was said, 'breaketh no bones'; but the 'cockering', i.e. indulging, of them, could be dangerous to their happiness. Most children were given Scriptural names or even sentences, such as 'The Lord is near'; they were expected to be seen rather than heard; to be submissive to all their elders; to be apprenticed to godly masters, who would not only ensure that they worked hard and learned their trade thoroughly, but were brought up in a strait-laced Scriptural discipline. This last consisted not only of a thorough knowledge of the 'pure Word' of God in the Bible, but also of the puritanical Catechisms, of which there were many in print; all exhorting their readers to obey their superiors, to love their neighbours, to be charitable and compassionate to all men, and to 'walk diligently' in their occupations, since he who 'will not sweat on earth shall sweat in hell'. But it was the Bible itself that meant most to the puritan. His prayers were composed almost entirely of Scriptural phrases; every task he performed, every journey he undertook, even every thought and idea he harboured in his mind, had to be heart-searchingly surveyed and scrutinised to see if it conformed with the commandments of God's holy 'Word'. For if he loathed and abominated the Catholic practice of auricular confession, yet in the privacy of his own chamber, alone with his Maker, he himself would indulge in the most rigorous and torturing of self-examinations. 'Labour daily more and more', Bayly wrote, 'to see thine own misery through unbelief, self-love and wilful breaches of God's law'; and exhorted him to pour out his heart before Christ in prayer, who was the one and only true intercessor with God for Man. The idea that the Virgin Mary or any of the saints could undertake this rôle was laughed to scorn. 'There is no mention in Scripture of them for this purpose', declared Richard Sibbes, 'but behold My Servant whom I have chosen'.

This rigorous self-examination and purification of the soul was accompanied by a like disciplining of the body through fasting, keeping it chaste and temperate, and by resisting the temptations of the devil to engage in unlawful sports and pastimes. For the puritan, in fact, the following minimal and indispensable qualities were required for a life of true holiness: unwearying prayer, deep humility, the patient bearing of wrongs, a merciful disposition, bountiful liberality, a scrupulous honesty that made it a sin even to steal a pin, a thorough knowledge and unceasing study of the Bible, and above all 'constancy in his whole course'. The deadly sins that undermined such a godly way of life included : 'roaving fancies', i.e. uncontrolled sexual thoughts and impulses; an unwholesome desire for financial gain; 'worldliness'; 'spiritual dullness'; an over indulgence of the body in food, drink or sleep; pride and anger; a want of true charity or of genuine sympathy towards the needs and interests of other people; and 'over much myrth'.

In his *Directions for Christians*, published in 1603, Richard Rogers demanded regular times 'everie day' for private meditation and prayer, besides family and group devotions. He also urged the keeping of a diary in order to hold 'the attention fixed on the goal'. This 'goal' was not simply, as many historians have supposed, the expectation of heavenly rewards in the life to come, but rather the joy which came to him here and now for being in the right kind of relationship with God. This 'godliness' in fact brought its own exquisite reward; but it was also 'burdensome', since it involved a constant and unending struggle to resist temptation and refuse to yield to one's lower nature. Rogers himself, who was minister at Wethersfield in Essex during the latter half of Elizabeth's reign, spent as much as nine or ten hours a day in his study. Even so he was not satisfied :

> I further espy in myselfe, [he wrote in his diary on 21 July 1589] much untowardnes to study and meditation as to such lik godly things, and hardly finding the cause, doe yet perswade myselfe that I see some cause of it. Want of stricter diet, and the taking of too much liberty in godes lawful blessings, and contenting myselfe to kepe a common course and takeing to much ease.

This flogging of oneself towards perfectionism was helped in Rogers's case by the example set him by certain outstanding contemporary puritan ministers and laymen, and in particular John Knewstubs, Rector of Cockfield, Suffolk :

> First in prayer [recorded Rogers] he is unwearyed, if it were to passe the most parts of the dayes and nightes in it. . . . Then his merveilous love to all in diverse sortes, as the persons are. His rare humility ioined with so great knowledge, wisdom. His bearing of wrongues, his bountiful liberality with mercifullness, where he seeth cause, litl account makeing of

any thinge that he hath, or keepinge any stock, and his con-
tcnation in a sol lif, theise, with such a constancy in his whole
cause, to walke with the lord, and such a preventinge of the
devils subtilties that he may not be unsettled by them . . . I
perceive not that any thing, almost, toucheth him greatly
to disquiet or distemper him, but so handleth and ordreth
him selfe that he proceedeth in evry good course and part of
his life with merveilous fittness thereto. This glass I desire
to set before mine eies dayly.

The contemporary diary of Samuel Ward, written whilst a
young layman at Christ's College, Cambridge, is equally concerned with his own unworthiness; and is also intended as a spur
to encourage him in a more godly life. He complains in it of his
spiritual 'dullness', his 'wandering mynd . . . at prayers . . . at
communion tyme', his 'gluttony', pride and 'negligence in stirring
up my brethren in Christianity,' of his failure to rise early enough
in the morning or study long enough at night, and over indulgence
in 'the transitory pleasures of the world'. In particular he seems
to have been addicted to the eating of fruit, and unable to curb
his appetite in this direction![3]

My crapula (surfeit) in eating peares in a morning . . . as
also my much gluttony at dinner tyme . . . my immoderate
eating of walnuts and cheese after supper, whereby I did
distemper my body . . . Also think how intemerate thow
was in eating so many plums before supper. . . . Also my long-
ing after damsens when I made my vow not to eat in the
orchard.

Strong drink, on the other hand, gave him comparatively little
trouble, and only once is he driven to confess to 'my too much
drinking after supper'. It is worth noting in passing that even
today the Evangelical churchman is far more likely to fall a victim
to gluttony than to drunkenness; while the Anglo-Catholic is
usually sparing of his diet, but fond of good liquor. It is reported
that when a modern bishop was arranging a gathering of his
clergy the caterer asked him whether they were 'High' or 'Low'.

---

[3] Richard Baxter in his *Autobiography* also confessed to an over-fondness
for fruit: 'I was much addicted to the excessive gluttonous eating of apples
and pears . . . I have oft gone into other men's orchards and stolen their
fruit, when I had enough at home', p. 5.

'Why', inquired the puzzled Diocesan, 'what difference can that make?' 'Well', was the reply, 'if they're High they drinks more, if they're Low they always eats more'.

Tudor and Stuart records of domestic piety are necessarily almost entirely confined to the educated classes in society. The private religious observances and practices of the very poor are much more a matter of conjecture. An entry from John Evelyn's *Diary*, however although of a date outside our period, throws light on what was going on in some English cottages. Speaking of a Berkshire woman in 1685, he wrote :

> There was amongst them a maiden of primitive life, the daughter of a poor labouring man, who had sustained her parents (sometime since dead) by her labours, and has for many years refused marriage, or to receive any assistance from the parish, besides a little hermitage which my Lady Clarendon gives her rent free; she lives on four pence a day which she gets by spinning; says she abounds and can give alms to aothers, living in great humility and content, without any apparent affectation or singularity; she is continually working, praying or reading, gives a good account of her knowledge in religion; visits the sick; is not in the least given to talk; very modest, of a simple but not unseemly behaviour; of a lowly countenance, clad very plain but clean and tight. In sum she appears a saint of an extraordinary sort, in so religious a life, as is seldom met with in villages now-a-days.

The pious Englishman, then, of the sixteenth and early seventeenth centuries, whether of Anglican or puritan tendencies and loyalties, refused to renounce the world, although he would if he could, convert the world to his way of thinking. He would mortify and discipline his flesh in order to control it, but he never regarded it as an enemy to be tortured and maltreated because of its incorrigible sinfulness and corruption. He accepted the need for marriage, home and family; and did not as a rule regard the single life, dedicated to God, in lonely isolation from its fellows, as being of any particular merit. In fact he was usually suspicious and afraid of it. But like the medieval monk he himself found an established routine of spiritual exercises essential for the maintenance of the godly life; and so he substituted for the Catholic pilgrimage and the laying of gifts on the shrines of famous saints, the taking of the Covenant, which, like that of Ancient Israel, represented an agreement with the Almighty whereby in exchange for His Grace and Favour he would obey His most holy Will and Commandments, and walk in the ways of Scriptural righteousness all the days of his life.

BIBLIOGRAPHY

'ABUSES of excommunication and decline in ecclesiastical discipline under Queen Elizabeth,' *English Historical Review*. LVII, 1942.

A Collection of Letters from the Original MSS : ed. L. Howard. 1753.

Addy, John, *The Archdeacon and Ecclesiastical Discipline in Yorkshire 1598-1714: Clergy and Churchwardens*. 1963.

A Hampshire Miscellany. I. Metropolitical Visitation of Winchester 1607-1608 : ed. A. J. Willis. 1963.

An Episcopal Visitation in 1593 : ed. J. F. Williams. Norfolk and Norwich Archaeological Society. Vol. XXVII.

'A Puritan Survey of the Church in Staffordshire', ed. A. Peel. *English Historical Review*. XXVI. 1911.

Archdeacon's Court. 1584, ed. E. R. C. Brinkworth. Oxfordshire Record Society, 2 vols. 1942-46.

Ashley, Maurice, *Life in Stewart England*, 1964.

Atchley, C., *The Parish Clerk and his right to read the Liturgical Epistle*. Alcuin Club Tracts. IV. 1904.

Autobiography of Richard Baxter : ed. J. M. Lloyd Thomas. 1925.

Autobiography of Sir John Bramston, Camden Society, 1825.

Autobiography of Henry Newcombe : ed. R. Parkinson. Chetham Society. 2 vols. 1852.

BABBAGE, S. Barton, *Puritanism and Richard Bancroft*. 1962.

Barclay, R., *The Inner Life of the Religious Societies of the Commonwealth*. 2nd. edn., 1877.

Barratt, D. M., *The Condition of the Parochial Clergy between the Reformation and 1660*. Unpublished D.Phil. thesis, Oxford University.

Bewes, W. A., *Church Briefs*. 1896.

Beard, C. A., *The Office of Justice of the Peace in England in its Origin and Development*. 1904.

Bishop Redman's Visitation. 1597 : ed. J. F. Williams. Norfolk Record Society. 1946.

'Bishop Hooper's Visitation of Gloucester 1551 :' ed. James Gairdner. *English Historical Review*. XIX. 1904.

Braithwaite, W. C., *The Beginnings of Quakerism*, 1955.

Brand, J., *Popular Antiquities of Great Britain* : ed. W. C. Haslitt. 2 vols. 1870.

Brinkworth, E. R. C., 'The Laudian Church in Buckinghamshire.' *University of Birmingham Historical Journal*. Vol. V. 1955/6.

CALDER, Isabel, *The Activities of the Puritan Faction of the Church of England. 1625-1633*. 1957.

Calendar of the Committee of Compounding. 1643-1660. 2 vols. 1889-1890.

Calendar of State Papers Domestic : Elizabeth I, James I., Charles I, Commonwealth and Protectorate: 1558-1660. 1856-1886.

Campbell, M., *The English Yeomen under Elizabeth and the early Stuarts*. 1942.

Cardwell, E., *Documentary Annals*. 2 vols. 1839.

    Synodolia. 2 vols. 1842.

Chadwick, Owen, *The Reformation*. 1964.

Chanter, J. F., *The Parish Clerks of Barnstaple. 1500-1900*. Reports and Transactions of the Devonshire Association for the Advancement of Science, Literature and Art. Vol. XXXVI. 1904.

Churchwardens' Accounts of Croscombe, Pilton, Patton, Tintinhull, Morebath and St Michael's, Bath : ed. Bishop Hobhouse. Somerset Record Society. 1890.

Churchwardens' Presentments in 17th century. Parts I & II. The Archdeaconry of Chichester : ed. Hilda Johnstone. Sussex Record Society. 1947/8 and 1948/9.

Church and Parish of St Nicholas, Abingdon : ed. A. E. Preston. Oxfordshire Record Society. 1935.

Coate, Mary, *Social Life in Stuart England*. 1924.

Collectanea II : ed. T. F. Palmer. Somerset Record Society. 1928.

Condition of the Archdeaconry of Norwich in 1603. Norfolk and Norwich Archaeological Society. Vol X. Part 1.

Constitutions and Canons Ecclesiastical 1604 : ed. H. A. Wilson. 1923.

Correspondence of John Cosin. Surtees Society. 2 vols. 1869.

Cox, J. C., *Churchwardens' Accounts*. 1913.

Cropper, Margaret, *Flame Touches Flame*. 1951.

DAVIES, Horton, *The Worship of the English Puritans*. 1928.

Depositions and other Ecclesiastical Proceedings from the Courts of Durham. Surtees Society. 1845.

Diary of John Manningham : ed. J. Brice. Camden Society. 1868.

Diary of the Revd. Ralph Josselin : ed. E. Hockliffe. 1616-1683. Camden Society. 1908.

Diary of Sir Henry Slingsby of Scriven : ed. D. Parsons. 1836.

Dictionary of National Biography.

Ditchfield, P. H., *The Parish Clerk.* 1907.

Dodd, A. H., *Life in Elizabethan England.* 1961.

Durham Parish Books. 1580-1700. Surtees Society. 1888.

Ecclesiastical Proceedings of Bishop Barnes. 1575-1587 : ed. J. Raines. Surtees Society. 1850.

Elizabethan Churchwardens' Accounts : ed. J. E. Farmiloe and R. Nixeseamen. Bedfordshire Record Society. 1952.

English History from Essex Sources: ed. A. C. Edwards, 2 vols. 1952.

'Essex Churches : Notes contributed by R. H. Browne concerning the condition of some Essex Churches, furniture and grave-yards in the 16th and 17th centuries.' *Essex Review.* Vol. XV. 1906.

Essex Parish Records, 1240-1894. Essex Record Society. 1950.

Extracts from the Act Books of the Archdeacons of Nottingham : ed. R. F. B. Hodgkinson. Transactions of the Thornton Society. 1925.

FIRTH, C. H., and Rait, R. S., *Acts and Ordinances of the Interregnum.* 3 vols. 1911.

Frere, W. H., *The English Church in the Reigns of Elizabeth and James I.* 1904.

Frere, W. H., and Douglas, C. E., *Puritan Manifestos,* 1907.

Frere, W. H., and Kennedy, W. M., *Visitation Articles and Injunctions of the Period of the Reformation.* 3 vols. Alcuin Club Collections. 1910.

Fuller, Thomas, *The Holy State and the Profane State.* 1642.

GEE, H. and Hardy, W., *Documents illustrative of English Church History.* 1921.

Gee, H., *The Elizabethan Clergy.* 1898.

The Elizabethan Prayer Book. 1902.

HALLER, W., *The Rise of Puritanism.* 1938.

Liberty and Reformation in the Puritan Revolution. 1955.

Harrison's Description of England in Shakespeare's Youth : ed. F. J. Furnival. 2 vols. 1877.

Harrison, Molly, and Royston, O. M., *How They Lived. 1485-1700.* 1963.

o

Hardy, W. J. 'Remarks on the history of seat reservation in churches.' *Archaeologia.* 2nd series. Vol. III. 1892.

Hart, A. Tindal, *The Country Clergy in Elizabethan and Stuart Times.* 1958. *The Country Priest in English History.* 1959.

Heales, Alfred, *History of the Law of church seats and pews.* 2 vols. 1872.

Henry Best's Farming Book ; ed. C. B. Robinson. Surtees Society. 1857.

Higham, Florence, *Catholic and Reformed.* 1559-1662. 1962.

Hill, Christopher, *Economic Problems of the Church.* 1956. *The Century of Revolution.* 1961. *Society and Puritanism in Pre-Revolutionary England.* 1964.

Hinde, William, *A Faithfull Remonstrance of the Holy Life and Happy Death of John Bruen of Bruen Stapelford.* 1641.

Hole, C., *English Home Life.* 1947.

Hoskins, W. G., *The Midland Peasant.* 1957. *Provincial England.* 1963.

Jordan, W. K., *The Charities of Rural England. 1480-1660.* 1961.

Journal of Nicholas Assheton. 1617-1618. Chetham Society : ed. F. R. Raines. 1848.

Kennedy, W. P. M., *Elizabethan Episcopal Administration.* 3 vols. Alcuin Club Collections. 1924.

Knappen, M. M., *Tudor Puritanism.* 1939. *Two Elizabethan Puritan Diaries.* 1933.

Lambeth Churchwardens' Accounts : ed. C. Drew. Surrey Record Society. 1941.

Layman in Church History, The : ed. Stephen Neile and Hans-Ruedi. 1963.

Leach, A. F., *The English Schools at the Reformation.* 1896.

Leicestershire : 'The Metropolitical Visitation of Archbishop Laud.' *The 65th Report of the Associated Architectural Societies.* Vol. XXIX. Part II. 1908.

Life of Marmaduke Rawdon of York : ed. R. Davies. Camden Society. 1863.

Lincoln Episcopal Records in the time of Thomas Cooper Bishop of Lincoln. 1571-1584. Lincoln Record Society. 1912.

Linn, F. H., *Holy Households in the 17th Century.* Uncompleted thesis for B.Litt. Oxford University.

Magee, Brian, *The English Recusants.* 1938.

Marchant, R., *The Puritans and the Church Courts in the Diocese of York. 1560-1642.* 1960.

Marriage Contracts and Espousals in the reign of Queen Elizabeth :
ed. A. Percival Moore. Associated Architectural Societies
Reports and Papers. 1909.

Marsden, J. B., *The History of the Early Puritans.* 1860.

Matthews, A. G., *Walker Revised.* 1948.

Montague, Richard, *Visitation Articles for the Diocese of Norwich,*
1638.

NEALE, Daniel, *The History of the Puritans.* 5 vols. 1822.

New, J. F. H., *Anglican and Puritan.* 1964.

Nottinghamshire County Records in the 17th century : ed. H. H.
Copnall. 1915.

Official Papers of Sir Nathaniel Bacon of Stiffkey, J.P. 1580-1620 :
ed. H. W. Saunders. Camden Society. 1915.

Oxfordshire Peculiars : ed. S. A. Peyton. Oxfordshire Record Society.
1928.

PEACOCK, E., *Lincoln Episcopal Visitations.* 1884.

Pearson, A. E. F., *Thomas Cartwright and Elizabethan Puritanism.*
1925.

Pemberton, W. A., *Studies in the Ecclesiastical Court and Archdeaconry of Nottingham. 1660-1689.* Unpublished D. Phil.
thesis. University of Nottingham.

Perry, E. W., *Under Four Tudors.* 1964 edn.

Peters, Robert, *Oculi Episcopi: Administration in the Archdeaconry
of St. Albans, 1580-1625.* 1963.

Ponsonby, Arthur, *English Diaries.* 1923. *More English Diaries.*
1927.

Powicke, F. J., *The Life of the Revd. Richard Baxter.* 1924.

*Presbyterian Movement in the Reign of Queen Elizabeth as Illus-
trated by the Minute Book of the Dedham Classis. 1582-
1589* : ed. R. G. Usher. Camden Society. 1905.

'Primary Visitation of the Diocese of Lincoln by Bishop Neile. A.D.
1614' : ed. Rev. Precentor Venables. *The 38th Report of
the Associated Architectural Societies.* Vol. XVI. Part I.
1881.

Proceedings Primarily in the County of Kent : ed. L. B. Larking.
Camden Society. 1862.

Prothero, G. W., *Select Statutes . . . reigns of Elizabeth and James I.*
1906.

Prynne, William, *A Breviate of the Prelates intolerable Usurpations.*
1637.

Purvis, J. S., *Tudor Parish Documents of the Diocese of York.* 1948.

Quarter Sessions Records of the County of Northampton. 1630-58 :
    ed. Joan Wake. 1921/2.
Quarter Sessions, the Records of the North Riding Court of : ed.
    J. C. Atkinson.

ROUTLEY, Erik, *English Religious Dissent*. 1960.
Rowse, A. L., *Ralegh and the Throckmortons*. 1962.

SELDEN, *Table Talk*. 1638.
Shaw, W. A., *A History of the English Church during the Civil
    Wars and under the Commonwealth*. 2 vols. 1900.
Smith, H., *The Ecclesiastical History of Essex*. 1932.
Smith, H. Maynard, 'The Pious Englishman 1600-1800' *Church
    Quarterly Review*. 1927.
Smith, J. Toulmin., *The Parish*. 1857.
State of the Church in the Reigns of Elizabeth and James I. Lincoln
    Record Society : ed. C. W. Foster. 1926.
Stowe, A. R. M., *English Grammar Schools in the reign of Queen
    Elizabeth*. 1908.
Strutt, Joseph, *Sports and Pastimes*. 1838.
Strype, John, *Annals of the Reformation*. 2 vols. 1824 edn.
    History of the Life and Acts of Edmund Grindal. 1821 edn.
    The Life and Acts of Matthew Parker. 1821 edn.
    The Life and Acts of John Aylmer. 1821 edn.
    The Life and Acts of John Whitgift. 1882 edn.
    Memorials of Thomas Cranmer. 1848 edn.
Stubbs, Philip, *Anatomie of Abuses*. 1583.
'Surplice in Essex, The,' *Essex Review* Vol. XLV. 1936.

TATE, W. E., *The Parish Chest*. 1946.
Tatham, G. B., *The Puritans in Power*. 1913.
Tawney, R. H., *The Agrarian Problem in the 16th Century*. 1912.
    Religion and the Rise of Capitalism. 1927.
Tilney Churchwardens' Accounts : ed. A. D. Stallard. 1914.
Trevelyan, G. M., *English Social History*. 2nd edn. 1946.
Trotter, E., *Seventeenth Century Life in the Country Parish*. 1919.

USHER, R. G., *The Reconstruction of the English Church*. 2 vols.
    1910.

VENN, J. A., *The Foundation of Agricultural Economics*, 2nd. edn.
    1933.
Verney Papers. Camden Society : ed. John Bruce. 1845.

Victoria County History: Berkshire. Vol. II; *Lancashire.* Vol. II; *Leicestershire.* Vol. III; *Lincolnshire.* Vol. II; *Oxfordshire.* Vol. I.

Vincent, W. A. L., *The State and School Education. 1640-1660.* 1950.

'Visitation of the Archdeaconry of Colchester. 1588.' *Essex Review.* Vol. XXII. 1923.

WAKEFIELD, G. S., *Puritan Devotion.* 1957.

Waters, R. E. Chester, *Parish Registers in England.* 1883.

Walton, Isaak, *The Lives of Mr Richard Hooker etc.* 1895 edn.

Ware, S. L., *The Elizabethan Parish in its Ecclesiastical and Financial Aspects.* 1908.

Warne, Arthur, *The Church and Society in 18th Century Devon.* Unpublished thesis for D. Phil. degree. Leeds University.

Webb, S. & B., *English Local Government: The Parish and the County.* 1906.

West, F. H., *Rude Forefathers. 1600-66.* 1949.
 Sparrows of the Spirit. 1957.

Whitaker, W. B., *Sunday in Tudor and Stuart Times.* 1933.

Williams, J. E., *The Early Churchwardens Accounts of Hampshire.* 1913.

Winchester Consistory Court Depositions. 1561-1602 : ed. A. J. Willis. Hampshire Record Society. 1960.

Wingfield-Stratford, E., *The Squire and his Relations.* 1956.

Wood, A., and Richardson, R., *Parochial Collections.* Vols. II, IV, XI, Oxfordshire Record Society. 1920-29.

Wood, N., *The Reformation in English Education.* 1931.

Index